THE ANGLO-AMERICAN TRADITION IN FOREIGN AFFAIRS

The Anglo-American Tradition
in Foreign Affairs

READINGS FROM THOMAS MORE TO WOODROW WILSON

Edited with an introduction and commentary

by ARNOLD WOLFERS

STERLING PROFESSOR OF INTERNATIONAL RELATIONS, YALE UNIVERSITY

and LAURENCE W. MARTIN

INSTRUCTOR IN POLITICAL SCIENCE, YALE UNIVERSITY

NEW HAVEN: *Yale University Press, 1956*

LONDON: GEOFFREY CUMBERLEGE, OXFORD UNIVERSITY PRESS

PREFATORY NOTE

THE READINGS contained in this volume are intended to provide a comprehensive picture of four centuries of outstanding English and American writing on the general problems of international relations. We have examined the works which have established an important place in Anglo-American political thought and from these numerous sources we have assembled what seem to be the significant observations on foreign affairs. The authors are arranged in chronological order without relating them or their ideas one to another. Commentaries which introduce and accompany the text direct the reader's attention to the chief points of interest in the passages placed before him but, so far as possible, refrain from editorializing in order not to prejudice his own interpretation. It is our hope that these selections will prove enlightening in themselves and also stimulate intensive studies of political theory pertaining to international relations.

Full bibliographical references are given for the convenience of students who wish to read more widely. All omissions and insertions have been conventionally indicated except where, in a few cases, we have modernized spelling and the use of italics and capitals by some earlier authors whose usage was distracting to the modern eye. Whenever we have left out one or more whole paragraphs, we signify the omission by four spaced periods at the end of the previous paragraph.

We are grateful to Mrs. William E. Scott and Mrs. Katherine B. Sohler, who both contributed to early stages of this project. For permission to quote from copyrighted works, our thanks are due to Mrs. Woodrow Wilson, Mr. Lyle Evans Mahan and the following publishers: Appleton-Century-Crofts, Inc., George Allen and Unwin, Ltd., Harper and Brothers, and The Clarendon Press. Finally, we acknowledge a special debt of gratitude for the support of Yale University, without which this book could not have been compiled.

A. W.
L. W. M.

CONTENTS

Prefatory Note   v

Introduction: Political Theory and International Relations   ix

1.	Sir Thomas More	1
2.	Francis Bacon	11
3.	Thomas Hobbes	26
4.	John Locke	41
5.	Bolingbroke	55
6.	David Hume	63
7.	Adam Smith	78
8.	Adam Ferguson	94
9.	Edmund Burke	109
10.	Thomas Paine	126
11.	Alexander Hamilton	139
12.	Thomas Jefferson	155
13.	William Godwin	166
14.	Jeremy Bentham	180
15.	Richard Cobden	192
16.	John Stuart Mill	206
17.	Herbert Spencer	221
18.	Alfred Thayer Mahan	234
19.	John Atkinson Hobson	248
20.	Woodrow Wilson	263
	Index	281

INTRODUCTION

Political Theory and International Relations
BY ARNOLD WOLFERS

NOWHERE in English-speaking countries would the study of government and politics be considered complete that did not include political
theory; in fact, at many universities theory is regarded as the very
foundation on which all other aspects of the subject should be made
to rest. This does not hold true, however, for the study of international
politics. What a student of international relations may happen to learn
about political thinkers of earlier centuries usually comes to him from
outside the program of his specialty, and if he takes a course in political theory he is not likely to hear much about earlier thought on
foreign policy.[1]

A cleavage exists between international relations and political theory, and it is a two-way affair. If specialists in international politics
with rare exceptions have neglected political theory, the political
theorists in turn, departing from older tradition, have paid little attention to what the thinkers of the past—Machiavelli not always excepted
—have had to say on international relations. From reading the current
histories of political doctrine, particularly as they deal with the political and moral philosophers representing the Anglo-American tradition,

1. As far as the literature on international relations is concerned—and the same
is true for the teaching in the field—there are exceptions to this rule of silence
on political theory. There is Frank M. Russell, *Theories of International Relations*
(New York, D. Appleton-Century, 1936) and notably the more recent book of
readings by Hans J. Morgenthau and Kenneth W. Thompson, *Principles and Problems of International Politics,* New York, Alfred A. Knopf, 1950. These authors have
chosen their material with a view to a series of topical subjects and have included
both contemporary and earlier authors, Continental as well as English and American writers, statesmen as well as philosophers. The present volume, on the other
hand, is a selection of the contributions well known English and American philosophers and "statesmen-philosophers" have made to the theory of international politics in the four centuries between 1516 and 1919.

one might be led to believe that these thinkers had been interested in domestic problems exclusively.

Such mutual neglect, if that is what it should be called, is not a matter of accident. It has deep roots in the political experience of England and the United States and in the way this experience has been intellectually absorbed. The question today, however, is whether the reasons which explain this divorce between the two fields also justify its continuation; if they do not, the early "remarriage" which this book is meant to promote may commend itself to both parties.

As is well known, international relations as a special field of study made its appearance on the academic scene only after the close of World War I. It came as a fruit of Wilsonian idealism and the founding of the League of Nations. On the grounds that a "new era" had been ushered in and that the League if properly used and implemented would mark the end of European power politics, the study of international relations was meant to promote the cause of peace and international cooperation by showing how the new peace machinery should be used and developed. It was centered, therefore, on the "ought" of a better future order rather than on the "is" and "was" of the sorry conditions to which policy makers and their advisors had traditionally addressed themselves. Under these circumstances only those earlier thinkers deserved to be studied who, like Sully, Kant, Penn, or Bentham, had proposed schemes of international organization for peace and could thus qualify as precursors of the new prophets.

When in the 1930's disillusionment and a sharp reaction against this Wilsonian approach set in, the new realist school of thought, dominant today in academic circles, had reasons of a different kind for paying no attention to the doctrines of the past. The effort was now directed toward building up an empirical or causal science of international politics. Because its subject was now to be the "is" and "was" rather than the "ought" of external state behavior, the new program left even less incentive for concern with what was believed to be the exclusively normative outlook of political and moral philosophers of the past, Machiavelli alone being placed in a different category. Even if it had been realized that past thinkers on the subject had been anything but inarticulate about what they considered to be the actual workings of the state-system, their observations and generalizations on this aspect of the subject would probably have been discounted because of their lack of scientific methodology.

As in the 1930's, the climate of thought is undergoing another important change today, this time in a direction that may prove far more favorable to the study of political doctrine. It is no longer so confidently expected that an empirical science of international politics can meet all our needs; with new and growing interest in the theoretical bases of scientific work in this field, attention is being drawn to normative thought and philosophical speculation. Moreover, doubts have arisen whether new methods of investigation really allow the political scientist of today to dispense with such traditional tools as impressionistic observation, historical analogy, and common sense judgment, on which through the ages his predecessors relied for the validation of their assertions. Thus the road is being opened for a new appreciation of earlier contributions to the knowledge of international affairs.

The non-normative aspects of earlier thinking on the subject deserve to be emphasized first because they are less obvious. Much of the time the political philosophers of the past were preoccupied with the way statesmen and nations should behave toward each other. Yet they could not have felt justified in offering advice on rules to be followed had they not believed that they possessed knowledge of what would happen if their advice were accepted. This means, then, that some causal theorizing, however inadequate, was at least implicit in much of their normative effort. Thus Godwin states views about the way nations actually behave by declaring it "an improbable supposition" to conceive of a nation being attacked "so long as its own conduct is sober, acceptable and moderate." Hamilton's admonition not to continue wars to the point of the enemy's surrender if compromise should be possible, advice that deserves to be taken seriously in our time, rests on the explicit assertion that such surrender will cause the subsequent peace to be less secure. Some theorists quoted in this volume will be found to have made explicit propositions concerning some such cause and effect relationships; others have made them by implication. Hume's chapter on the balance of power offers a good illustration of a study directed primarily at empirical rather than normative theory. While Hume can be said to imply that governments should aim at balanced power in the world, his reasoning is based on generalizations concerning the way states as a rule have behaved in the past and are likely to behave in the future, the emphasis being on factors that induce them to push beyond the point of equilibrium. The bulk of the discussion of international relations by both Hobbes and Locke is of a similar kind. Because it serves them merely as an illustration of the state of nature, it is clearly directed toward a generalized description of what to them seemed to be the way sovereigns behave toward each other in fact; it was not intended as advice in matters of foreign policy.

Without any doubt, most of the sweeping generalizations that run through the writings of the political philosophers of the past are open to severe criticism. They are often crude, in many cases patently prejudiced, and as a rule presented without even the claim of meticulous verification. Hobbes "proves" to his own satisfaction that war coalitions cannot last beyond victory—a shrewd and prophetic hunch—by deducing his conclusion from premises he can hardly be said to have substantiated. Neither he nor others have been able to prove that men and nations are by nature enemies of one another and can therefore cooperate only as long as they are threatened by a common foe. Also from a scientific point of view, there is not one theorist or philosopher who cannot be blamed for a lack of clearly stated hypotheses and for the failure to validate them by means less open to prejudice than mere random experience and arbitrary choice of historical illustrations.

Yet before turning away contemptuously from the inadequate work of his predecessors, the social scientist of today who is struggling with the problems of international relations should ask himself how much better he is able to validate the hunches on which he is forced to base himself. He would have to remain within a narrow circle of rather marginal problems if he excluded all but scientifically unimpeachable investigations, particularly of the controlled-experiment or quantitative kind. For example, significant scientific work has been undertaken by psychologists and sociologists in recent years on the effects of insecurity and frustration on human behavior, some of it applicable to the behavior of nations. However, a political scientist called upon to evaluate the effects on foreign policy of frustration suffered by a nation in the wake of a punitive peace settlement, or of feelings of insecurity arising out of recollections of past invasions, while he would hardly refuse to express a scholarly opinion on the ground that there is no way open to him to "prove" his contentions, would have to rely heavily on personal experience and observations to supplement and qualify his tenuous scientific insight. Like the political philosophers before him, then, he would find himself mustering all the evidence which history, personal experience, introspection, common sense, and the gift of logical reasoning put at his disposal. If there is any difference between him and his predecessors—who, like himself, were confronted with such problems as alliance policy, the balancing of power, intervention in the affairs of other countries, and the pursuit of ideological goals—one would hope it might lie in a keener realization of the controversial and tentative nature of his reply, in a greater effort to consider alternative answers, and in a more conscious attempt to remain dispassionate and objective. Sometimes the scientifically minded scholar of today may turn out to be merely more pedantic in his formulations and less afraid of belaboring the obvious. In any case, analyses of national conduct undertaken by men of keen insight into human behavior and wide experience in the affairs of the political world cannot fail to be valuable to anyone seeking to understand what makes the clock tick in international relations. The reflections of the thinkers of the past—quoted in this volume on such matters as the advantages and weaknesses of the balance of power, the peculiarities of insular location, and the dangers of preventive war—are far removed from amateurish guesswork; the arguments as well as the evidence offered to sustain them are, in kind at least, the same as those used today in even the most scholarly debates on the same subjects.

Whether the political philosophers of the past have contributed much or little to empirical theory, the main test of their importance to the student of international relations today must rest on the continued value of their normative thought, which was undoubtedly their chief concern. They were seeking to decide when it is right or wrong for a nation to participate in "other peoples' wars," to interfere in the domestic affairs of others, to keep faith with allies, or to expand into new territory. They were also concerned with what they called the prudence of certain types of action, prudence meaning expediency guided and moderated by morality and wise judgment. To a considerable extent they were expressing value preferences—often couched in the form of "laws of nature"—and inquiring into the consequences which follow when nations fail to act in conformity with these preferences.

More and more it is coming to be appreciated that such moral preferences as well as broad assumptions about man and his motives are an inescapable starting point for even the most strictly empirical enterprise in matters of national behavior. Attempts to escape from this scientific dilemma merely lead to a lack of awareness of one's own presuppositions or to a failure to make them explicit. The very words that are used—self-preservation, aggression, imperialism, national interest—are loaded with emotional connotations, moral judgment, and prescientific assumptions. There might never have been any study of how to outlaw and prevent "aggressive" war had it not been for the tacit assumption that any *status quo* is morally preferable to a resort to international violence. It would make no sense to say or assume that nations must seek power adequate for survival if high value were not placed on the existence of independent nations. No expectations regarding the conduct of nations can be formulated that are not affected by either the optimistic hunch of a Locke, who entertained the belief that "calm reason and conscience" would guide the behavior of most men, or the pessimistic hunch of a Hobbes, to whom man appeared obsessed by fear and greediness. While the pessimist is likely to expect that peace will be maintained only if the power of all nations is held in check by a balance of their respective power, the optimist fears war only at times when the exceptional aggressor nations are not met with the unchallengeable predominance and solidarity of the great majority of peace-loving peoples. In this sense, all students in the field, consciously or unconsciously, belong to schools of moral and philosophical thought.

If this be so, the normative and speculative ideas of the great thinkers of the past are worthy of even more attention than are their clearly impressionistic insights into the realities and laws which explain the actual behavior of nations. Here is a wealth of explicit formulations and judgments concerning most of the problems of moral choice and prudence which plague the thinkers and practitioners of our time. Today there is still heated discussion of the respective values of the general human interest and the particular national interest, as Burke called them, and of the line to be drawn between justifiable and unjustifiable resistance to the demands of others. What this indicates is a search for standards, rational and moral, by which to judge policy— one's own and that of others—and by which to be guided in reaching decisions.

Although it is regrettable that value judgments in the past, as in the present, are often presented with assertions of fact as if there were no fundamental difference between them, the theorists which are included here left no doubt that most of the time they were seeking to guide statesmen and nations in choosing their ends and means with a view to maximizing desirable values or minimizing their sacrifice. If this meant treating the subject of values extensively, as in discussions about justice, weighing values against one another, and bringing them into conscious and discriminating perspective, it was an exercise which no policy science can avoid if it is to be useful.

While the student of international politics has every reason, then, to bridge the gulf which has separated him from political theory, it remains to be asked—remarriage requiring the consent of both sides— whether contemporary teachers of theory or of the history of doctrine may not have equally good reasons to break the silence they have maintained in respect to political matters transcending national boundaries.

Three factors may account for the lack of interest which political theorists are currently showing for anything but domestic government and politics: the first is the persistent impact of what until quite recently could be called the strategic insularity of both the British Isles and the American continent; the second is the striking contrast that exists for both countries between the internal and the external political scene; the third is a difference in the degree of moral opportunity offered by the domestic and the foreign field of political activity.

As long as the relative insular security of Britain and the United States lasted—or was thought to exist—it was possible to conceive of the development of institutions at home as being entirely separate from and independent of the events occurring beyond the frontiers of the nation. Where propinquity rather than isolation was characteristic of the relations between states, as on the Continent of Europe, domestic affairs could hardly be conceived except in interdependence with foreign affairs. In fact, the main emphasis was on the so-called primacy of foreign policy. In sharp contrast to this attitude the insular political theorists could choose to concentrate on internal politics, overlooking or leaving to the tender mercy of others the unsavory problems of international power politics and anarchy. Now that insular security has gone, this justification for aloofness from external problems has vanished too.

The second factor is also a phenomenon peculiar to Britain, the United States, and, in this instance, a few democracies in Western Europe. In these countries domestic political conditions stand in striking contrast to the conditions these nations face in their external relations: the domestic conditions are characterized by order, lawfulness, and peace arising from popular consensus on principles—a consensus so marked that some believe coercion has practically ceased to play a role here; but the external relations continue to be full of bitter struggle, violence, and Machiavellian practices. Obviously, no such contrast is experienced by peoples whose country is the frequent scene of revolution and domestic violence or suffers the cruel terrors of tyranny; to them "civil society," or "order under government," if it is experienced at all, possesses most of the objectionable features we attribute to international anarchy. The sharper the contrast between the domestic and the international scene, the greater, then, will be the inclination to treat the two fields of political activity separately and to overlook the traits they have in common. It is not a happy sign that much of what has been occurring in this century militates against the continued separation of the two fields. For the difference between them has been reduced, even to the observer in countries of democratic orderliness, not primarily because the international arena has taken on new and striking traits of lawfulness and order under government but because tyrannical suppression and persecution as well as revolutionary strife have come to be the order of the day in wide areas of the world. Thus government no longer appears as the safe panacea against the evils of Machiavellian practice or violence that set domestic affairs in sharp and unmistakable contrast to international anarchy. Working to lessen the contrast, but from the opposite side, has been the experience that the lack of supranational government, for example in the case of the British Commonwealth, has not prevented close and friendly cooperation within this "anarchical" partnership. It would therefore seem that the two poles of the political continuum, civil society and international anarchy or power politics, are not so far apart in reality as they appeared at times, which suggests that a comprehensive theory of politics, including both foreign and domestic affairs, would make good sense.

This leads to the third, though closely related, factor: the difference in "moral opportunity." During the modern age England and the United States, together with a few Western countries, managed to put their sovereign control of internal affairs to excellent use for the progressive development of institutions of lawful government and civil liberty. This occurred in the course of the same four centuries during which the very existence of national sovereignty produced externally a multistate system with all the conflict, struggle, and war that this implies. Therefore, for political and moral philosophers the internal scene with its opportunity to promote the good life under civil government was as encouraging as the external scene was frustrating. One can hardly wonder that teachers of political theory, in the end, should have come to be interested far more in the way the theorists of the past had helped to solve the problems of government at home than in what they had to say about the comparatively barren and stagnant power politics of the multistate system. The more clearly normative their concern with politics, the more incentive they had to concentrate on the field in which sovereign control gave each people and government, individually, a high degree of power and opportunity to conduct itself according to its own moral precepts. There cannot fail to be a difference in moral opportunity between a realm in which every nation is at the mercy of the acts of others and one in which the course of events is predominantly shaped by its own decision. If there is to be less separation in the treatment of the two realms, the change must come from a growing realization that, after all, the single mind and will of the nation even at home is more fictitious than real and that moral opportunity is not so radically lacking in external politics as some impatient perfectionists of our time, impressed by the horrors of two world wars, are inclined to maintain.

If one may look forward, then, to a growing readiness to draw international relations and political theory closely together—as moral and political philosophers in past centuries were accustomed to do—the question is whether the student of international relations, awakened to this need, would do well to focus his attention, first, on the political thought of men with a particular national background and of a particular historical period. The readings contained in this volume imply that the answer should be in the affirmative; they point to the desirability of giving priority to English and American theorists and to a period running roughly from the beginning of the 16th to the early part of the 20th century. This choice requires justification.

Theory pertaining to foreign policy is not an invention of the modern age. For obvious reasons the topic became a matter of live interest whenever the political arena was occupied by more than one sovereign political unit, thereby giving rise to inter-unit relations and foreign policies clearly distinct from the domestic affairs within these units. This situation did not exist at all times, however. There was little occasion for theoretical thought on foreign policy in the days of the Roman Empire once it had disposed of all of its serious competitors. There is no medieval theory on the subject of international relations properly speaking, because under what has been called the theory of universal community political activity within European Christendom was not conceived in terms of a dichotomy between domestic and foreign policy; theoretically, relations between pope and emperor and between feudal kings were expected to follow the same rules and moral principles as those between kings and subordinate feudal lords, or between kings and their subjects. If in fact conduct deviated, often radically, from these precepts, it did so no less in internal than in external relations.

All of which means, then, that political theorists writing in periods of multiple sovereignty are of major if not of exclusive interest to the study of international relations; and among them preference will necessarily go to those who since the age of Machiavelli and More were dealing with the behavior of political units similar in most respects to the nation-states of our own day.

This of course does not preclude the possibility that at some future time speculations and observations of medieval thinkers like Saint Augustine, Thomas Aquinas, or Dante will become relevant again in matters of world politics. Even today it is not fantastic to speak of recent changes within the international arena as pointing toward a kind of "new medievalism." The trend would seem to be toward complexities that blur the dividing lines between domestic and foreign policy. We are faced once again with double loyalties and overlapping realms of power—international communism versus nation-state, transnational affinity versus nationalism—as well as with wars like those recently fought in Korea and Indo-China that partake of the character of international and civil war simultaneously. Yet despite these novel developments, which deserve theoretical as well as practical attention, the traditional problems of interstate or intersovereign relations, predominant over the last four centuries, continue to occupy the center of the political stage whenever relations transcending national boundaries come into play. From this it follows that the theories dealing with interstate relations are at the present time most pertinent.

If drastic change has occurred in recent times, it has not taken the form of bringing to a close the modern era of interstate power politics, as many had hoped; it has merely brought to an end the "European Age" of such politics. The character of international relations has not been revolutionized, rendering obsolete earlier thought on these relations. The entry of the United States and other non-European countries as actors into the company of the world's leading powers has merely made past theory of international politics directly relevant to the United States, as it was all along to the European nations to whom it was originally addressed. If one were looking for a reason why the readings in this volume should end with Woodrow Wilson's speeches of 1919, one might cite the fact that this makes them coincidental with the European Age. Thomas More wrote at the time when, with the discovery of America, the great powers of Europe were starting on their course of world predominance; Woodrow Wilson spoke at the close of World War I when, partly because of him, American leadership in world affairs was asserting itself for the first time. Since then, any theory of international politics, though dealing with the same set of problems, must be concerned with the global multistate system that has taken the place of its European predecessor.

While it makes sense, therefore, to draw insight primarily from those who have lived to see the modern multistate system at work, the question remains whether English and American thinkers deserve special attention. Obviously, theoretical discussion of international politics has not been the preserve of the English-speaking peoples. In fact, in matters of international relations the works of Continental authors such as Machiavelli, Grotius, Spinoza, and Kant have received much more attention than those of their Anglo-Saxon contemporaries. But the very silence that surrounds the latter provides one good reason for paying special attention to them.

There are other, still more cogent, reasons for doing so. If it can be shown that their response to the challenging issues raised by the multistate system differs from that of the Continentals, knowledge of their views should serve at least two important purposes: it should help explain some of the peculiarities of the contemporary British and American approach to world affairs, which often puzzle the foreign observer and lead him either to praise the special virtues of Anglo-Saxon policy or condemn what he considers its hypocritical wrappings; it should also help to promote critical self-understanding within the English-speaking world, making for more awareness of its moral presuppositions and of the deeply ingrained traditional habits of thought which inevitably color conduct in a field where emotion and value judgment play an important role. These are the chief reasons why an attempt is made here to arouse special interest in the Anglo-American tradition of thought. It might be added that by paying respect to an impressive intellectual ancestry, contemporary Anglo-American study in the field of international relations should also gain in philosophical depth, historical perspective, and academic respectability.

If insular security has been responsible, at least in part, for the divorce between political theory and international relations, it has had yet another and more important effect, this one bearing on the substance of the theory itself. It may be dangerous to lump together into two distinct categories all Anglo-American theorists on the one hand and all Continental theorists on the other, as if agreement within each camp had been the rule. On most points it has not. Yet in one vital respect it would seem permissible to so generalize about the two groups, even at the risk of doing injustice to exceptions.

It would be grossly misleading to suggest that all Continental thought in matters of international politics has been Machiavellian; passionate opposition to the views expressed in Machiavelli's *Prince* was voiced throughout the centuries that followed its publication. Friedrich Meinecke in his book on *Staatsräson,*[2] has given a brilliant account of the Continental debate between Machiavellians and anti-Machiavellians. Yet his discussion of Continental thought on foreign policy justifies the contention that Continental theory centered around the idea of the "necessity of state," which was the core of Machiavelli's argumentation. As the Continental political philosophers saw it, the main problem presented by conditions of multiple sovereignty was that of a deep conflict between morality and *raison d'état*. This was in line with the experience common to all Continental countries which in the face of constant external threats to their national existence believed themselves exposed to the compelling impact of forces beyond their control. The main question as they saw it was whether statesmen and nations were under moral obligation to put up resistance against these "compelling" demands of state necessity. While not all were ready, fatalistically or cynically, to advocate sheer resignation, there was ever present a feeling that nations were puppets in the hands of demonic forces, with little leeway if any to rescue moral values from a sea of tragic necessity.

English and American thought and experience traveled a different road. Even the concepts of necessity of state or reason of state remained foreign to the political philosophers of the English-speaking world. While the Continentals were arguing about the dilemma of statesmen faced by the irreconcilable demands of necessity and morality, English and American thinkers in turn were engaged in a debate about the best way of applying accepted principles of morality to the field of foreign policy. Here the assumption was that statesmen and nations enjoyed considerable freedom to choose the right path in their external conduct as they did in their internal policies. If there was any question about the compatibility of service to the national interest on the one hand and the avoidance of evil on the other, there was

2. Friedrich Meinecke, *Die Idee der Staatsräson*, Munich, 1925.

surely room, it was held, to decide for the good ends and to pursue them with the least evil of the available means.

This was a philosophy of choice, then, which was bound to be ethical, over against a philosophy of necessity, in which forces beyond moral control were believed to prevail. Choice presupposes freedom to decide what goals to pursue and what means to use in accordance with one's desires and convictions. Not to follow the dictates of moral conviction becomes a matter of guilt and subject to moral judgment. Thus from Thomas More to Woodrow Wilson the recurrent topics of concern and debate were questions such as the right of self-defense and its limits, the right and duty to intervene or not to intervene in the affairs of others, or the extent to which colonial rule and territorial expansion were justified under given circumstances.

Whereas the philosophy of necessity tends to lead to resignation, irresponsibility, or even to the glorification of amorality, the philosophy of choice lends itself to excessive moralism and self-righteousness as if the leeway for choice were unlimited and were of the same dimension for all. What saved most of the theorists of England and America from the pitfalls of such excesses was the care with which they defined to themselves the limitations that the need for national self-preservation—or the duty of self-defense as they might call it—sets on the freedom of choice. Nations were not being advised to sacrifice themselves on the altar of humanity or human liberty or to set the general interest above the national interest of self-preservation. There was no inclination to forget the rules of prudence for the rules of morality, prudence that taught men to use common sense and wise judgment in deciding where the duty of self-defense deserved primacy over other duties. Prudence also meant husbanding one's means and staying within these means even in the pursuit of good causes. There was room for hypocrisy in this argument. If there is a place for moral choice only within the limits set by a prudent concern for self-preservation, it becomes tempting to interpret and thus to justify, as a means of sheer self-preservation, almost anything seemingly reprehensible that one's own country may undertake in foreign affairs. Moreover, if in order to receive moral approbation every resort to violence must be strictly a matter of self-defense, there is much incentive to accuse others of evil aggression when they use force, while justifying one's own acts as purely defensive. On the whole it will be found, however, that the moral philosophers in question, rather than posing as apologists of their nation, placed themselves in the creditable role of serving as the conscience of the nation, reminding statesmen of the dictates of justice and reason.

Also, English and American theorists were not blind to the exceptional freedom of choice which insularity gave to their respective countries. Long before there was any science of geopolitics, More, Bolingbroke, Jefferson, and others praised the privileges offered their countries by the fact of insular location. The advantage, it was suggested, lay in the freedom to remain aloof from many international struggles without a sacrifice of national security, and thus in the chance of keeping one's hands clean of many of the morally more obnoxious vicissitudes of power politics to which others were subjected.

There may be some question whether all the thinkers whose work is presented below can be said to belong to the school of thought described here as typically Anglo-American. About a Locke, Godwin, Jefferson, or Wilson there can be little doubt. They were not merely urging nations to apply the Golden Rule in the conduct of their foreign policy to the maximum compatible with a moderate, prudent policy of self-preservation—they were confident that this was the road to peace and human happiness. But what about men like Hobbes, Bacon, Bolingbroke, Hamilton, or Mahan, usually characterized as conservatives, realists, and pessimists? In many respects they will be found to have stood closer to Machiavelli than to the moralists of their own countries, and to have concurred with views of their Continental contemporaries. Bacon speaks of wars—though of just and honorable wars—as being "the true exercise to a kingdom or sovereignty"; Hobbes sees nations "in the position of gladiators one against the others"; to Bolingbroke self-love is the determining principle in international relations; and Hamilton declares harmony to be impossible "among unconnected sovereignties." The conclusions to which these men are led are not made to please those who expect "good" nations to be capable in time of eliminating the use of force from international politics except as it might be needed to stop and punish the exceptional criminal disturber of the peace.

Yet even among these representative exponents of what is now often referred to as the power political school of thought we find Bacon asserting that he would "never set politics against ethics," Hobbes maintaining that the state of nature when applied to sovereign nations allows for moderation in war and for self-restraint, Bolingbroke advising against acquisition of territory, and Hamilton agreeing with Locke that even the state of nature is "governed by moral law perceivable by reason" and advocating a foreign policy of moderation and vigilance in the exclusive service of self-preservation. Hume deserves to be mentioned as representing a middle road. He maintains that "the obligation to justice is less strong among nations than among individuals," thus suggesting a double standard of morality, one for individuals, the other for nations; but he leaves no doubt that his support of the balance of power, for example, is based on moral considerations as offering the best chance for "moderation and the preservation of the liberties of mankind."

Thus pessimists and optimists, realists and idealists, emphasize the moral aspects of political choice. While all of them take the right of national self-defense for granted, nowhere do they suggest that competition for power, conflict, struggle, or war could be regarded as signs of national health or heroism. If there is any awareness of a moral dilemma arising out of the conflicting demands of self-preservation on the one hand and the obedience to moral principle on the other, it is resolved, without apparent strain on the conscience, by reference to the analogous case of the individual who is considered morally justified in defending himself by force against external attack. This analogy is the weakest point in the argument. It fails to take into account how far more extensive and arbitrary than in the case of individuals are the claims that nations can label as self-defense. The emphasis placed on moderation and self-restraint indicates some awareness of this moral pitfall.

Moreover, for the two "island" countries external attack or invasion were unlikely contingencies most of the time, so that self-preservation in a strict sense of the term rarely came to place restrictions on the leeway they enjoyed in respect to other policy objectives. In matters of colonial expansion, for example, or of the spread of ideologies by means of intervention—often even of efforts to influence the outcome of other peoples' wars—there was much freedom to choose the road that appeared most consistent with one's scale of values. Here the door was wide open for soul-searching as well as for the exercise of wise judgment. Political theory in the Anglo-American tradition was full of such soul-searching, though the enjoyment of relative national security and an abiding confidence in reasonableness and common sense took much of the sting out of it.

It can be argued that however lofty the ideas and however noble the advice proffered to their governments by these philosophers, much of it in sharp contrast to what Machiavelli laid down in the admonitions to his

Prince, they may have been deluding themselves about their chances of being heard or about the true motives by which statesmen of their countries were actually guided. Thomas More faced up to this problem at the very start of the modern era and appears to have reached the conclusion that while sovereigns cannot be swayed by counsels of perfection, "indirect" advice by philosophers may induce them to take the path of lesser evil. His successors, at least the more realistic among them, may well have concurred with this view. After all, most of them held responsible public office themselves, if they were not leading statesmen at some period of their life. Unless they had sensed the need for guiding principles in reaching decisions and believed moral guidance no less important than advice on expediency, they would hardly have wasted so much of their energies figuring out what is right and wrong in foreign policy. In any case, their mode of approach has so molded the outlook and expectations of the peoples of the two countries that it has become in itself a powerful factor in world affairs.

Inasmuch as the English and American theorists of the past applied a philosophy of choice to both internal and external politics, they had every reason to devote attention to both and to consider them closely related. Yet the two fields of policy differ in one important respect, with a cleavage within the theory of politics remaining to be noted. Since the dawn of the modern nation-state, domestic politics, particularly in the English-speaking world, constituted a gradual and progressive evolution from absolutism to constitutional government and democracy. Theory addressed itself here to a series of problems which presented themselves consecutively in the course of this historical process and found a solution as time went on. The theory that dealt with issues such as the relative place of church and state, the separation of powers, or the rights of the individual, all-important at some period, is on the whole a matter of historical and philosophical rather than of contemporary political interest, though it may again become pertinent in the latter sense within some new context. This accounts for the practice of treating the theory of internal politics as a history of political thought with emphasis on the interdependence between specific theories and the specific conditions prevailing at successive historical periods.

No similar evolution has taken place in international politics during the same four centuries in which the nation-state underwent its internal transformation. The essential features of the multistate system and of the conduct of its members had changed little by the time Woodrow Wilson made his speeches from what they were when Thomas More wrote his *Utopia* in 1516. As a consequence, theorists contemplating the international scene have been responding throughout this period to one and the same pattern of events and addressing themselves on the whole to the same set of problems.

Because of this lack of evolutionary development there would seem to be no need to study the views of past theorists on international politics in the historical manner that is customary in matters of domestic politics. Theory here is related not to a particular period of the multistate system but to a single persistent historical situation now extending back over more than four centuries. In this sense the theorists of this entire period must be considered contemporaries. The problems of self-preservation in the light of external danger, of expansion into new territories or of contraction, of intervention in the affairs of others, of alliances, peacemaking, and the conduct of wars are as much matters of concern and controversy today as they were when a More, Hume, or Bentham put their minds to them.

This contemporaneousness has its positive as well as its negative sides. To start with the latter, the inability of nations to fashion the world according to their wishes and thus to dispose of worrisome problems once and for all has meant that the theorists cannot generally be said to have moved step by step to the discovery of solutions of ever greater perfection. There is little reason to expect here the kind of accumulation of knowledge or increasing depth of insight that characterizes other parts of political theory. Had Hume written his classic chapter on the balance of power two centuries later, it is not likely that his treatment would have appeared outdated any more than Woodrow Wilson's argument in favor of a peace without victory would have seemed strange if stated a few centuries earlier.

For the student of international politics there is a great advantage, however, in what from other angles may seem to represent sheer stagnation and a source of frustration. Even if his interests were focused exclusively on the contemporary scene and the policy problems that statesmen of his own age are facing, he could still turn with profit to the discussions of theorists of the past. Except for one significant change in external conditions which will be discussed in a moment, and with one qualification necessitated by this change, the theorists of the last four centuries looked out on the same kind of world that he does and were seeking answers to the same questions which occupy his mind today. In this sense they are his contemporaries, too. To study their views is not a diversion satisfying a purely historical or what some might consider an antiquarian interest. Any reader will find himself on familiar ground in most of the texts reproduced in this volume if only he is prepared to take a few semantic and stylistic hurdles, like translating "kings and subjects" into "decision-makers and the public," or to recognize that if, for example, the old colonialism is coming to an end, territorial expansion of control continues to present a serious problem today.

But there is one qualification to this statement which needs to be emphasized and put in the form of a warning. If it was correct to relate the peculiar outlook of the English-speaking theorists—their philosophy of moral choice—to the insular security that their countries enjoyed, the disappearance of this security in our time, now an acknowledged fact, may call for a significant modification of the traditional philosophy. The leeway for choice which the two countries enjoyed in the past has been gravely curtailed. For all practical purposes they have become "Continental" in terms of the dangers and compulsions pressing upon them from the outside. While the multistate system has remained what it was before, their place in it has radically changed. The question is how they will and should adapt to this new situation not only their foreign policy but their way of thinking.

There are two extreme ways open to them, both tempting, both dangerous. One consists in swinging over to the Continental philosophy in its most extreme form, meaning the acceptance without qualification of a philosophy of necessity. All major decisions in foreign policy would then be conceived as dictated by external circumstances beyond human control, statesmen and people alike being absolved as a consequence from all moral responsibility. With resignation, anger, or glee the old quest for moral guidance would be laid aside to give free play to expediency and the concern for power. In this case the ideas of the old theorists would come to appear no less obsolete than the former, insular policies with which they coincided; they would be condemned as naive and moralistic.

The other departure from tradition, more subtle than the first, would consist in closing one's eyes to the diminution of leeway that has taken place and to pretend that in doing under strong compulsion what was considered evil when undertaken by others was no longer evil when done by oneself. Thus if it became necessary to participate in wars in remote places, to threaten the use of force, or to build up military alliances in peace time, theory would provide the suitable moral labels, catering thereby to the sense of self-righteousness.

The lesson that can be learned from the theorists of the Anglo-American tradition points toward neither such cynicism nor such hypocrisy. As mentioned earlier, it was never suggested that national self-preservation itself should be sacrificed to moral principle. Instead, statesmen were urged to combine two basic goals: one, the primary though prudently conceived objective of self-preservation—call it the vital national security interest—the other, implied in such prudence, a fulfillment of the moral law to the maximum compatible with the primary duty of defense. If national security has come to occupy a much larger place in the policy of the two countries which have lost the advantages of insular remoteness, a break with tradition need not follow. Even now survival is not always at stake. Even now there is freedom of choice between more or less moderation, more or less concern for the interests of others, more or less effort to preserve the peace, more or less respect for justice, more or less of a sense of responsibility for the whole of mankind. In other words, there may be plenty of opportunity even now to justify the belief implicit in much of what is said in this volume that a wise interpretation and responsible pursuit of the national interest will be found to conform with the principles of morality, reasonably applied, and to the broader interests of mankind. If by the study of the theorists of the past the spirit which they expressed in happier days continues to influence Anglo-American thinking, it may prevent the adjustment which is imperative from leading to extremist theories; it may even help to keep the ship of English and American statecraft on an even keel.

1. SIR THOMAS MORE

1478-1535

SIR THOMAS MORE *was at once a great political figure and a leading English Humanist. After being removed from Oxford because of his unusual determination to learn Greek, More remained intimate with the devotees of "new learning" at the University. He was a close friend of Erasmus, who wrote his* In Praise of Folly *at More's house. In 1504, More was returned to Parliament and earned some dangerous distinction by leading the Commons' resistance to one of Henry VII's demands for a grant of money. More continued to rise in prominence as a lawyer and in 1510 became Under Sheriff of London. In 1515 he served on a trade mission to Flanders. It was on this mission that he wrote the original parts of Utopia, completing the rest on his return to England the next year. In November of that year the book was published in Latin at Louvain. Two years later he succumbed to the requests of Henry VIII and accepted a place in the King's Council. On the death of Wolsey in 1529 More became Lord Chancellor, to resign three years later because of differences with the King's settlement of the religious question. In 1535 these differences brought More to the scaffold.*

Utopia is the only one of More's writings which continues to receive much attention as political philosophy. More wrote almost all of Book II and part of Book I in Flanders. On his return to England he added the main part of Book I and a very brief conclusion for Book II.

Book I is chiefly a discussion, in the form of a dialogue between More and a fictitious person, Raphael Hythloday, as to whether a philosopher should serve as counselor to a ruler. In this connection Raphael, who has visited the island of Utopia [Nowhere] describes in blackest terms and condemns the foreign policy as well as the domestic government of contemporary Europe.

Book II contains Raphael's account of the island of Utopia. Raphael

---

The edition used is *Utopia* trans. and ed. H. V. S. Ogden, New York, Appleton-Century-Crofts, 1949.

describes in detail the domestic institutions, customs, and policies of the Utopians. According to the philosophy of the Utopians the proper purpose of a commonwealth is to secure for the whole population a life of "security and felicity." To attain corporate happiness each man must subordinate private pleasure to public interest. In particular greed and pride must be suppressed. Utopian education and institutions are designed for this purpose. It is assumed that a society can be directed into rational cooperative behavior by proper training and environment. At the heart of the system is complete community of property and absolute standardization of consumption.

Raphael then proceeds to discuss the foreign policy of Utopia and its methods of warfare. Thus both Books consider international relations. In the first More describes international politics in the Europe of his day. These politics are characterized by a furious pursuit of conquest and glory without regard to morality or the welfare of the people. Constant wars destroy all semblance even of domestic order. Distracted rulers cannot attend to their distended empires and consequently not one part of them is well governed.

The problem of the philosopher, a man of purest ideals according to Raphael, who seeks to advise a ruler, is whether he can do so without being either ineffective or corrupted. In order to illustrate the contrast between what morality demands and the actual practice of rulers, Raphael describes the way in which the King of France conducts his foreign policy, a policy of war and conquest in which the French peoples' "blood was sacrificed to their king's glory, though their peace was none the more secure." [1]

"But suppose I should go on to tell the King's council of the law of the Macarians, a people who live not far from Utopia. On the day that their king begins to reign, he must take an oath confirmed by solemn ceremonies never to have more than a thousand pounds of gold in his treasury, or the equivalent to that in silver. They say that an excellent king, who cared more for the prosperity of his country than for his own wealth, made this law as a barrier against heaping up so much treasure as to impoverish his people. He thought that sum would suffice, whether the ruler had occasion to use it against rebels or to protect the kingdom against the invasion of an enemy, but would not be enough to encourage the ruler to invade foreign countries. This last was his chief purpose in

1. *Utopia,* p. 19.

making the law. He also thought that by this provision there would not be a shortage of money for use in daily business. And when a king must distribute among the people whatever comes into his treasury above the legal amount, he will not be disposed to oppress his subjects. Such a king as this will be a terror to evil-doers and will be loved by all good men. If I should press these views on men strongly inclined to the contrary, how deaf they would be to it all!"

"Stone deaf, no doubt," I said, "and no wonder! To tell the truth, it seems to me that you should not offer advice which you know will not be considered. What good could it do? How could such a bold discourse influence men whose minds are prepossessed and deeply imbued with contrary aims? Such academic philosophy is not unpleasant among friends in free conversation, but in the King's council, where official business is being carried on, there is no room for it."

"That is what I was saying," Raphael replied. "There is no place for philosophy in the councils of princes."

"Yes, there is," I said, "but not for the speculative philosophy which thinks all things suitable for all occasions. There is another philosophy that is more urbane, that takes its proper cue and fits itself to the drama being played, acting its part aptly and well. This is the philosophy you should use. When one of Plautus's comedies is being played and the slaves are joking together, what if you should suddenly appear on the stage in a philosopher's garb and repeat Seneca's speech to Nero from the *Octavia?* Would it not be better to say nothing than to make a silly tragicomedy by mixing opposites? You ruin a play when you add irrelevant and jarring speeches, even if they are better than the play. So go through with the drama in hand as best you can, and do not spoil it because another more pleasing comes into your mind.

"So it is in a commonwealth and in the councils of princes. If evil opinions cannot be quite rooted out, and if you cannot correct habitual attitudes as you wish, you must not therefore abandon the commonwealth. Don't give up the ship in a storm, because you cannot control the winds. And do not force unheard-of advice upon people, when you know that their minds are different from yours. You must strive to guide policy indirectly, so that you make the best of things, and what you cannot turn to good, you can at least make less bad. For it is impossible to do all things well unless all men are good, and this I do not expect to see for a long time." [2]

2. *Ibid.,* pp. 22–3.

"Imagine me at the court of the King of France. Suppose I were sitting in his council with the King himself presiding, and that the wisest men were earnestly discussing by what methods and intrigues the King might keep Milan, recover Naples so often lost, then over-throw the Venetians and subdue all Italy, and add Flanders, Brabant, and even all Burgundy to his realm, besides some other nations he had planned to invade. One man urges him to make an alliance with the Venetians (to last as long as expedient), to share plans with them, and even give them some of the spoils, which can be got back when things work out according to plan. One proposes hiring German mercenaries and paying the Swiss to be neutral. Another suggests propitiating His Imperial Majesty with gold, as with a holy sacrifice. Still others think that peace should be made with the King of Aragon, and Navarre restored to him to cement the peace. Another man thinks that the Prince of Castile ought to be ensnared with the hope of an alliance, and some of his courtiers won over to the French interest with pensions. The hardest problem of all is what to do with England. A treaty of peace must be negotiated with them, as strong as possible, since a weak alliance must be bound by the strongest possible bonds. They must be called friends, but suspected as enemies, and the Scots must be kept in readiness to attack them, in case they stir ever so little. Also a banished nobleman who has pretensions to the English crown must be secretly supported (treaties prevent its being done openly), as a means of bringing pressure to bear on the English King and holding him to the treaty.

"Now in this great ferment, with so many brilliant men planning together how to carry on war, imagine so modest a man as myself standing up and urging them to change all their plans, to leave Italy alone and stay at home, since the kingdom of France is indeed greater than one man can govern well, so that he ought not to think of adding others to it. Then imagine that I should tell them about the great decree of the Achorians, who live near the island of Utopia to the southeast. Long ago these people engaged in a war to gain another kingdom for their king, who inherited an ancient claim to it through marriage. When they had conquered it, they found that keeping it was as hard as getting it. Their new subjects were always rebelling or being invaded by foreign aggressors, so that the Achorians were always at war either for them or against them, and thus could never disband their army. In the meantime taxes lay heavy on them, money went out of their kingdom and their blood was sacrificed to their king's glory, though their peace was none the more secure. Their morals were corrupted by war. Their thirst for plunder and violence became confirmed. Their laws were falling into contempt, because their king, distracted with the cares of the two kingdoms, was unable to give adequate care to either. When they saw that there would be no end of these evils, they agreed to make a humble address to their king, desiring him to choose which of the kingdoms he had the greatest mind to keep, since he could not hold them both. They were too numerous a people, they said, to be governed by half a king. A man would not even share his mule-driver with another. So this good prince was constrained to be content with his old kingdom, and give his new one to a friend (who was not long after driven out).

"Finally imagine that I told the French King's council that these wars would throw whole nations into social chaos, would exhaust the King's treasury and destroy his own people, and yet in the end through some mischance might all be fought for nothing. I would urge the King to tend his ancestral Kingdom and improve it as much as he could. He should love his people and be loved by them. He should live among them and govern them gently, and let other kingdoms alone, since his own is big enough, if not too big for him. Pray how do you think such a speech as this would be taken?"

"I admit, not very well," I said.[3]

In sharp contrast to the vile domestic and foreign policy of contemporary rulers More sets his description of Utopia. The Utopian foreign policy refuses to accept the premise that nations are "bound by no tie of nature, but were born natural enemies." [4] For this reason they do not enter into alliances or treaties which are based on the assumption that nations would attack each other unless restrained by treaties.

Whereas other nations are continually making alliances, breaking them, and then renewing them, the Utopians make no alliances with any nation. If nature, they say, will not make man friendly with man, will an alliance do so? Will a man who scorns nature respect mere words? They have been confirmed in this view all the more, because among neighboring nations the alliances and pacts of princes are usually so carelessly observed.

In Europe, especially where the Christian religion prevails, treaty agreements are sacred and inviolable. This is partly owing to the justice and goodness of princes, and partly owing to the reverence and fear they feel toward the popes, who themselves observe their agreements

3. *Ibid.*, pp. 18–20.
4. *Ibid.*, p. 63.

very religiously. The popes order all other chiefs of state to abide by their promises, even bringing pressure upon evaders by pontifical censure. And the popes rightly point out that it would be most ignominious if men who are specifically called "the faithful" were faithless to their treaties.

But in this new world, which is as far from us in distance as our customs are different from theirs, no confidence is put in alliances, even though they are contracted with the most sacred ceremonies. The greater the formalities, the sooner the treaty may be dissolved by twisting the words, which are often purposely ambiguous. A treaty can never be bound with chains so strong, but that a government can somehow evade it and thereby break both the treaty and its faith. If statesmen found such craftiness and fraud in the contracts of business men, they would scornfully brand them as sacrilegious and worthy of the gallows. These very statesmen, however, take pride in giving just such counsel to princes. Thus justice seems to be a low and humble virtue, one which dwells far beneath the high dignity of kings. Or there may be two kinds of justice, one the people's justice, mean, lowly, bound by fetters on every side so that it cannot jump the fences, the other the justice of princes, which is more majestic and so much freer than the other that it may take whatever it wants.

This practice of keeping treaties so badly is the reason why the Utopians made no alliances. They might indeed change their minds if they lived here. However, they think it a bad custom to make treaties at all, even if they are well observed. To do so makes it seem as if men who are separated by only a hill or a river were bound by no tie of nature, but were born natural enemies and therefore rightly attacked each other unless restrained by treaties. Moreover they see that these alliances do not cement friendship; the two countries still have licence to prey upon each other, unless sufficient caution is used in making the treaty to see that there is no loophole in the wording. The Utopians' view is that no man should be esteemed an enemy if he has done no injury, that the fellowship of nature among men serves instead of a treaty, and that men are bound more adequately by good will than by pacts, more strongly by their hearts than by their words.[5]

The Utopians detest war and particularly repudiate the notion that there is anything noble about fighting. Yet they keep themselves in a state of constant preparedness and will fight what they consider just wars. Of these More lists five:

5. *Ibid.*, pp. 62–3.

*1. Wars to defend their territory. If they believe an enemy is mount-
ing an attack against them, the Utopians do not meekly await the onset
but "at once attack him in strength outside their own territory."* [6]

2. Wars in defense of their friends, if an enemy invades their territory.

*3. Wars to avenge injury to their friends; if consulted the Utopians
will fight "against the aggressor."* [7]

4. Wars to help "some of their neighbors gain freedom from tyrants." [8]

*5. Wars for what the Utopians count as "a very just cause of war,"
namely to conquer territory which others hold "idle and uncultivated"* [9]
while the Utopians have more people than their land can support.

They hate and detest war as a thing manifestly brutal, and yet prac-
ticed by man more constantly than by any kind of beast. Contrary to
almost all other peoples they consider nothing so inglorious as the glory
won in war. Nevertheless both the men and the women of Utopia
regularly practice military exercises on certain days, so that they will
be prepared when the need arises. They go to war cautiously and reluctantly, only to protect their own territory or that of their friends if an
enemy has invaded it, or to free some wretched people from tyrannous
oppression and servitude. They help their friends not only in defense,
but also to avenge injuries. They do this only if they are consulted in
the whole affair, if the facts are proved, and if the stolen plunder is
not returned. Then they think they should wage war against the aggressor. They decide on this policy when booty is taken from their
friends by force or when the merchants of one country are oppressed
in another country by unjust laws or by twisting good laws. This they
think is a greater evil than direct attack. . . . .

If the Utopians themselves are cheated in this way, they carry their
anger only to the point of cutting off trade with that country, provided
no bodily injury is done. Not that they care less for their own citizens
than for their neighbors, but they think it worse for their neighbors'
property to be seized than their own. The neighbors' merchants suffer a
great injury because they lose their own property but the Utopians
think little of their loss, for only common goods have been lost. Besides
whatever is exported must be in superfluous abundance at home, or it
would not be shipped out. So they think it cruel to avenge a relatively
unimportant loss by killing many men, whose death would only affect

6. *Ibid.*, p. 70.
7. *Ibid.*, p. 63.
8. *Ibid.*, p. 61.
9. *Ibid.*, p. 38.

the lives and livelihood of others. But if any Utopian citizens are un-justly hurt or killed, whether by private or public policy, they send envoys demanding that the guilty persons be handed over to them. If that is refused, they declare war. If the guilty men are given up, their punishment is death or bondage.[10]

If there is too great an increase throughout the entire island, they take a certain number of citizens from the different cities and plant a colony on the adjoining mainland, where the inhabitants still have more land than they can well cultivate. If the natives wish to live with the Utopians, they are taken in. Since they join the colony willingly, they quickly adopt the same institutions and customs. This is advantageous for both peoples. For by their policies and practices the Utopians make the land yield an abundance for all, which before seemed too small and barren for the natives alone. If the natives will not conform to their laws, they drive them out of the area they claim for themselves, waging war if they meet resistance. Indeed they account it a very just cause of war if a people possess land that they leave idle and uncultivated and refuse the use and occupancy of it to others who according to the law of nature ought to be supported from it.

If the population of any of their cities happens to decline so much that it cannot be made good from other parts of the island without reducing the size of the other cities too much, then the population is built up with citizens from the colonies. This has happened only twice in all their history, both times the result of a devastating plague. They prefer their colonies to die off rather than allow any of their island cities to grow too small.[11]

In the conduct of war the Utopians do all they can to reduce its destructive effects, especially on their own nation. They make subsidies to their friends and hire mercenaries so as to withold their own troops from battle. They limit their objectives to correcting the immediate causes of the war. Moreover they try to reduce bloodshed by making use of subversion and propaganda. There has been much dispute as to whether More really approved these tactics. The greater weight of evidence seems to justify taking this part of Utopia *at its face value. It is worth noting that in another part of* Utopia *More declared, "nothing in the world can be of equal value with a man's life."* [12]

10. *Ibid.*, pp. 63–4.
11. *Ibid.*, pp. 37–8.
12. *Ibid.*, p. 12.

The Utopians are troubled and ashamed when they gain a bloody victory, like merchants who have paid too high a price for what they have bought. If they overwhelm the enemy by skill and cunning, they exult and celebrate a public triumph, and erect a memorial for a victory efficiently won. When they win a victory by the strength of understanding (as only men can), they pride themselves on acting bravely and manfully. Bears, lions, boars, wolves, dogs, and other wild beasts fight with their bodies, and many of them surpass us in strength and ferocity as much as we surpass them in understanding and reason.

The Utopians have this one aim in war, to accomplish what they would gladly have achieved without war if just terms had been granted in time. Or if that cannot be done, they aim to exact so severe a revenge from those that have injured them that they will be afraid to do it again. Their policies are directed to these ends, which they strive toward in such a way as to avoid danger rather than to attain glory and fame.

As soon as war is declared, they at once arrange to have many small notices, which are marked with their official seal, set up by stealth in the most conspicuous places in the enemy's country. In these proclamations they promise great rewards to any one who will kill the enemy's king, and smaller rewards (but still very great) for killing those whom they regard as most responsible after the king for plotting aggression against them. They double the reward for anyone who brings in the proscribed man alive. Also they offer like rewards, as well as exemption from punishment, to any of the proscribed men who turn against their countrymen. As a result the proscribed men soon suspect everyone, distrust each other, and become distracted by their danger. . . . Though this manner of waging war by bidding for and buying enemies may seem like the cruel villainy of an ignoble mind, it is considered by the Utopians as a wise and praiseworthy policy, since it enables them to wage great wars without any battle at all. They even think themselves humane and merciful, because by the death of a few bad men they spare the lives of many innocent men who would otherwise die in battle, some fighting on their own side, some on the enemy's. Indeed they pity the mass of enemy soldiers no less than their own, for they know that they do not fight willingly, but are driven to it by the madness of their rulers.

If this method does not succeed, they sow the seeds of discord among the enemy by inciting the king's brother or some member of the nobility to plot for the crown. If these internal factions languish, then they arouse the neighboring people against the enemy and induce them to revive some old claims, such as kings never lack. . . . . .

If possible they use only their mercenaries and so avoid sending their own citizens to battle. When this is impossible and they must take part in the fighting themselves, they join battle with a boldness as great as their prudence in avoiding it. . . . They are free from the cares which often weaken noble spirits. Their own security at home and their confidence in their children's welfare make them stout-hearted and too proud to be conquered. Moreover their skill in warfare increases their valor, and the sound ideas instilled into them in childhood by instruction and the wise institutions of their commonwealth add to their courage. They do not hold life so cheap that they waste it, nor do they hold it so dear that they avidly and shamefully grasp it when duty bids them give it up. . . .

When they win a battle, they are more ready to take prisoners than to make a great slaughter. . . . . .

When the Utopians agree to a truce, they observe it so religiously that they will not violate it even though provoked. They do not lay waste the enemy's country nor burn his grain. In their marches they take care that neither the men nor the horses trample down the grain, for they may need it themselves. They attack no man who is disarmed unless he is a spy. When cities are surrendered, they take them under their protection. If they carry a place by storm, they do not plunder it, but kill those who opposed the surrender and reduce the rest of the garrison to bondage, leaving the inhabitants unharmed. If the Utopians find any of the inhabitants who recommended surrender, they share with them part of the property of those who have been condemned, and then divide the rest among the auxiliary troops. None of the Utopians themselves want any of the spoils.

When a war is ended, they charge the cost to the conquered, not to the friends for whom they undertook it.[13]

13. *Ibid.*, pp. 64–9.

2. FRANCIS BACON

1561-1626

FRANCIS BACON *had two interests in life which he was never wholly successful in reconciling. He aimed at and achieved eminence in politics and he sought to establish a new system of learning on what he considered sound foundations. As the son of the Lord Keeper and the nephew of Lord Burghley, Bacon was in a position to beg favors at court, a practice he never abandoned. He became an eminent lawyer and eventually Lord Chancellor of England. His career ended in disgrace in 1621, when he was impeached and convicted of corruption for practices which were quite normal in his day but which were used as a lever by his enemies.*

As a scholar Bacon devoted himself to a reform of the educational system. He wanted to establish a unified science to explain all of nature. Despite the scholastic flavor of this idea Bacon was a "modern" thinker who subscribed to a thoroughgoing naturalism. He believed in the divorce of revealed theology and philosophy. His method of study was that of extensive observation and experiment, to the results of which he applied an improved inductive method of his own invention. Following these methods he arrived at some remarkably advanced ideas, reducing matter to terms of space-time and correctly divining that the phenomenon of heat was caused by rapidly moving particles. There were serious flaws in his technique, but he is undoubtedly an eminent figure in the development of modern scientific method.

Bacon conceived of learning as the basis for practical operations useful to mankind. This desire for usefulness pervaded his political writings, which were largely concerned with practical statecraft. He

The editions used are *The Works of Francis Bacon,* ed. James Spedding, R. L. Ellis and D. D. Heath, 14 vols. London, Longman and Company, 1857–74; *The Letters and the Life of Francis Bacon,* ed. James Spedding, 7 vols. London, Longman, Green, Longman and Roberts, 1861–74.

believed that political success could be achieved by careful study of political conditions. In Bacon's day England was combatting a powerful Spain, meeting the Armada, and painfully struggling to her position of naval supremacy. It was not surprising that Bacon should have shared the widespread interest in foreign affairs. This interest was aroused when his father, who had once designed a college for diplomats, sent him as secretary to Sir William Paulet, Ambassador to France. In that period of strife and under the influence of the Ambassador, a shrewd and ruthless diplomatist, Bacon was impressed by the elements of struggle in international affairs. On his return to England he kept up his interest in foreign policy and was at one time an important link in Elizabeth's elaborate foreign intelligence service.

Bacon saw man as "full of savage and unreclaimed desires, of profit, of lust, of revenge." Men often restrain these impulses and "give ear to precepts, to laws, to religion." But at other times these restraints prove inadequate and "all things dissolve into anarchy and confusion." [1] *Bacon applied this view to international relations and put little faith in treaties. Such instruments were only reliable when they truly reflected power relationships. He therefore believed that a state could only achieve security by being powerful, and that a general peace could only be preserved by a balance of power.*

. . . Whatever be the solemnity and sanctity of the oath they [treaties] are confirmed with, yet they are little to be depended on; insomuch that they are used in fact rather with an eye to reputation and fame and ceremony, than for confidence and security and effect. And even when the ties of relationship (which are as the sacraments of nature) or of mutual good services come in to aid, yet in most cases all are too weak for ambition and interest and the licence of power: the rather because princes can always find plenty of plausible pretexts (not being accountable to any arbiter) wherewith to justify and veil their cupidity and bad faith. There is adopted therefore but one true and proper pledge of faith; and it is not any celestial divinity. This is Necessity (the great god of the powerful), and peril of state, and communion of interest. Now Necessity is elegantly represented under the figure of Styx; the fatal river across which no man can return. This is the deity which Iphicrates the Athenian invoked to witness treaties; and since he was one that spoke out plainly what most men think and keep to themselves, his words are worth quoting. Finding that the Lacedaemonians were

1. "The Advancement of Learning," *Works*, 3, 302.

devising and propounding various cautions and sanctions and securities and bonds to hold the treaty fast, *There is only one bond and security* (said he, interrupting them) *that can hold between you and us:—you must prove that you have yielded so much into our hands that you cannot hurt us if you would.* And so it is that if the means of hurting be taken away, or if a breach of the treaty would endanger the existence or the integrity of the state and revenue,—then the treaty may be considered to be ratified and sanctioned and confirmed as by the oath of Styx: for then it is upon peril of being interdicted from the banquets of the gods; which was the ancient expression for the rights and prerogatives of empire, and wealth, and felicity.[2]

Kings have to deal with their neighbours, their wives, their children, their prelates or clergy, their nobles, their second-nobles or gentlemen, their merchants, their commons, and their men of war; and from all these arise dangers, if care and circumspection be not used.

First for their neighbours; there can no general rule be given (the occasions are so variable,) save one, which ever holdeth; which is, that princes do keep due sentinel, that none of their neighbours do overgrow so (by increase of territory, by embracing of trade, by approaches, or the like), as they become more able to annoy them than they were. And this is generally the work of standing counsels to foresee and to hinder it. During that triumvirate of kings, King Henry the Eighth of England, Francis the First King of France, and Charles the Fifth Emperor, there was such a watch kept, that none of the three could win a palm of ground, but the other two would straightways balance it, either by confederation, or, if need were, by a war; and would not in any wise take up peace at interest.[3]

Bacon regarded it as quite natural that a state would pursue its own power interests and that war would be a normal instrument of policy. He did not, however, renounce all self-restraint in foreign affairs. Princes, he said, should "preserve . . . sacred and inviolate . . . the life and good name each of other. For the wars are no massacres and confusions; but they are the highest trials of right . . ." [4] He distinguished wars which were necessary to the preservation of the state from "ambitious predatory wars." Some wars were just and others unjust. Just wars were those which were defensive. Bacon used the word

2. "Of the Wisdom of the Ancients," *Works*, 6, 706–7.
3. "The Essays or Counsels, Civil and Moral," *Works*, 6, 420.
4. "Observations on a Libel," *Works*, 8, 146.

defensive broadly and applied it to preventive war—a concept he propounded at length. He opposed intervention in the internal affairs of other nations and, in keeping with his efforts to promote a religious settlement in England, he frowned upon wars to propagate religion.

Apparently Bacon condemned unjust wars for two reasons. In the first place he objected to the injustice itself. He declared he would "never set politics against ethics." [5] A good end could never justify bad means, for the evil of the means was certain, the good of the end, speculative. Secondly, he seems to have believed that an unjust war was inexpedient because the people would not support a war without at least a "specious"—that is, a credible—justification. But though he rejected the idea that foreign policy should be designed on the theory that might makes right he maintained that, to be successful, a state must be highly suspicious of others and quick to resent any threat to its security. To appeasement, which he frequently called "peace at interest," he was unalterably opposed.

Wars (I speak not of ambitious predatory wars) are suits of appeal to the tribunal of God's justice, where there are no superiors on earth to determine the cause: and they are (as civil pleas are) plaints or defences. . . . wars preventive upon just fears are true defensives, as well as upon actual invasions: and again . . . wars defensive for religion (I speak not of rebellions) are most just; though offensive wars for religion are seldom to be approved, or never, unless they have some mixture of civil titles. . . .

Concerning the . . . "proposition [that a just fear (without an actual invasion or offence) is a sufficient ground of a war, and in the nature of a true defensive]" it is good to hear what time saith. Thucydides, in his inducement to his story of the great war of Peloponnesus, sets down in plain terms, that the true cause of that war was *the overgrowing greatness of the Athenians, and the fear that the Lacedaemonians stood in thereby;* and doth not doubt to call it *a necessity imposed upon the Lacedaemonians of a war;* which are the very words of a mere defensive: adding, that the other causes were but specious and popular. . . . "The truest cause of this war, though least voiced, I conceive to have been this; that the Athenians, being grown great, to the terror of the Lacedaemonians, did impose upon them a necessity of a war; but the causes that went abroad in speech were these," etc.

Sulpitius Galba, consul, when he persuaded the Romans to a preven-

5. "Considerations Touching a War with Spain," *Letters,* 7, 478.

tive war with the latter Philip King of Macedon, in regard of the great preparations which Philip had then on foot, and his designs to ruin some of the confederates of the Romans, confidently saith, that they who took that for an offensive war understood not the state of the question. . . . "Ye seem to me (ye Romans) not to understand, that the consultation before you is not, whether you shall have war or peace (for Philip will take order you shall be no choosers, who prepareth a mighty war both by land and sea), but whether you shall transport the war into Macedon, or receive it into Italy." . . . .

Clinias the Candian (in Plato) speaks desperately and wildly, as if there were no such thing as peace between nations; but that every nation expects but his advantage to war upon another. But yet in that excess of speech there is much that may have a civil construction; namely, that every state ought to stand upon his guard, and rather prevent than be prevented. His words are . . . "That which men for the most part call peace, is but a naked and empty name; but the truth is, that there is ever between all estates a secret war." I know well this speech is the objection and not the decision, and that it is after refuted; but yet (as I said before) it bears thus much of truth, that if that general malignity and predisposition to war (which he untruly figureth to be in all nations) be produced and extended to a just fear of being oppressed, then it is no more a true peace, but a name of a peace.

As for the opinion of Iphicrates the Athenian, it demands not so much towards a war as a just fear, but rather cometh near the opinion of Clinias; as if there were ever amongst nations a brooding of a war, and that there is no sure league but impuissance to do hurt. For he, in the treaty of peace with the Lacedaemonians, speaketh plain language; telling them, there could be no true and secure peace, except the Lacedaemonians yielded to those things, which being granted, it would be no longer in their power to hurt the Athenians, though they would. And to say truth, if one mark it well, this was in all memory the main piece of wisdom in strong and prudent counsels, to be in perpetual watch that the states about them should neither by approach nor by increase of dominion, nor by ruining confederates, nor by blocking of trade, nor by any the like means, have it in their power to hurt or annoy the states they serve: and whensoever any such cause did but appear, straightways to buy it out with a war, and never to take up peace at credit and upon interest. It is so memorable, as it is yet as fresh as if it were done yesterday, how that triumvirate of kings, Henry the eighth of England, Francis the first of France, and Charles the fifth, Emperor and king of Spain, were in their times so provident, as scarce a palm of ground could be gotten by either of the three, but that the other two would be sure to do their best to set the balance of Europe upright again. And the like diligence was used in the age before by that league . . . which was contracted between Ferdinando King of Naples, Lorenzo of Medici Potentate of Florence, and Lodovico Sforza Duke of Milan, designed chiefly against the growing power of the Venetians; but yet so, as the confederates had a perpetual eye one upon another, that none of them should overtop.

To conclude therefore; howsoever some schoolmen (otherwise reverend men, yet fitter to guide penknives than swords) seem precisely to stand upon it, that every offensive war must be *ultio;* a revenge, that presupposeth a precedent assault or injury; yet neither do they descend to this point (which we now handle) of a just fear; neither are they of authority to judge this question against all the precedents of time. For certainly, as long as men are men . . . and as long as reason is reason, a just fear will be a just cause of a preventive war; but especially if it be part of the case that there be a nation that is manifestly detected to aspire to monarchy and new acquests, then other states (assuredly) cannot be justly accused for not staying for the first blow, or for not accepting Polyphemus' courtesy, to be the last that shall be eaten up.[6]

Incident to this point is for a state to have those laws or customs which may reach forth unto them just occasions or at least pretexts for making war. For there is that justice imprinted in the nature of men, that they enter not upon wars (whereof so many calamities do ensue), but upon some weighty, at the least specious, grounds and quarrels. The Turk has at hand for the cause of war the propagation of his law or sect; a quarrel that he may always command. The Romans, though they esteemed the extending the limits of their empire to be great honour to their generals when it was done, yet they never rested upon that alone to begin a war. First therefore, let nations that pretend to greatness have this, that they be quickly sensible of wrongs, either upon borderers, merchants, or public ministers; and that they sit not too long upon a provocation. Secondly, let them be prompt and ready to give aids and succours to their confederates and allies, as it ever was with the Romans; insomuch, as if the confederate had leagues defensive with divers other states, and upon invasion offered did implore their aids severally, yet the Romans would ever be the foremost and leave

6. *Ibid.,* pp. 470–7.

it to none other to have the honour. As for the wars which were anciently made on the behalf of a kind of party or tacit conformity of estate, I do not see how they may be well justified; as when the Romans made a war for the liberty of Greece; or when the Lacedaemonians and Athenians made wars, to set up or pull down democracies and oligarchies; or when wars were made by commonwealths and princes, under the pretence of justice or protection, to deliver the subjects of others from tyranny and oppression, and the like. Let it suffice for the present, that no estate expect to be great that is not awake upon any just occasion of arming.[7]

The emphasis which Bacon laid on national power led him to analyze its elements. He thought this analysis essential because the power of nations was frequently misjudged. Perhaps because he looked at the world from a small, embattled England, Bacon listed national courage, strategic location, and sea power as the prime factors in national strength. He urged that the national spirit be kept up by wise government, avoiding overtaxation and any oppression of the rank and file, and promoting an interest in military affairs. As for sea power, he referred both to its defensive advantages, which secure the homeland and permit a nation "to take as much or as little of the war" as it wishes, and to its offensive potentiality for commanding commerce and colonies. Consistent with his minimization of territory as a power factor, Bacon approved of colonies only if kept strictly proportionate to the mother country's ability to control them.

The greatness of kingdoms and dominions in bulk and territory doth fall under measure and demonstration that cannot err: but the just measure and estimate of the forces and power of an estate is a matter than the which there is nothing among civil affairs more subject to error, nor that error more subject to perilous consequences. For hence may proceed many inconsiderate attempts and insolent provocations in states that have too high an imagination of their own forces: and hence may proceed, on the other side, a toleration of many grievances and indignities, and a loss of many fair opportunities, in states that are not sensible enough of their own strength . . . I have thought good, as far as I can comprehend, to make a true survey and representation of the greatness of this your kingdom of Britain. . . . first by confuting the errors or rather correcting the excess of certain immoderate opinions, which ascribe too much to some points of greatness which are not so

7. "De Augmentis Scientiarum," *Works,* 5, 85–6.

essential, and by reducing those points to a true value and estimation: then by propounding and confirming those other points of greatness which are more solid and principal, though in popular discourse less observed . . .

Of these the former part . . . (branches) into these articles:

First, That in the measuring or balancing of greatness, there is commonly too much ascribed to largeness of territory.

Secondly, That there is too much ascribed to treasure or riches.

Thirdly, That there is too much ascribed to the fruitfulness of the soil, or affluence of commodities.

And fourthly, That there is too much ascribed to the strength and fortification of towns or holds.

The latter will fall into this distribution:

First, That true greatness doth require a fit situation of the place or region.

Secondly, That true greatness consisteth essentially in population and breed of men.

Thirdly, That it consisteth also in the valour and military disposition of the people it breedeth: and in this, that they make profession of arms.

Fourthly, That it consisteth in this point, that every common subject by the poll be fit to make a soldier, and not only certain conditions or degrees of men.

Fifthly, That it consisteth in the temper of the government fit to keep subjects in heart and courage, and not to keep them in the condition of servile vassals.

And Sixthly, That it consisteth in the commandment of the sea.

And let no man so much forget the subject propounded, as to find strange that there is no mention of religion, laws, policy. For we speak of that which is proper to the amplitude and growth of states, and not of that which is common to their preservation, happiness, and all other points of well-being.[8]

. . . let us consider . . . what is the true greatness of kingdoms and states and how it can be obtained. It is a subject indeed fit for princes to have ever in their hands and carefully to consider; to the end that neither by over-measuring their forces they may engage in vain enterprises beyond their power; nor on the other hand by undervaluing them they may demean themselves to timid and pusillanimous counsels.

8. "Of the True Greatness of the Kingdom of Britain," *Works*, 7, 47–9. Italics omitted.

The greatness of an empire as regards its size and territory falls under measure; as regards its revenue under computation. The number of the population may be taken by a census; the number and greatness of cities and towns by maps and surveys. But yet there is nothing among civil affairs more subject to error than the forming a true and right valuation of the power and forces of an empire. The kingdom of heaven is likened not to an acorn or any larger nut, but to a grain of mustard seed; which is the smallest of all seeds, but yet has within itself a certain property and spirit hastily to get up and spread. So there are some kingdoms and states very great in extent of territory, and yet not apt to enlarge or command; and some that have but a small dimension of stem, and yet are apt to be the foundations of great monarchies.

Walled towns, stored arsenals and armouries, goodly races of horse, chariots of war, elephants, ordnance, artillery, and the like; all this is but a sheep in a lion's skin, except the breed and disposition of the people be stout and warlike. Nay, number itself in armies is not much advantage, where the people are of weak courage; for, as Virgil says, it never troubles the wolf how many the sheep be. . . . Many are the examples of the great odds between number and courage; so that it may be set down as a sure and tried rule, that the principal point of greatness in any state is that the people itself be by race and disposition warlike. Neither is money the sinews of war, as it is trivially said, where the sinews of men's arms in base and effeminate people are failing. For Solon said well to Croesus, when in ostentation he showed him his gold, "Sir, if any other come that has better iron than you, he will be master of all this gold." Therefore let any prince or state think soberly of his forces, except his militia of natives be of good and valiant soldiers. And let princes, on the other side, who have subjects of martial disposition, know their own strength, unless they be otherwise wanting unto themselves. As for mercenary forces, (which is the usual help in this case,) all examples show, that whatsoever state or prince rests upon them, he may spread his feathers for a time, but he will mew them soon after.

The blessing of Judah and Issachar will never meet; that the same people or nation should be both the lion's whelp, and the ass between burdens. Neither will it be that a people over-laid with taxes should ever become valiant and martial. It is true that taxes levied by consent of the state do abate men's courage less; as it has been seen notably in the excises of the Low Countries; and, in some degree, in the subsidies of England. For you must note, that we speak now of the heart and not of the purse. So that although the same tribute and tax, laid by consent or by imposing, be all one to the purse, yet it works differently upon the courage. So that you may conclude that no people over-charged with tribute is fit for empire. . . . .

By all means it is to be looked to, that the trunk of Nebuchadnezzar's tree of monarchy be great enough to bear the branches and the boughs; that is, that the natural subjects of the crown or state bear a sufficient proportion to the stranger subjects that they govern. Therefore all states that are liberal of naturalization towards strangers are fit for empire. For to think that an handful of people can, with the greatest courage and policy in the world, embrace too large extent of dominion, it may hold for a time, but it will fail suddenly. The Spartans were a difficult and jealous people in point of naturalization; whereby, while they kept their compass, they stood firm; but when they did spread, and their boughs were become too great for their stem, they became a windfall upon the sudden. Never was any state in this point so open to receive strangers into their body as were the Romans; therefore it sorted with them accordingly, for they grew to the greatest monarchy. Their manner was to grant naturalization, which they called the right of citizenship, and to grant it in the highest degree, that is, not only the right of commerce, the right of marriage, the right of inheritance; but also, the right of voting, and the right of bearing office; and this not to single persons alone, but likewise to whole families; yea, to cities, and sometimes to nations. Add to this their custom of plantation of colonies, whereby the Roman plant was removed into the soil of other nations: and putting both constitutions together, you will say, that it was not the Romans that spread upon the world, but it was the world that spread upon the Romans: and that was the surest way of greatness. . . . .

No body can be healthful without exercise, neither natural body nor politic; and certainly to a kingdom or state a just and honourable war is the true exercise. A civil war indeed is like the heat of a fever; but a foreign war is like the heat of exercise, and serves most of all to keep the body in health. For in a slothful peace both courage will effeminate and manners corrupt. But howsoever it be for happiness, without all question for greatness, it makes to be still for the most part in arms; and the strength of a veteran army (though it be doubtless a costly business), always on foot, is that which commonly gives the law, or at least the reputation amongst all neighbour states, as may be well seen in Spain; which has had, in one part or other, a veteran army almost continually, now by the space of six-score years.

To be master of the sea, is an abridgment of a monarchy. Cicero writing to Atticus of Pompey's preparation against Caesar, says, "Pom-

pey's counsel is plainly that of Themistocles, for he thinks that whoever is master of the sea is master of the empire." And without doubt
Pompey had tired out and reduced Caesar, if upon vain confidence he
had not left that way. We see the great effects of battles by sea from
many instances. The battle of Actium decided the empire of the world.
The battle of Lepanto arrested the greatness of the Turk. There be
certainly many examples where seafights have put an end to the war;
but this is, when princes or states have risked their whole fortune upon
the battles. But thus much is certain, that he that commands the sea
is at great liberty, and may take as much and as little of the war as he
will; whereas those that be strongest by land are many times nevertheless in great straits. Surely at this day with us of Europe the advantage
of strength at sea (which is one of the principal dowries of this kingdom of Great Britain) is great; both because most of the kingdoms of
Europe are not merely inland, but girt with the sea most part of their
compass; and because the wealth and treasures of both Indies seem in
great part but an accessory to the command of the sea. . . . . .

To conclude: no man can, by taking thought, as the Scripture saith,
"add one cubit to his stature" in this little model of a man's body; but in
the great frame of kingdoms and commonwealths it is in the power of
princes or states to add amplitude and greatness to their kingdoms.
For by wisely introducing such ordinances, constitutions, and customs,
as we have now touched, and others like them they may sow greatness
to their posterity and succession. But these counsels are commonly not
observed, but left to take their chance.[9]

Upon the breaking and shivering of a great state and empire, you
may be sure to have wars. For great empires, while they stand, do
enervate and destroy the forces of the natives which they have subdued,
resting upon their own protecting forces; and then when they fail also,
all goes to ruin, and they become a prey. So was it in the decay of the
Roman empire; and likewise in the empire of Almaigne, after Charles the
Great, every bird taking a feather; and were not unlike to befal to Spain,
if it should break. The great accessions and unions of kingdoms do
likewise stir up wars: for when a state grows to an over-power, it is
like a great flood, that will be sure to overflow. . . . Look when the
world hath fewest barbarous peoples, but such as commonly will not
marry or generate, except they know means to live, (as it is almost everywhere at this day, except Tartary,) there is no danger of inundations

9. "De Augmentis," Works, 5, 80–7.

of people: but when there be great shoals of people, which go on to populate, without foreseeing means of life and sustentation, it is of necessity that once in an age or two they discharge a portion of their people upon other nations; which the ancient northern people were wont to do by lot; casting lots what part should stay at home, and what should seek their fortunes. When a warlike state grows soft and effeminate, they may be sure of a war. For commonly such states have grown rich in the time of their degenerating; and so the prey inviteth, and their decay in valour encourageth a war.[10]

Bacon summed up his advice on international conflict in a parable based on the story of Perseus. In this parable can be found his precepts of foresight and preparedness, his insistence on a just cause capable of arousing enthusiasm and his argument in favor of a careful estimate of relative power. He also advises certain additional policies, including secrecy, speed, unity of command, espionage and subversion.

Perseus, an Eastern man, was sent, it is said, by Pallas to destroy Medusa, who was a grievous plague to many nations of the West in the furthest parts of Spain. She was a monster, otherwise huge and savage, and of an aspect so foul and hideous that her look alone turned men into stones. Now Medusa was one of the Gorgons, and the only mortal amongst them, the others not being subject to death. Perseus then, equipping himself for so noble an enterprise, borrowed arms as presents from three of the gods; from Mercury wings,—fitted to the ankles, not the shoulders; from Pluto a helmet; from Pallas a shield and mirror. Nevertheless (though he was now so well furnished) he did not go direct to Medusa, but turned aside to the Grææ. These were the half-sisters of the Gorgons; and were grey-headed from their birth, and like old women. They had but one eye and one tooth among them all; which, as they had occasion to go abroad, each wore by turns and put off again when she came back. This eye and this tooth they lent to Perseus. And now judging himself sufficiently armed to effect his purpose, he went against Medusa with all haste, flying. Her he found sleeping; but not daring to meet her gaze (in case she should wake), he turned his face away, and looking into the mirror of Pallas to direct his blow, cut off her head. From her blood spilt upon the ground immediately sprang forth Pegasus the winged horse. But the severed head Perseus transferred to the shield of Pallas, and fixed it there; where it

10. "The Essays or Counsels, Civil and Moral," *Works,* 6, 515–16.

still retained its former virtue, that whoever gazed upon it became as it were thunder or planet struck.

This fable seems to have been devised with reference to method and prudence in making war. And first, the undertaking of every war ought to be as a mission from Pallas; not from Venus (as the Trojan war was), or for any other slight motive; for resolutions respecting wars ought to be based on solid counsels. Secondly, with regard to the kind of war to be chosen, the fable propounds three very wholesome and important precepts. The first is, not to make too great a point of subjugating the neighbouring nations. For the method of enlarging a patrimony and an empire is not the same. In private estates contiguity of lands is taken into account, but in the extension of empire, occasion and facility for making war and fruit of conquest ought to be regarded in place of contiguity. . . . The second precept is, that there must be a cause of war, just, pious, honourable, and popular. For this begets alacrity as well in the soldiers, as in those who provide the funds, opens the way to alliances, and conciliates friends, and has many other advantages. Now among the causes of war few are more popular than the putting down of tyrannies, beneath whose yoke the spirit and energy of the people are worn down and prostrated, as by the head of Medusa; a thing which gained Hercules divine honours. Certainly the Romans made it a great point of duty to hasten with all speed to succour their allies when in any way attacked. Wars also undertaken for a just revenge have almost always been successful; as the war against Brutus and Cassius to avenge the murder of Caesar; of Severus to avenge the death of Pertinax; of Junius Brutus to avenge the death of Lucretia. In a word, whosoever either relieves or avenges by war the calamities and injuries of men, bears arms under Perseus. The third precept is, that in every war a true estimate of strength must be taken, and it must be duly considered whether the war be such as can be carried through and brought to an issue; so that one may not engage in pursuit of vast and boundless projects. For of the Gorgons (which are the representatives of wars) Perseus wisely chose her alone who was of mortal nature, nor did he attempt impossibilities. Such then is the advice which the fable gives touching the things that require deliberation in undertaking war; the rest relate to the carrying it on.

In war those three gifts of the gods are of all things the most important; insomuch that they commonly command and carry with them fortune itself. For Perseus received speed from Mercury, secrecy of counsels from Orcus, and foresight from Pallas. And it is not without allegory, and that of the wisest sort, that those wings of speed (seeing speed is of much avail in war) were attached to the feet and not to the shoulders; because celerity is required not so much in the first onsets of war as in the pursuit and following up thereof. For no error in war is more common than this, that the prosecutions and subsidiary actions correspond not to the energy of the first commencements. And the helmet of Pluto (which used to render men invisible) is a manifest parable. For next to speed in war secrecy of counsels is of the greatest moment; of which indeed speed itself is a great part; for speed anticipates the disclosures of counsels. To the helmet of Pluto belongs also this: that there should be one commander in a war, with free instructions; for consultations held with many savour more of the crests of Mars than the helmet of Pluto. Variety of pretexts, ambiguous directions, rumours spread abroad, which either blind or avert men's eyes and involve the real designs in obscurity, refer to the same. So also diligent and suspicious precautions respecting despatches, ambassadors, deserters, and many like matters, are wreathed round the helmet of Pluto. But it is of no less importance to discover the counsels of the enemy than to conceal our own. To the helmet of Pluto therefore must be added the mirror of Pallas, whereby to discern the strength or weakness of the enemy, their secret partisans, their discords and factions, their movements and designs. But since there is so much of chance in war, that no great confidence can be placed either in discovering the designs of the enemy, or in concealing our own, or even in speed itself, we must take special care to be armed with the shield of Pallas, that is, of foresight, so as to leave as little as possible to fortune. To this belong the exploring of roads before a march, the careful fortification of the camp (which in modern warfare has fallen almost into disuse, whereas the camps of the Romans were like a fortified town, to fall back upon in case of defeat), a firm and well drawn up line of battle, not trusting too much to light troops, or even to cavalry; in a word, everything which relates to a sound and careful system of defensive war; for the shield of Pallas is generally of more avail in war, than the sword of Mars itself. But Perseus, however furnished with forces and courage, has still need of one thing more, of the greatest possible importance, before he commences the campaign; he must turn aside to the Grææ. Now the Grææ are Treasons, which are the Sisters of War, though not indeed own sisters, but as it were of less noble birth. For wars are noble and generous; treasons degenerate and base. . . . Wherefore Perseus must conciliate these Grææ, and bring them into alliance with him, especially that they may lend him their eye and tooth; the eye to gain information; the tooth to spread rumours, raise envy, and gain over the minds of men. But when everything has been arranged in order for war, we must take special care, like Perseus, to find Medusa asleep; for he who undertakes a war wisely will almost always attack his enemy unprepared and in security. Lastly, in the very actions and onsets of war the mirror of Pallas must be resorted to; for there are many who before the time of danger can take a clear and accurate survey of the position of the enemy, but in the very moment of peril they are either stupified with terror, or look their dangers too rashly in the face; and so rush madly into them, bent on overcoming, not on avoiding them. Neither of which things should be done; but we should turn aside the head and look into the mirror of Pallas, that the onset may be rightly directed without either terror or fury.

From the conclusion of the war and victory follow two effects, first, the birth and springing up of Pegasus, which evidently enough signified Fame that flies abroad and proclaims the victory, and so makes what remains of the war easy and satisfactory; secondly, the carrying of Medusa's head on the shield; to which for excellence no other kind of defence can be compared. For one great and memorable enterprise successfully carried out paralyses every movement of the enemy, and stupifies disaffection itself.[11]

11. "De Augmentis," *Works*, 5, 327–32.

3. THOMAS HOBBES

1588-1679

SHORTLY *after leaving Oxford, Thomas Hobbes became tutor to William Cavendish, later second Earl of Devonshire, and by means of his long and close connection with that family he was provided with the leisure for scholarship. Upon his return from a trip to the continent in 1610, he began his literary career with a translation of Thucydides; at this same time an acquaintanceship with Francis Bacon led to the translation into Latin of three of Bacon's essays. On the eve of civil war in England, in 1640, Hobbes went to France and remained there for eleven years, the period of his major philosophic output. He associated with the brilliant circle of philosophers and scientists which centered around the friar Marin Mersenne; and while the English royal court was in exile in Paris he served as tutor in mathematics to the Prince of Wales, later Charles II. In 1651 he returned to England, and in that year* Leviathan *was published. Much of the writing of the later part of his life was given to controversy in defense of his religious views, but he also produced a history of the English civil war and a translation of Homer.*

Hobbes did not set out to develop a theory of international politics but he arrived at such a theory indirectly. In order to explain the need for civil and, in fact, absolute government he asked in what condition mankind would be in the absence of government or in what he called "a condition of mere nature." Conceding that such a condition probably never existed generally between individuals, he pointed to existing relations between kings—that is, international relations—as an illustration. Thus what Hobbes says about the "condition of mere nature" constitutes a discussion of international politics.

The edition used is *The English Works of Thomas Hobbes of Malmesbury,* Sir William Molesworth, 11 vols. London, John Bohn, 1841.

According to him the condition of nature is a state of war of all against all. This follows from the nature of man. By nature, man lives in constant fear of losing his life by the action of other men. He therefore dreads and distrusts other men and seeks to preserve himself. At the same time, man, driven by his passions, has continual desires and appetites for material things and for power, which is the ability to gratify desire. It is because men seek the same things that fear and distrust of each other arise and are justified. Even if a majority of men were seeking only security and had no desire to hurt others, they too, would have to use "force and wiles," suspecting all others of hostile designs.

. . . in the first place I set down for a principle, by experience known to all men, and denied by none, to wit, that the dispositions of men are naturally such, that except they be restrained through fear of some coercive power, every man will distrust and dread each other; and as by natural right he may, so by necessity he will be forced to make use of the strength he hath, toward the preservation of himself. You will object perhaps, that there are some who deny this. Truly so it happens, that very many do deny it. But shall I therefore seem to fight against myself, because I affirm that the same men confess and deny the same thing? In truth I do not; but they do, whose actions disavow what their discourses approve of. We see all countries, though they be at peace with their neighbours, yet guarding their frontiers with armed men, their towns with walls and ports, and keeping constant watches. To what purpose is all this, if there be no fear of the neighbouring power? We see even in well-governed states, where there are laws and punishments appointed for offenders, yet particular men travel not without their sword by their sides for their defences; neither sleep they without shutting not only their doors against their fellow subjects, but also their trunks and coffers for fear of domestics. Can men give a clearer testimony of the distrust they have of each other, and all of all? Now, since they do thus, and even countries as well as men, they publicly profess their mutual fear and diffidence. But in disputing they deny it; that is as much as to say, that out of a desire they have to contradict others, they gainsay themselves. Some object that this principle being admitted, it would needs follow, not only that all men were wicked, (which perhaps though it seem hard, yet we must yield to, since it is so clearly declared by holy writ) but also wicked by nature, which cannot be granted without impiety. But this, that men are evil by nature, follows not from principle. For though the wicked were fewer than the righteous, yet because we cannot distinguish them, there is a necessity of suspecting, heeding, anticipating, subjugating, self-defending, ever incident to the most honest and fairest conditioned. . . . The foundation therefore which I have laid, standing firm, I demonstrate, in the first place, that the state of men without civil society, which state we may properly call the state of nature, is nothing else but a mere war of all against all; and in that war all men have equal right unto all things.[1]

All men in the state of nature have a desire and will to hurt, but not proceeding from the same cause, neither equally to be condemned. For one man, according to that natural equality which is among us, permits as much to others as he assumes to himself; which is an argument of a temperate man, and one that rightly values his power. Another, supposing himself above others, will have a license to do what he lists and challenges respect and honour, as due to him before others; which is an argument of a fiery spirit. This man's will to hurt ariseth from vain glory, and the false esteem he hath of his own strength; the other's from the necessity of defending himself, his liberty, and his goods, against this man's violence. . . . . .

But the most frequent reason why men desire to hurt each other, ariseth hence, that many men at the same time have an appetite to the same thing; which yet very often they can neither enjoy in common, nor yet divide it; whence it follows that the strongest must have it, and who is strongest must be decided by the sword.[2]

. . . Felicity is a continual progress of the desire, from one object to another; the attaining of the former, being still but the way to the latter. The cause whereof is, that the object of man's desire, is not to enjoy once only, and for one instant of time; but to assure for ever, the way of his future desire. And therefore the voluntary actions, and inclinations of all men, tend, not only to the procuring, but also to the assuring of a contented life; and differ only in the way: which ariseth partly from the diversity of passions, in divers men; and partly from the difference of the knowledge, or opinion each one has of the causes, which produce the effect desired.

So that in the first place, I put for a general inclination of all mankind, a perpetual and restless desire of power after power, that ceaseth only in death. And the cause of this, is not always that a man hopes for a more intensive delight, than he has already attained to; or that he

1. "De Cive," *Works,* 2, xiv–xvii.
2. *Ibid.,* pp. 7–8.

cannot be content with a moderate power: but that he cannot assure the power and means to live well, which he hath present, without the acquisition of more.[3]

Thus it is as a result of their craving for security, as well as for gain and prestige, that men in a state of nature, and states which are always in a condition of nature in relation to one another, become enemies continually disposed to fighting one another.

. . . there is no way for any man to secure himself, so reasonable, as anticipation; that is, by force, or wiles, to master the persons of all men he can, so long, till he see no other power great enough to endanger him: and this is no more than his own conservation requireth, and is generally allowed. Also because there be some, that taking pleasure in contemplating their own power in the acts of conquest, which they pursue farther than their security requires; if others, that otherwise would be glad to be at ease within modest bounds, should not by invasion increase their power, they would not be able, long time, by standing only on their defence, to subsist. And by consequence, such augmentation of dominion over men, being necessary to a man's conservation, it ought to be allowed him.

Again men have no pleasure, but on the contrary a great deal of grief in keeping company, where there is no power able to overawe them all, For every man looketh that his companion should value him, at the same rate he sets upon himself: and upon all signs of contempt, or undervaluing, naturally endeavours, as far as he dares, (which amongst them that have no common power to keep them in quiet, is far enough to make them destroy each other), to extort a greater value from his contemners, by damage; and from others, by the example.

So that in the nature of man, we find three principal causes of quarrel. First, competition; secondly, diffidence; thirdly, glory.

The first maketh men invade for gain; the second, for safety; and the third, for reputation. The first use violence, to make themselves masters of other men's persons, wives, children, and cattle; the second, to defend them; the third for trifles, as a word, either direct in their persons, or by reflection in their kindred, their friends, their nation, their profession, or their name.

Hereby it is manifest, that during the time men live without a common power to keep them all in awe, they are in that condition which is called war; and such a war, as is of every man, against every man.

3. "Leviathan," *Works, 3,* 85–6.

For WAR, consisteth not in battle only, or the act of fighting; but in a tract of time, wherein the will to contend by battle is sufficiently known: and therefore the notion of *time* is to be considered in the nature of war; as it is in the nature of weather. For as the nature of foul weather, lieth not in a shower or two of rain; but in an inclination thereto of many days together: so the nature of war, consisteth not in actual fighting; but in the known disposition thereto, during all the time there is no assurance to the contrary. All other time is PEACE.

Whatsoever therefore is consequent to a time of war, where every man is enemy to every man; the same is consequent to the time, wherein men live without other security, than what their own strength, and their own invention shall furnish them withal. In such condition, there is no place for industry; because the fruit thereof is uncertain: and consequently no culture of the earth; no navigation, nor use of the commodities that may be imported by sea; no commodious building; no instruments of moving, and removing, such things as require much force; no knowledge of the face of the earth; no account of time; no arts; no letters; no society; and which is worst of all, continual fear, and danger of violent death; and the life of man, solitary, poor, nasty, brutish and short. . . . .

But though there had never been any time, wherein particular men were in a condition of war one against another; yet in all times, kings, and persons of sovereign authority, because of their independency, are in continual jealousies, and in the state and posture of gladiators; having their weapons pointing, and their eyes fixed on one another; that is, their forts, garrisons, and guns upon the frontiers of their kingdoms; and continual spies upon their neighbours; which is a posture of War.[4]

In this state of constant enmity men have a right to use any means which will effectively preserve them. Each man has the right to judge what are the most efficient means. Hobbes specifically points out that independent states have the same right to do whatever seems necessary to maintain their security.

Among so many dangers therefore, as the natural lusts of men do daily threaten each other withal, to have a care of one's self is so far from being a matter scornfully to be looked upon, that one has neither the power nor the wish to have done otherwise. For every man is desirous of what is good for him, and shuns what is evil, but chiefly the chiefest of natural evils, which is death; and this he doth, by a certain

4. *Ibid.*, pp. 111–15.

impulsion of nature, no less than that whereby a stone moves downward. It is therefore neither absurd nor reprehensible neither against the dictates of true reason, for a man to use all his endeavours to preserve and defend his body and the members thereof from death and sorrows. But that which is not contrary to right reason, that all men account to be done justly, and with right. Neither by the word *right* is anything else signified, than that liberty which every man hath to make use of his natural faculties according to right reason. Therefore the first foundation of natural right is this, *that every man as much as in him lies endeavour to protect his life and members.*

But because it is in vain for a man to have a right to the end, if the right to the necessary means be denied him, it follows, that since every man hath a right to preserve himself, he must also be allowed a right *to use all the means, and do all the actions, without which he cannot preserve himself.*

Now whether the means which he is about to use, and the action he is performing, be necessary to the preservation of his life and members, or not, he himself, by the right of nature, must be judge.[5]

To this war of every man, against every man, this also is consequent; that nothing can be unjust. The notions of right and wrong, justice and injustice have there no place. Where there is no common power, there is no law: where no law, no injustice. Force, and fraud, are in war the two cardinal virtues. Justice, and injustice are none of the faculties neither of the body, nor mind. If they were, they might be in a man that were alone in the world, as well as his senses, and passions. They are qualities, that relate to men in society, not in solitude. It is consequent also to the same condition, that there be no propriety, no dominion, no *mine* and *thine* distinct; but only that to be every man's, that he can get; and for so long, as he can keep it. And thus much for the ill condition, which man by mere nature is actually placed in; though with a possibility to come out of it, consisting partly in the passions, partly in his reason.[6]

The liberty of the commonwealth . . . is the same with that which every man then should have, if there were no civil laws, nor commonwealth at all. And the effects of it also be the same. For as amongst masterless men, there is perpetual war, of every man against his neigh-

5. "De Cive," *Works,* 2, 8–9.
6. "Leviathan," *Works,* 3, 147.

bour; no inheritance, to transmit to the son, nor to expect from the
father; no propriety of goods, or lands; no security; but a full and absolute liberty in every particular and so in states, and comonwealths
not dependent on one another, every commonwealth, not every man,
has an absolute liberty, to do what it shall judge, that is to say, what
that man, or assembly that representeth it, shall judge most conducing
to their benefit. But withal they live in the condition of a perpetual war,
and upon the confines of battle, with their frontiers armed, and cannons planted against their neighbours round about.[7]

*In this war of all against all none can find safety, for even the strongest
may fall a prey to the cunning of the weak. Men come to regard this
perpetual insecurity as a "hateful condition," and their "right reason"
suggests certain rules of mutual conduct, otherwise called the law of
nature, which will increase their chance of survival. The first of these
laws which "are but conclusions, or theorems concerning what con-
duceth to the conservation and defence of themselves,"[8] enjoins men
to seek peace and mitigate the universal struggle wherever possible.
Should others fail to respond men must continue to use whatever means
come to hand for self-preservation.*

But it is easily judged how disagreeable a thing to the preservation
either of mankind, or of each single man, a perpetual war is. But it is
perpetual in its own nature; because in regard of the equality of those
that strive, it cannot be ended by victory. For in this state the conqueror
is subject to so much danger, as it were to be accounted a miracle,
if any, even the most strong, should close up his life with many years
and old age. . . . . .

Yet cannot men expect any lasting preservation, continuing thus in
the state of nature, that is, of war, by reason of that equality of power,
and other human faculties they are endued withal. Wherefore to seek
peace, where there is any hopes of obtaining it, and where there is none,
to enquire out for auxiliaries of war, is the dictate of right reason, that
is, the law of nature.[9]

And because the condition of man, as hath been declared . . . is a
condition of war of every one against every one; in which case every one
is governed by his own reason; and there is nothing he can make use of,

7. *Ibid.*, pp. 110–11.
8. *Ibid.*, p. 147.
9. "De Cive," *Works, 2, 13.*

that may not be a help unto him, in preserving his life against his enemies; it followeth, that in such a condition, every man has a right to every thing; even to one another's body. And therefore, as long as this natural right of every man to every thing endureth, there can be no security to any man, how strong or wise soever he be, of living out the time, which nature ordinarily alloweth men to live. And consequently it is a precept, or a general rule of reason, that every man, ought to endeavour peace, as far as he has hope of obtaining it; and when he cannot obtain it, that he may seek, and use, all helps, and advantages of war. The first branch of which rule, containeth the first, and fundamental law of nature; which is, to seek peace, and follow it. The second, the sum of the right of nature; which is, by all means we can, to defend ourselves.

From this fundamental law of nature, by which men are commanded to endeavour peace, is derived this second law; that a man be willing, when others are so too, as far-forth, as for peace, and defence of himself he shall think it necessary, to lay down this right to all things; and be contented with so much liberty against other men, as he would allow other men against himself. For as long as every man holdeth this right, of doing anything he liketh; so long are all men in the condition of war. But if other men will not lay down their right, as well as he; then there is no reason for any one to divest himself of his: for that were to expose himself to prey, which no man is bound to, rather than to dispose himself to peace. This is that law of the Gospel; whatsoever you require that others should do to you, that do ye to them.[10]

The only way by which men can escape from the state of war is by a mutual surrender of the right to all things. This escape can only be certain if all are assured that each party will observe the compact. The only way to obtain such assurance, and thus the only way to find reliable peace and security, is for the "right to all things" to be surrendered and also transferred to an absolute sovereign.

It follows that states cannot put an end to the state of war in international relations and must take all steps necessary for national self-preservation. Under these circumstances it is the duty of every government to provide defense against foreign power and to use all available means to this end. In addition to building up the strength of their own state, sovereigns may add to the preponderance of power needed to deter others by entering into leagues and covenants of mutual aid.

10. "Leviathan," *Works, 3,* 117–18.

These means, however, like all agreements not made under sovereign power, must remain unreliable and can last only temporarily: "a League being a connexion of men by covenants, if there be no power given to any one man or assembly, as in the condition of mere nature, to compel them to performance, is so long only valid, as there ariseth no just cause of distrust." [11]

For the laws of nature, as *justice, equity, modesty, mercy,* and, in sum, *doing to others, as we would be done to,* of themselves, without the terror of some power, to cause them to be observed, are contrary to our natural passions, that carry us to partiality, pride, revenge, and the like. And covenants, without the sword, are but words, and of no strength to secure a man at all. Therefore notwithstanding the laws of nature, which every one hath then kept, when he has the will to keep them, when he can do it safely, if there be no power erected, or not great enough for our security; every man will, and may lawfully rely on his own strength and art, for caution against all other men. And in all places, where men have lived by small families, to rob and spoil one another, has been a trade, and so far from being reputed against the law of nature, that the greater spoils they gained, the greater was their honour; and men observed no other laws therein, but the laws of honour; that is, to abstain from cruelty, leaving to men their lives, and instruments of husbandry. And as small families did then; so now do cities and king-doms which are but greater families, for their own security, enlarge their dominions, upon all pretences of danger, and fear of invasion, or assistance that may be given to invaders, and endeavour as much as they can, to subdue, or weaken their neighbours, by open force, and secret arts, for want of other caution, justly; and are remembered for it in after ages with honour.[12]

Now all the duties of rulers are contained in this one sentence, *the safety of the people is the supreme law.* For although they who among men obtain the chiefest dominion, cannot be subject to laws properly so called, that is to say to the will of men, because to be chief, and sub-ject, are contradictories; yet is it their *duty* in all things, as much as possibly they can, to yield obedience unto right reason, which is the natural, moral, and divine law. But because dominions were constituted for peace's sake, and peace was sought after for safety's sake; he, who being placed in authority, shall use his power otherwise than to the

11. *Ibid.,* p. 223.
12. *Ibid.,* pp. 153–4.

safety of the people, will act against the reasons of peace, that is to say, against the laws of nature.[13]

But in vain do they worship peace at home, who cannot defend themselves against foreigners; neither is it possible for them to protect themselves against foreigners, whose forces are not united. And therefore it is necessary for the preservation of particulars, that there be some one council or one man, who hath the right to arm, to gather together, to unite so many citizens, in all dangers and on all occasions, as shall be needful for common defence against the certain number and strength of the enemy; and again, as often as he shall find it expedient, to make peace with them. We must understand, therefore, that particular citizens have conveyed their whole right of war and peace unto some one man or council; and that this right which we may call *the sword of war*, belongs to the same man or council, to whom the sword of justice belongs. For no man can by right compel citizens to take up arms and be at the expenses of war, but he who by right can punish him who doth not obey. Both swords therefore, as well this of war as that of justice, even by the constitution itself of a city and essentially do belong to the chief command. . . . .

Furthermore, since the affairs of the city both those of war and peace, cannot possibly be all administered by one man or one council without officers and subordinate magistrates; and that it appertaineth to peace and common defence, that they to whom it belongs justly to judge of controversies, to search into neighbouring councils, prudently to wage war, and on all hands warily to attend the benefit of the city, should also rightly exercise their offices; it is consonant to reason that they depend on, and be chosen by him who hath the chief command both in war and in peace.[14]

Nor is it the joining together of a small number of men, that gives them this security; because in small numbers, small additions on the one side or the other, make the advantage of strength so great, as is sufficient to carry the victory; and therefore gives encouragement to an invasion. The multitude sufficient to confide in for our security, is not determined by any certain number, but by comparison with the enemy we fear; and is then sufficient, when the odds of the enemy is not of so visible and conspicuous moment, to determine the event of war, as to move him to attempt.

13. "De Cive," *Works*, 2, 166–7.
14. *Ibid.*, 2, 75–8.

And be there never so great a multitude; yet if their actions be directed according to their particular judgments, and particular appetites, they can expect thereby no defence, nor protection, neither against a common enemy, nor against the injuries of one another. For being distracted in opinions concerning the best use and application of their strength, they do not help but hinder one another; and reduce their strength by mutual opposition to nothing; whereby they are easily, not only subdued by a very few that agree together; but also when there is no common enemy, they make war upon each other, for their particular interests. For if we could suppose a great multitude of men to consent in the observation of justice, and other laws of nature, without a common power to keep them all in awe; we might as well suppose all mankind to do the same; and then there neither would be, nor need to be any civil government, or commonwealth at all; because there would be peace without subjection.

Nor is it enough for the security, which men desire should last all the time of their life, that they be governed, and directed by one judgment, for a limited time; as in one battle, or one war. For though they obtain a victory by their unanimous endeavour against a foreign enemy; yet afterwards, when either they have no common enemy, or he that by one part is held for an enemy, is by another part held for a friend, they must needs by the difference of their interests dissolve, and fall again into a war amongst themselves.[15]

There are two things necessary for the people's defence *to be warned and to be forearmed*. For the state of commonwealths considered in themselves, is natural, that is to say, hostile. Neither if they cease from fighting, is it therefore to be called peace; but rather a breathing time, in which one enemy observing the motion and countenance of the other, values his security not according to the pacts, but the forces and counsels of his adversary. And this by natural right . . . from this, that contracts are invalid in the state of nature, as oft as any just fear doth intervene. It is therefore necessary to the defence of the city, first that there be some who may, as near as may be, *search into* and *discover* the counsels and motions of all those who may prejudice it. For *discoverers* to ministers of state, are like the beams of the sun to the human soul. And we may more truly say in vision political, than natural, that the sensible and intelligible species of outward things, not well considered by others, are by the air transported to the soul; that is to say, to them who have

15. "Leviathan," *Works*, 3, 154–6.

the supreme authority: and therefore are they no less necessary to the preservation of the state, than the rays of the light are to the conservation of man. Or if they be compared to spider's webs, which, extended on all sides by the finest threads, do warn them, keeping in their small holes, of all outward motions; they who bear rule, can no more know what is necessary to be commanded for the defence of their subjects without *spies*, than those spiders can, when they shall go forth, and whether they shall repair, without the motion of those threads.

Furthermore, it is necessarily requisite to the people's defence, that they be *forearmed*. Now to be forearmed is to be furnished with soldiers, arms, ships, forts, and monies, before the danger be instant; for the lifting of soldiers and taking up of arms after a blow is given, is too late at least, if not impossible. In like manner, not to raise forts and appoint garrisons in convenient places before the frontiers are invaded, is to be like those country swains, (as Demosthenes said), who ignorant of the art of fencing, with their bucklers guarded those parts of the body where they first felt the smart of the strokes. But they who think it then seasonable enough to raise monies for the maintenance of soldiers and other charges of war, when the danger begins to show itself, they consider not, surely, how difficult a matter it is to wring suddenly out of close-fisted men so vast a proportion of monies. For almost all men, what they once reckon in the number of their goods, do judge themselves to have such a right and propriety in it, as they conceive themselves to be injured whensoever they are forced to employ but the least part of it for the public good. Now a sufficient stock of monies to defend the country with arms, will not soon be raised out of the treasure of imposts and customs. We must therefore, for fear of war, in time of peace hoard up good sums, if we intend the safety of the commonwealth. Since therefore it necessarily belongs to rulers, for the subjects' safety to discover the enemy's counsel, to keep garrisons, and to have money in continual readiness; and that princes are, by the law of nature, bound to use their whole endeavour in procuring the welfare of their subjects: it follows, that it is not only lawful for them to send out spies, to maintain soldiers, to build forts, and to require monies for these purposes; but also not to do thus is unlawful. To which also may be added, whatsoever shall seem to conduce to the lessening of the power of foreigners whom they suspect, whether by slight or force. For rulers are bound according to their power to prevent the evils they suspect; lest peradventure they may happen through their negligence.[16]

16. "De Cive," *Works*, 2, 169–71.

Despite the general insecurity of international politics, that part of the law of nature which recommends mitigation of the universal struggle as a means of self-preservation remains as applicable to states as to individuals. Thus, though states must always be prepared to meet force with force, they are still obliged to "seek peace, and follow it" whenever possible, and can do this with some success. The predicament of the condition of nature is not so acute for states as for individuals, because by reason of their organization states can protect a large part of their members from the immediate impact of war. Thus, "there does not follow from [war] that misery, which accompanies the liberty of particular men," [17] *and therefore states, more than individuals, are able to observe certain restraints, such as the acceptance of reparation and moderation in war.*

It is a proverbial saying, *inter arma silent leges*. There is a little therefore to be said concerning the laws that men are to observe one toward another in time of war, wherein every man's being and well-being is the rule of his actions. Yet thus much the law of nature commandeth in war, that men satiate not the cruelty of their present passions, whereby in their own conscience they foresee no benefit to come. For that betrayeth not a necessity, but a disposition of the mind to war, which is against the law of nature.[18]

The last thing contained in that supreme law, *salus populi*, is their defence; and consisteth partly in the obedience and unity of the subjects, of which hath been already spoken, and in which consisteth the means of levying soldiers, and of having money, arms, ships, and fortified places in readiness for defence; and partly, in the avoiding of unnecessary wars. For such commonwealths, or such monarchs, as affect war for itself, that is to say, out of ambition, or of vain-glory, or that make account to revenge every little injury, or disgrace done by their neighbours, if they ruin not themselves, their fortune must be better than they have reason to expect.[19]

Lawyer. Do you think it lawful for a lord, that is the sovereign ruler of his family, to make war upon another like sovereign lord, and dispossess him of his lands?
Philosopher. It is lawful, or not lawful, according to the intention of him

17. "Leviathan," *Works, 3*, 115.
18. "De Corpore Politico," *Works, 4*, 118.
19. *Ibid.*, pp. 219–20.

that does it. For, first, being a sovereign ruler, he is not subject to any law of man; and as to the law of God, where the intention is justifiable, the action is so also. The intention may be lawful in divers cases by the right of nature; one of those cases is, when he is constrained to it by the necessity of subsisting. . . . And as their preservation, so also is their security a just pretence of invading those whom they have just cause to fear, unless sufficient caution be given to take away their fear: which caution, for anything I can yet conceive, is utterly impossible. Necessity and security are the principal justifications before God, of beginning war. Injuries received justify a war defensive; but for reparable injuries, if reparation be tendered, all invasion upon that title is iniquity.[20]

It is of itself manifest that the actions of men proceed from the will, and the will from hope and fear, insomuch as when they shall see a greater good or less evil likely to happen to them by the breach than observation of the laws, they will wittingly violate them. The hope therefore which each man hath of his security and self-preservation, consists in this, that by force or craft he may disappoint his neighbour, either openly or by stratagem. Whence we may understand, that the natural laws, though well understood, do not instantly secure any man in their practice; and consequently, that as long as there is no caution had from the invasion of others, there remains to every man that same primitive right of self-defence by such means as either he can or will make use of, that is, a right to all things, or the right of war. And it is sufficient for the fulfilling of the natural law, that a man be prepared in mind to embrace peace when it may be had.

It is a trite saying, that all laws are silent in the time of war, and it is a true one, not only if we speak of the civil, but also of the natural laws, provided they be referred not to the mind, but to the actions of men . . . And we mean such a war as is the mere state of nature; although in the war of nation against nation, a certain mean was wont to be observed.[21]

. . . *upon caution of the future time, a man ought to pardon the offences past of them that repenting, desire it.* For PARDON is nothing but granting of peace; which though granted to them that persevere in their hostility, be not peace but fear; yet not granted to them that give caution of the future time, is sign of an aversion to peace; and

20. "A Dialogue of the Common Laws," *Works,* 6, 147–8.
21. "De Cive," *Works,* 2, 63–4.

therefore contrary to the law of nature. . . . *in revenges,* that is, retribution of evil for evil, *men look not at the greatness of the evil past, but the greatness of the good to follow.* Whereby we are forbidden to inflict punishment with any other design, than for correction of the offender, or direction of others. For this law is consequent to the next before it, that commandeth pardon, upon security of the future time. Besides, revenge without respect to the example, and profit to come, is a triumph, or glorying in the hurt of another, tending to no end; for the end is always somewhat to come; and glorying to no end, is vain-glory, and contrary to reason, and to hurt without reason, tendeth to the introduction of war; which is against the law of nature: and is commonly styled by the name of *cruelty.*[22]

22. "Leviathan," *Works, 3,* 139–40.

4. JOHN LOCKE

1632-1704

THROUGHOUT *a great part of his career as a philosopher and scientist, John Locke was actively engaged in government service. During the second Dutch War he accompanied Sir Walter Vane on a diplomatic mission to the Elector of Brandenburg, but upon his return to England in 1666 he declined an opportunity to go to Spain as secretary to the English ambassador there. Three years later he entered the household of the Whig leader, Lord Ashley, as physician and friend. After Ashley became Earl of Shaftesbury and Lord Chancellor in 1672, Locke was given a position in the government. For four years after 1675 he lived in France, and from 1683 until the Revolution of 1688 he was in political exile in Holland. It was during these years abroad that most of his philosophical works took shape; they were published in quick succession after 1689 and made Locke one of the influential figures in Whig circles. Again declining ambassadorial appointments offered him by William III, he served as Commissioner of Appeals and then as a commissioner to the Board of Trade and Plantations, retiring from public life in 1704. His writings make him one of the most important contributors to philosophy and political thought.*

Like Thomas Hobbes, Locke was chiefly concerned with the origins and wise ordering of civil government and did not profess a theory of international politics. But, following the custom of the seventeenth century, he began his study with a discussion of what men's relations with each other would be in the absence of government, a condition to which he applied the conventional term "state of nature," and asserted that rulers of "independent governments" were in such a condition of nature vis a vis *each other. Thus Locke's discussion of the state of nature is also a consideration of international relations. In addition*

The edition used is *The Works of John Locke,* 12th ed. 9 vols. London, Longman, 1824.

*to this, he paid rather more attention than Hobbes to the conduct of
foreign policy by a civil government. In this connection he touched
upon both the content of such a policy and the way in which it should be
formulated. Locke considered this function of government sufficiently
important to deserve the special name of the "federative" power.*

*According to Locke the state of nature is one of freedom. It is not,
however, a state of complete license, because there is a law of nature
to govern it. This law of nature, which is the "will of God" perceived by
reason, obliges men and states to do all they can to preserve the whole
of mankind as long as their own survival is not endangered. The state
of nature, then, is one not of war but of peace and good will.*

But though this be a state of liberty, yet it is not a state of licence:
though man in that state have an uncontrolable liberty to dispose of
his person or possessions, yet he has not liberty to destroy himself, or
so much as any creature in his possession, but where some nobler use
than its bare preservation calls for it. The state of nature has a law
of nature to govern it, which obliges every one: and reason, which is
that law, teaches all mankind, who will but consult it, that being all
equal and independent, no one ought to harm another in his life, health,
liberty, or possessions: for men being all the workmanship of one omnip-
otent and infinitely wise Maker; all the servants of one sovereign
master, sent into the world by his order, and about his business; they
are his property, whose workmanship they are, made to last during
his, not another's pleasure: and being furnished with like faculties,
sharing all in one community of nature, there cannot be supposed any
such subordination among us, that may authorize us to destroy another, as if we were made for one another's uses, as the inferior ranks
of creatures are for ours. Every one, as he is bound to preserve himself,
and not to quit his station wilfully, so by the like reason, when his own
preservation comes not in competition, ought he, as much as he can,
to preserve the rest of mankind, and may not, unless it be to do justice
to an offender, take away or impair the life, or what tends to the preservation of life, the liberty, health, limb, or goods of another. . . . . .

It is often asked as a mighty objection, "where are, or ever were there
any men in such a state of nature?" To which it may suffice as an answer
at present, that since all princes and rulers of independent governments,
all through the world, are in a state of nature, it is plain the world never
was, nor ever will be, without numbers of men in that state. I have
named all governors of independent communities, whether they are,

or are not, in league with others: for it is not every compact that puts
an end to the state of nature between men, but only this one of agreeing
together mutually to enter into one community, and make one body
politic; other promises and compacts men may make one with another,
and yet still be in the state of nature. The promises and bargains for
truck, etc. between the two men in the desert island . . . or between
a Swiss and an Indian, in the woods of America, are binding to them,
though they are perfectly in a state of nature, in reference to one another: for truth and keeping of faith belongs to men as men, and not as
members of society.[1]

I will not dispute now, whether princes are exempt from the laws
of their country; but this I am sure, they owe subjection to the laws
of God and nature. Nobody, no power, can exempt them from the obligations of that eternal law. Those are so great, and so strong, in the case
of promises, that omnipotency itself can be tied by them. Grants,
promises, and oaths, are bonds that hold the Almighty: whatever some
flatterers say to princes of the world, who, all together, with all their
people joined to them, are in comparison of the great God, but as a
drop of the bucket, or a dust on the balance, inconsiderable, nothing.[2]

*However men are "no strict observers of equity and justice" and they
often break the law of nature by forcibly encroaching on the liberty of
others. This "use of force without authority, always puts him that uses
it into a state of war, as the aggressor."* [3] *In such cases the men or states
who are attacked may defend themselves with violence, for "in all states
and conditions the true remedy of force without authority, is to oppose
force to it."* [4]

The state of war is a state of enmity and destruction: and therefore
declaring by word or action, not a passionate and hasty, but a sedate
settled design upon another man's life, puts him in a state of war with
him against whom he has declared such an intention, and so has exposed
his life to the other's power to be taken away by him, or any one that
joins with him in his defence, and espouses his quarrel; it being reasonable and just, I should have a right to destroy that which threatens me
with destruction; for, by the fundamental law of nature, man being to

1. "Of Civil Government," Bk. II, *Works, 4*, 341–6.
2. *Ibid.*, p. 454.
3. *Ibid.*, p. 430.
4. *Ibid.*

be preserved as much as possible, when all cannot be preserved, the safety of the innocent is to be preferred: and one may destroy a man who makes war upon him, or has discovered an enmity to his being, for the same reason that he may kill a wolf or a lion; because such men are not under the ties of the common law of reason, have no other rule, but that of force and violence, and so may be treated as beasts of prey, those dangerous and noxious creatures, that will be sure to destroy him whenever he falls into their power.

And hence it is, that he who attempts to get another man into his absolute power, does thereby put himself into a state of war with him; it being to be understood as a declaration of a design upon his life: for I have reason to conclude, that he who would get me into his power without my consent, would use me as he pleased when he had got me there, and destroy me too when he had a fancy to it; for nobody can desire to have me in his absolute power, unless it be to compel me by force to that which is against the right of my freedom, i.e. make me a slave. To be free from such force is the only security of my preservation; and reason bids me look on him, as an enemy to my preservation, who would take away that freedom which is the fence to it; so that he who makes an attempt to enslave me, thereby puts himself into a state of war with me. . . .

This makes it lawful for a man to kill a thief, who has not in the least hurt him, nor declared any design upon his life, any farther than, by the use of force, so to get him in his power, as to take away his money, or what he pleases, from him; because using force, where he has no right, to get me into his power, let his pretence be what it will, I have no reason to suppose, that he who would take away my liberty, would not, when he had me in his power, take away everything else. And therefore it is lawful for me to treat him as one who has put himself into a state of war with me, i.e. kill him if I can; for to that hazard does he justly expose himself, whoever introduces a state of war, and is aggressor in it.

And here we have the plain "difference between the state of nature and the state of war," which however some men have confounded, are as far distant, as a state of peace, good-will, mutual assistance and preservation; and a state of enmity, malice, violence and mutual destruction are one from another. Men living together according to reason, without a common superior on earth, with authority to judge between them, is properly the state of nature. But force, or a declared design of force upon the person of another, where there is no common superior on earth to appeal to for relief, is the state of war; and it is the want of such an appeal gives a man the right of war even against an aggressor . . . Want of a common judge with authority, puts all men in a state of nature: force without right, upon a man's person, makes a state of war, both where there is, and is not, a common judge.[5]

When an instance of aggression occurs the law of nature must be enforced if it is to have any effect at all. The law of nature therefore prescribes certain rules for dealing with an aggressor. Even if an offender against the law of nature directly damages only one other, he injures all by renouncing those rules of conduct which conduce to the good of all. Thus, although only the direct sufferer has a right to reparation, everyone may assist in extracting the reparation and in punishing the offender. This punishment should not be severer than necessary to extract due recompense and provide a deterrent against future offenses.

And that all men may be restrained from invading others rights, and from doing hurt to one another, and the law of nature be observed, which willeth the peace and preservation of all mankind, the execution of the law of nature is, in that state, put into every man's hands, whereby every one has a right to punish the transgressors of that law to such a degree as may hinder its violation: for the law of nature would, as all other laws that concern men in this world, be in vain, if there were nobody that in the state of nature had a power to execute that law, and thereby preserve the innocent and restrain offenders . . .

And thus, in the state of nature, "one man comes by a power over another;" but yet no absolute or arbitrary power, to use a criminal, when he has got him in his hands, according to the passionate heats, or boundless extravagancy of his own will; but only to retribute to him, so far as calm reason and conscience dictate, what is proportionate to his transgression; which is so much as may serve for reparation and restraint: for these two are the only reasons, why one man may lawfully do harm to another, which is what we call punishment. In transgressing the law of nature, the offender declares himself to live by another rule than that of reason and common equity, which is that measure God has set to the actions of men for their mutual security; and so he becomes dangerous to mankind. . . . . .

Besides the crime which consists in violating the law, and varying from the right rule of reason, whereby a man so far becomes degenerate,

5. *Ibid.*, pp. 347–8.

and declares himself to quit the principles of human nature, and to be a noxious creature, there is commonly injury done to some person or other, some other man receives damage by his transgression: in which case he who hath received any damage, has, besides the right of punishment common to him with other men, a particular right to seek reparation from him that hath done it: and any other person, who finds it just, may also join with him that is injured, and assist him in recovering from the offender so much as may make satisfaction for the harm he hath suffered.

. . . every man, in the state of nature, has a power to kill a murderer, both to deter others from doing the like injury, which no reparation can compensate, by the example of the punishment that attends it from everybody; and also to secure men from the attempts of a criminal, who having renounced reason, the common rule and measure God hath given to mankind, hath, by the unjust violence and slaughter he hath committed upon one, declared war against all mankind; and therefore may be destroyed as a lion or a tiger, one of those wild savage beasts, with whom men can have no society nor security: and upon this is grounded that great law of nature, "Whoso sheddeth man's blood, by man shall his blood be shed." . . .

By the same reason may a man in the state of nature punish the lesser breaches of that law. It will perhaps be demanded, with death? I answer, each transgression may be punished to that degree, and with so much severity, as will suffice to make it an ill bargain to the offender, give him cause to repent, and terrify others from doing the like. Every offence that can be committed in the state of nature, may in the state of nature be also punished equally, and as far forth, as it may in a commonwealth: for though it would be beside my present purpose, to enter here into the particulars of the law of nature, or its measures of punishment, yet it is certain there is such a law, and that too as intelligible and plain to a rational creature, and a studier of that law, as the positive laws of commonwealths: nay, possibly plainer, as much as reason is easier to be understood, than the fancies and intricate contrivances of men, following contrary and hidden interests put into words . . .[6]

This right of self-help in the absence of a common judge makes individuals, whether men or states, judges in their own case. Locke realised that this might be considered a "strange doctrine" and confessed that it was subject to grave objections. He admitted that civil government is

6. *Ibid.*, pp. 341–5.

the "proper remedy" but pointed out that this depends on the type of government. Self-help is less objectionable than an absolute government in which one ruler is judge in his own case against all others. Moreover an abuse of the right of self-help is itself a breach of the laws of nature and may be punished in the same way as other offenses. Thus the extension of civil government is not always preferable to the state of nature.

To this strange doctrine, viz. That "in the state of nature every one has the executive power" of the law of nature, I doubt not but it will be objected that it is unreasonable for men to be judges in their own cases, that self-love will make men partial to themselves and their friends; and on the other side, ill-nature, passion, and revenge will carry them too far in punishing others; and hence nothing but confusion and disorder will follow: and that therefore God hath certainly appointed government to restrain the partiality and violence of men. I easily grant, that civil government is the proper remedy for the inconveniences of the state of nature, which must certainly be great, where men may be judges in their own case; since it is easy to be imagined, that he who was so unjust as to do his brother an injury, will scarce be so just as to condemn himself for it: but I shall desire those who make this objection, to remember, that absolute monarchs are but men; and if government is to be the remedy of those evils, which necessarily follow from men's being judges in their own cases, and the state of nature is therefore not to be endured; I desire to know what kind of government that is, and how much better it is than the state of nature, where one man commanding a multitude, has the liberty to be judge in his own case, and may do to all his subjects whatever he pleases, without the least question or control of those who execute his pleasure? and in whatsoever he doth, whether led by reason, mistake, or passion, must be submitted to? much better it is in the state of nature wherein men are not bound to submit to the unjust will of another: and if he that judges, judges amiss in his own, or any other case, he is answerable for it to the rest of mankind.[7]

The most compelling reason for a number of men to form a state is defense against other groups rather than fear of each other; because "since . . . those, who liked one another so well as to join into society cannot but be supposed to have some acquaintance and friendship together, and some trust in another, they could not but have greater appre-

7. *Ibid.*, pp. 345–6.

*hensions of others than of one another; and therefore their first care
and thought cannot but be supposed to be, how to secure themselves
against foreign force."* [8] *Being in a condition of nature as regards each
other, states must provide their own defense and enforcement of the
law of nature. Consequently one of the chief functions of government
is "to employ the force of the community . . . abroad to prevent or
redress foreign injuries, and secure the community from inroads and
invasions."* [9]

There is another power in every commonwealth, which one may
call natural, because it is that which answers to the power every man
naturally had before he entered into society: for though in a commonwealth, the members of it are distinct persons still in reference to one
another, and as such are governed by the laws of the society; yet in
reference to the rest of mankind, they make one body, which is, as every
member of it before was, still in the state of nature with the rest of mankind. Hence it is, that the controversies that happen between any man
of the society with those that are out of it, are managed by the public;
and an injury done to a member of their body engages the whole in the
reparation of it. So that, under this consideration, the whole community
is one body in the state of nature, in respect of all other states or persons
out of its community.

This therefore contains the power of war and peace, leagues and
alliances, and all the transactions, with all persons and communities
without the commonwealth; and may be called federative, if any one
pleases. So the thing be understood, I am indifferent as to the name.

These two powers, executive and federative, though they be really
distinct in themselves, yet one comprehending the execution of the
municipal laws of the society within itself, upon all that are parts of it;
the other the management of the security and interest of the public
without, with all those that it may receive benefit or damage from; yet
they are always almost united. And though this federative power in the
well or ill management of it be of great moment to the commonwealth,
yet it is much less capable to be directed by antecedent, standing, positive laws, than the executive; and so must necessarily be left to the
prudence and wisdom of those whose hands it is in, to be managed for
the public good: for the laws that concern subjects one amongst another, being to direct their actions, may well enough precede them.

8. *Ibid.*, p. 401.
9. *Ibid.*, p. 414–15.

But what is to be done in reference to foreigners, depending much upon . . . them, to be managed by the best of their skill, for the advantage of the commonwealth.[10]

To carry out this defensive function, the executive must maintain the "inward strength" of the state. One important factor in national strength is wealth. Locke believed that his country in particular could best achieve wealth by trade rather than conquest, and that this method had the merit of being in accordance with the law of nature.

. . . forasmuch as men . . . entering into societies, grounded upon their mutual compacts of assistance, for the defence of their temporal goods, may nevertheless be deprived of them, either by the rapine and fraud of their fellow citizens, or by the hostile violence of foreigners: the remedy of all this evil consists in arms, riches, and multitudes of citizens; the remedy of others in laws: and the care of all things relating both to the one and the other, is committed by the society to the civil magistrate. This is the original, this is the use, and these are the bounds of the legislative, which is the supreme power in every commonwealth. I mean, that provision may be made for the security of each man's private possessions; for the peace, riches, and public commodities of the whole people; and, as much as possible, for the increase of their inward strength against foreign invasions.[11]

. . . Riches do not consist in having more gold and silver, but in having more in proportion than the rest of the world, or than our neighbours, whereby we are enabled to procure to ourselves a greater plenty of the conveniencies of life, than comes within the reach of neighbouring kingdoms and states, who, sharing the gold and silver of the world in a less proportion, want the means of plenty and power, and so are poorer. . . .

In a country not furnished with mines, there are but two ways of growing rich, either conquest or commerce. By the first the Romans made themselves masters of the riches of the world; but I think that, in our present circumstances, nobody is vain enough to entertain a thought of our reaping the profits of the world with our swords, and making the spoil and tribute of vanquished nations the fund for the supply of the charges of the government, with an overplus for the wants, and equally-craving luxury, and fashionable vanity of the people.

10. *Ibid.*, pp. 425–6.
11. "A Letter Concerning Toleration," *Works*, 5, 42–3.

Commerce, therefore, is the only way left to us, either for riches, or subsistence: for this the advantages of our situation, as well as the industry and inclination of our people, bold and skilful at sea, do naturally fit us: by this the nation of England has been hitherto supported, and trade left almost to itself, and assisted only by the natural advantages above-mentioned, brought us in plenty of riches, and always set this kingdom in a rank equal, if not superior to any of its neighbours; and would, no doubt, without any difficulty, have continued it so, if the more enlarged and better-understood interest of trade, since the improvement of navigation, had not raised us many rivals; and the amazing politics of some late reigns let in other competitors with us for the sea, who will be sure to seize to themselves whatever parts of trade our mismanagement, or want of money, shall let slip out of our hands: and when it is once lost, it will be too late to hope, by a mistimed care, easily to retrieve it again. For the currents of trade, like those of waters, make themselves channels, out of which they are afterwards as hard to be diverted, as rivers that have worn themselves deep within their banks.[12]

Locke, as a seventeenth-century Protestant and Whig, was deeply concerned with the rights of property. Though his belief that civil government must be based on consent made it natural for him to deny that authority can lawfully be founded on force of arms, it is largely as a question of property that he discusses and denies the existence of any right of conquest.

. . . Political power is that power, which every man having in the state of nature, has given up into the hands of the society, and therein to the governors, whom the society hath set over itself, with this express or tacit trust, that it shall be employed for their good and the preservation of their property. . . . .

Though governments can originally have no other rise than that before-mentioned, nor politics be founded on anything but the consent of the people; yet such have been the disorders ambition has filled the world with, that in the noise of war, which makes so great a part of the history of mankind, this consent is little taken notice of: and therefore many have mistaken the force of arms for the consent of the people, and reckon conquest as one of the originals of government. But con-

12. "Some Considerations of the Lowering of Interest and Raising the Value of Money," *Works*, 4, 13–14.

quest is as far from setting up any government, as demolishing a house is from building a new one in the place. Indeed, it often makes way for a new frame of a commonwealth, by destroying the former; but, without the consent of the people, can never erect a new one.

That the aggressor, who puts himself into the state of war with another, and unjustly invades another man's right, can, by such an unjust war, never come to have a right over the conquered, will be easily agreed by all men, who will not think, that robbers and pirates have a right of empire over whomsoever they have force enough to master; or that men are bound by promises, which unlawful force extorts from them. Should a robber break into my house, and with a dagger at my throat, make me seal deeds to convey my estate to him, would this give him any title? Just such a title, by his sword, has an unjust conqueror who forces me into submission. The injury and the crime is equal, whether committed by the wearer of the crown, or some petty villain. The title of the offender, and the number of his followers, make no difference in the offence, unless it be to aggravate it. The only difference is, great robbers punish little ones, to keep them in their obedience; but the great ones are rewarded with laurels and triumphs; because they are too big for the weak hands of justice in this world, and have the power in their own possession, which should punish offenders. What is my remedy against a robber that so broke into my house? Appeal to the law for justice. But perhaps justice is denied, or I am crippled and cannot stir, robbed and have not the means to do it. If God has taken away all means of seeking remedy, there is nothing left but patience. But my son, when able, may seek the relief of the law, which I am denied: he or his son may renew his appeal, till he recover his right. But the conquered, or their children, have no court, no arbitrator on earth to appeal to. Then they may appeal, as Jephthah did, to heaven, and repeat their appeal till they have recovered the native right of their ancestors, which was, to have such a legislative over them, as the majority should approve, and freely acquiesce in. If it be objected, this would cause endless trouble; I answer, no more than justice does, where she lies open to all that appeal to her. He that troubles his neighbour without a cause, is punished for it by the justice of the court he appeals to: and he that appeals to heaven must be sure he has right on his side; and a right too that is worth the trouble and cost of the appeal, as he will answer at a tribunal that cannot be deceived, and will be sure to retribute to every one according to the mischiefs he hath created to fellow-subjects; that is, any part of mankind: from whence it is plain, that he that "conquers in an unjust war, can thereby have no title to the subjection and obedience of the conquered."

But supposing victory favours the right side, let us consider a conqueror in a lawful war, and see what power he gets, and over whom.

First, it is plain, "he gets no power by his conquest over those that conquered with him." They that fought on his side cannot suffer by the conquest, but must at least be as much free men as they were before. . . .

But supposing, which seldom happens, that the conquerors and conquered never incorporate into one people, under the same laws and freedom; let us see next "what power a lawful conqueror has over the subdued:" and that I say is purely despotical. He has an absolute power over the lives of those who by an unjust war have forfeited them; but not over the lives or fortunes of those who engaged not in the war, nor over the possessions even of those who were actually engaged in it.

Secondly, I say then the conqueror gets no power but only over those who have actually assisted, concurred, or consented to that unjust force that is used against him: for the people having given to their governors no power to do an unjust thing, such as is to make an unjust war, (for they never had such a power in themselves) they ought not to be charged as guilty of the violence and injustice that is committed in an unjust war, any farther than they actually abet it; no more than they are to be thought guilty of any violence or oppression their governors should use upon the people themselves, or any part of their fellow-subjects, they having empowered them no more to the one than to the other. Conquerors, it is true, seldom trouble themselves to make the distinction, but they willingly permit the confusion of war to sweep all together: but yet this alters not the right . . .

Thirdly, the power a conqueror gets over those he overcomes in a just war, is perfectly despotical: he has an absolute power over the lives of those, who, by putting themselves in a state of war, have forfeited them; but he has not thereby a right and title to their possessions. This I doubt not but at first sight will seem a strange doctrine, it being so quite contrary to the practice of the world; there being nothing more familiar in speaking of the dominion of countries, than to say such an one conquered it; as if conquest, without any more ado, conveyed a right of possession. . . . .

But because the miscarriages of the father are no faults of the children, and they may be rational and peaceable, notwithstanding the brutishness and injustice of the father; the father, by his miscarriages and violence, can forfeit but his own life, but involves not his children in his guilt or destruction. His goods which nature, that willeth the preservation of all mankind as much as is possible, hath made to belong to the children to keep them from perishing, do still continue to belong to his children . . .

. . . Here then is the case: the conqueror has a title to reparation for damages received, and the children have a title to their father's estate for their subsistence: for as to the wife's share, whether her own labour, or compact, gave her a title to it, it is plain, her husband could not forfeit what was hers. What must be done in the case? I answer; the fundamental law of nature being, that all, as much as may be, should be preserved, it follows, that if there be not enough fully to satisfy both, viz. for the conqueror's losses, and children's maintenance, he that hath, and to spare, must remit something of his full satisfaction, and give way to the pressing and preferable title of those who are in danger to perish without it.

But supposing the charge and damages of the war are to be made up to the conqueror to the utmost farthing; and that the children of the vanquished, spoiled of all their father's goods, are to be left to starve and perish; yet the satisfying of what shall, on this score, be due to the conqueror, will scarce give him a title to any country he shall conquer: for the damages of war can scarce amount of the value of any considerable tract of land, in any part of the world, where all the land is possessed, and none lies waste. . . . No damage therefore, that men in the state of nature (as all princes and governments are in reference to one another) suffer from one another, can give a conqueror power to dispossess the posterity of the vanquished, and turn them out of that inheritance which ought to be the possession of them and their descendants to all generations. The conqueror indeed will be apt to think himself master: and it is the very condition of the subdued not to be able to dispute their right. But if that be all, it gives no other title than what bare force gives to the stronger over the weaker; and, by this reason, he that is strongest will have a right to whatever he pleases to seize on.

Over those then that joined with him in the war, and over those of the subdued country that opposed him not, and the posterity even of those that did, the conqueror, even in a just war, hath, by his conquest, no right of dominion: they are free from any subjection to him, and if their former government be dissolved, they are at liberty to begin and erect another to themselves. . . . .

From all which it follows, that the government of a conqueror, imposed by force, on the subdued, against whom he had no right of war, or who joined not in the war against him, where he had right, has no obligation upon them.[13]

13. "Of Civil Government," Bk. II, *Works*, 4, 441–51.

5. BOLINGBROKE

1678-1751

HENRY ST. JOHN, VISCOUNT BOLINGBROKE, *became a political essayist in* *an attempt to organize a successful opposition to Robert Walpole. In* *his youth he had a spectacularly successful political career, entering* *Parliament at the age of twenty-two and becoming Secretary of State* *in the Tory ministry of 1710. He combined these two careers with a* *social life which was distinguished for its easy morals even in his in-* *dulgent age. As Secretary of State he conducted a series of brilliant* *negotiations leading to the Treaty of Utrecht in 1714. Unfortunately for* *him the ascension of George I in that year brought the Whigs to power.* *The new Parliament passed a bill of attainder against Bolingbroke for* *his part in the peace negotiations. After exile, during which he planned* *to restore the Stuarts, Bolingbroke abandoned the Jacobite cause and* *was permitted to return to England. He was never again permitted to* *sit in the Lords but he conducted an active campaign to restore Tory* *influence. It was in this period that he produced his most important* *essays.*

Bolingbroke asserted that the "glory of a nation is to proportion the *end she proposes, to her interest and her strength."* [1] *This did not imply* *aggressiveness. Bolingbroke was a patriot but no modern nationalist in* *the sense of feeling hostile toward foreigners. "There is scarce any folly* *or vice," he wrote, "more epidemical among the sons of men, than that* *ridiculous and hurtful vanity by which the people of each country are* *apt to prefer themselves to those of every other."* [2]

These are the measures and proportions, according to which alone political societies ought to unite in alliances, and to assist one another.

1. "Letters on the Study and Use of History," *Works*, 2, 298.
2. *Ibid.*, p. 182.

The edition used is *The Works of Lord Bolingbroke*, 4 vols. Philadelphia, Carey and Hart, 1841.

There is a political, as well as a natural self-love; and the former ought to be, to every member of a commonwealth, the same determining principle of action, where public interest is concerned, that the latter will be to him most certainly wherever his private interest is concerned. I have heard it often said of one man, that he was a friend or an enemy to the house of Austria; and of another, that he was a friend or an enemy to the house of Bourbon. But these expressions proceed generally from passion and prepossession, as the sentiments they impute must proceed, whenever they are real, from these causes, or from one which is still worse, from corruption. A wise prince, and a wise people, bear no regard to other states, except that which arises from coincidence or repugnancy of their several interests; and this regard must therefore vary, as these interests do, in the perpetual fluctuation of human affairs. Thus Queen Elizabeth and her people opposed the house of Austria, and supported the house of Bourbon, in the sixteenth century. Thus Queen Anne and her people opposed the house of Bourbon, and supported the house of Austria, in the eighteenth.[3]

Bolingbroke admitted the importance of the balance of power but he believed this principle should not lead to a policy of frequent intervention in the affairs of Europe. Only major threats to the balance justified exertion to redress it. Even when the balance seemed in danger of being upset, nations should remember that it was only a means of securing the national interest. Only when that interest was endangered should a nation throw its weight in the scale.

Between all extremes there is a certain middle point, which men of genius perceive, and to which men of honor adhere in private and in public life.

Thus avarice and prodigality are at an immense distance; but there is a space marked out by virtue between them, where frugality and generosity reside together. Thus again, to abandon those, whom it is our interest to support, is an excess of folly; and to support the interests of other people, to the ruin of our own, is an excess of folly likewise. But there are lines described by prudence, between these two excesses, within which our common interests meet, and may proceed together.

It would be an invidious as well as tedious task, to go through all the instances which might be produced; wherein we have, under pretence of preserving a balance of power in Europe, gratified the pas-

3. "Some Reflections on the Present State of the Nation," *Works*, 2, 460–1.

sions of particular men, and served the turns of private interest, till we have rendered that principle, in a reasonable pursuit of which our safety and our glory consist, the occasion of real danger to the interest, and of reproach to the wisdom of our nation. . . . .

Whenever this balance is in real danger by the exorbitant growth of one power, or by the union of more, other princes and states will be alarmed of course. All of them ought, and most of them will take measures for their common security. But the wise council amongst them will . . . proportion their measures, and the engagements they enter into, not according to the nature of the danger considered generally, but according to the immediate or remote relation, which it has to each of them; and according to the strength, situation, or any other circumstances, which may be peculiar to each of them.

To do otherwise, would be to lose sight of our own particular interest in the pursuit of a common interest. It would be nothing better than setting up for the Don Quixotes of the world, and engage to fight the battles of all mankind. The state, which keeps its own particular interest constantly in view, has an invariable rule to go by; and this rule will direct and limit all its proceedings in foreign affairs; so that such a state will frequently take no share, and frequently a small share in the disputes of its neighbors, and will never exert its whole strength, but when its whole is at stake. But a state, who neglects to do this, has no rule at all to go by, and must fight to negotiate, and negotiate to fight again, as long as it is a state; because, as long as it is a state, there will be disputes among its neighbors and some of these will prevail at one time, and some at another, in the perpetual flux and reflux of human affairs.[4]

Bolingbroke thought his warning against too much reliance on the balance of power as a guide to foreign policy was reinforced by two failings in that system. First, there could never be an exact balance and efforts to maintain one would be interminable and doomed to failure. Indeed intervention might well lead to a greater imbalance. Second, calculations of national power were imprecise and it was often impossible to discern the actual state of the balance.

The scales of the balance of power will never be exactly poised, nor is the precise point of equality discernible or necessary to be discerned. It is sufficient in this, as in other human affairs, that the deviation be not

4. "The Occasional Writer, No. 2," *Works, 1,* 219–21.

too great. Some there will always be. A constant attention to these devia-tions is therefore necessary. When they are little, their increase may be easily prevented by early care and the precautions that good policy suggests. But when they become great for want of this care and these precautions, or by the force of unforeseen events, more vigor is to be exerted, and greater efforts to be made. But even in such cases, much reflection is necessary on all the circumstances that form the conjunc-ture; lest, by attacking with ill success, the deviation be confirmed, and the power that is deemed already exorbitant become more so; and lest, by attacking with good success, whilst one scale is pillaged, too much weight of power be thrown into the other. In such cases, he who has considered, in the histories of former ages, the strange revolutions that time produces, and the perpetual flux and reflux of public as well as private fortunes, of kingdoms and states as well as of those who govern or are governed in them, will incline to think, that if the scales can be brought back by a war, nearly, though not exactly, to the point they were at before this great deviation from it, the rest may be left to acci-dents, and to the use that good policy is able to make of them.[5]

The precise point at which the scales of power turn, like that of the solstice in either tropic, is imperceptible to common observation: and, in one case as in the other, some progress must be made in the new direction, before the change is perceived. They who are in the sinking scale, for in the political balance of power, unlike to all others, the scale that is empty sinks, and that which is full rises; they who are in the sinking scale do not easily come off from the habitual prejudices of superior wealth, or power, or skill, or courage, nor from the confidence that these prejudices inspire. They who are in the rising scale do not immediately feel their strength, nor assume that confidence in it which successful experience gives them afterwards. They who are the most concerned to watch the variations of this balance, misjudge often in the same manner, and from the same prejudices. They continue to dread a power no longer able to hurt them, or they continue to have no appre-hensions of a power that grows daily more formidable. Spain verified the first observation at the end of the second period, when, proud and poor, and enterprising and feeble, she still thought herself a match for France. France verified the second observation at the beginning of the third period, when the triple alliance stopped the progress of her arms, which alliances much more considerable were not able to effect afterwards.

5. "Use of History," *Works,* 2, 291.

The other principal powers of Europe, in their turns, have verified the third observation in both its parts, through the whole course of this period.[6]

The argument for abstention from international conflicts was especially strong in the case of an island. Bolingbroke granted that continental nations could be endangered by small movements in the balance but an island could afford to wait until major changes occurred. Meanwhile an island nation would do well to be friendly to all and engage in profitable trade. Above all it should not sacrifice its advantage by acquiring continental territory.

. . . Let us confine our reflections to some of those different means and objects, either of defence or offence, which nature, improved by art, presents to people who inhabit islands, or to people who inhabit the continent, according to their different situations. A powerful navy is of indispensable necessity to the former of these. Without it, they must be poor and exposed. With it, they may be rich and secure. Barriers of fortified towns, and great standing armies are of the same necessity to the latter. Without this security, they lie open to every inroad, and at the mercy of every neighbor. With it, they may be safe from foreign danger, and even terrible to those who live around them. . . . But farther: as particular families, by uniting together, formed larger societies, for their common defence, and gave rise to the kingdoms, and states, which have appeared in the world; so these larger societies have, ever since, found it necessary, or advantageous, to unite together in various manners; sometimes by an entire union, or an incorporation of different people into one body politic; sometimes by a partial, or federal union of distinct states in one common cause; and at all times by alliances, made on particular occasions, and suggested by a real or seeming conformity of interest. This occasional union, by alliances with other states . . . is so necessary to all the nations on the continent, that even the most powerful cannot subsist without it; and those who manage it best, are accounted wisest. . . . there always are, and always must be, systems of alliances subsisting among these nations; and therefore, as a change in some of the parts of one system necessarily requires a change in all the rest; so the alteration of one system necessarily requires an alteration of the others.

Thus are they always tossed from peace to war, and from war to

6. *Ibid.,* p. 258.

peace. Perpetual negotiation is the life and soul of their governments. Their well-being, nay their safety at home, requires that they should be always busy abroad. . . .

The interfering and clashing of their rights and pretensions, and the various obligations, by which they stand bound to one another, appear to be and are the immediate causes of all these disputes and contentions. But the principal and remote cause arises from the proximity and other circumstances of their situations. That necessity, or advantage, which gave occasion to the original engagements, has maintained and multiplied them since; and the last would not be reasonable, if the first had not been necessary.

Here then arises an essential difference between those objects which are proper to the policy of an island, and those which are so to the policy of the continent; a difference greatly to the advantage of the former; the circumstances of whose situation not requiring so constant and intimate a union with other states, either for defence or offence, render unnecessary a great part of the engagements which prove such heavy and lasting incumbrances on the latter.

An island under one government, advantageously situated, rich in itself, richer by its commerce, can have no necessity, in the ordinary course of affairs, to take up the policy of the continent; to enter into the system of alliances we have been speaking of; or, in short, to act any other part than that of a friendly neighbor and a fair trader. If an extraordinary crisis happens on the continent, which may endanger the safety even of those who are separated from it, such as we saw at the beginning of the present century, self-preservation will no doubt determine men, as it ought, to unite by stricter alliances with those powers with whom they are occasionally united by a more immediate interest; but even in this case, neither will self-preservation require, nor good policy suffer, that such a people should enter deep into the quarrels, or involve themselves intricately, much less continually, in the political schemes of the continent. We pass over offensive cases, because it is manifest that the people of an island can have no interest in making foreign acquisitions; and that therefore it would be absurd in them to spend their blood and treasure in acquiring only for others; or to attack any farther than is necessary to defend.

We confine ourselves to the case of defence before mentioned; and upon that we say, a people on the continent may have reason to engage as deeply in defence of another country, as if they defended the walls of their own towns, or the doors of their own houses; because another country may be the sole barrier of their own. But this can never be reasonably done by the people of an island, who have another, and a better barrier than any the continent can form for them. Such a people are to look on their engagements with other countries, as an outworks cast up in haste, which may serve to defeat a weak attack, or to delay and disappoint a strong one. But it would be the height of folly in them, even in one of those extraordinary conjunctures, which we now suppose, to lay the whole stress of their defence here; to spend their strength improperly; and to forego those advantages which nature has given them.[7]

Drawing on these principles, Bolingbroke outlined a foreign policy for Great Britain. He thought Britain should build up its sea power and stand aloof from European quarrels until its own interests were directly attacked or until a power arose which threatened all Europe. In this way Britain might preserve her forces as the decisive weight in the balance. Britain could be the guardian of a true balance, prepared to throw its weight into either scale, quick to withdraw when the scales swing back and never destroying its stabilizing influence by becoming permanently attached to any group of nations.

Great Britain is an island: and, whilst nations on the continent are at immense charge in maintaining their barriers, and perpetually on their guard, and frequently embroiled, to extend or strengthen them, Great Britain may, if her governors please, accumulate wealth in maintaining hers; make herself secure from invasions, and be ready to invade others when her own immediate interests, or the general interest of Europe requires it. Of all which Queen Elizabeth's reign is a memorable example, and undeniable proof. I said the general interest of Europe; because it seems to me that this, alone, should call our councils off from an almost entire application to their domestic and proper business. Other nations must watch over every motion of their neighbors; penetrate, if they can, every design; foresee every minute event; and take part by some engagement or other in almost every conjuncture that arises. But as we cannot be easily nor suddenly attacked, and as we ought not to aim at any acquisition of territory on the continent, it may be our interest to watch the secret workings of the several councils abroad; to advise, and to warn; to abet, and oppose; but it never can be our true interest easily and officiously to enter into action, much less into engagements that imply action and expense. Other nations, like the

7. "Remarks on the History of England," *Works, 1,* 385–7.

Velites or light-armed troops, stand foremost in the field, and skirmish perpetually. When a great war begins, we ought to look on the powers of the continent, to whom we incline, like the two first lines, the Principes and Hastati of a Roman army: and on ourselves, like the Triarii, that are not to charge with these legions on every occasion, but to be ready for the conflict whenever the fortune of the day, be it sooner or later, calls us to it, and the sum of things, or the general interest, makes it necessary.

This is that post of advantage and honor, which our singular situation among the powers of Europe determines us, or should determine us, to take, in all disputes that happen on the continent. If we neglect it, and dissipate our strength on occasions that touch us remotely or indirectly, we are governed by men who do not know the true interest of this island, or who have some other interest more at heart. If we adhere to it, so at least as to deviate little and seldom from it, as we shall do whenever we are wisely and honestly governed, then will this nation make her proper figure; and a great one it will be. By a continual attention to improve her natural, that is her maritime strength, by collecting all her forces within herself, and reserving them to be laid out on great occasions, such as regard her immediate interests and her honor, or such as are truly important to the general system of power in Europe; she may be the arbitrator of differences, the guardian of liberty, and the preserver of that balance, which has been so much talked of, and is so little understood.

. . . Occasionally too we must be soldiers, and for offence as well as defence; but in proportion to the nature of the conjuncture, considered always relatively to the difference here insisted upon between our situation, our interest, and the nature of our strength, compared with those of the other powers of Europe; and not in proportion to the desires, or even to the wants, of the nations with whom we are confederated. Like other amphibious animals, we must come occasionally on shore: but the water is more properly our element, and in it, like them, as we find our greatest security, so we exert our greatest force.[8]

8. "The Idea of a Patriot King," *Works, 2,* 417–18.

6. DAVID HUME

1711-1776

WHILE *studying in France from 1733 to 1737, David Hume wrote* A Treatise of Human Nature, *published 1739–40, before he was yet thirty years of age. In a series of subsequent essays (published in a collected edition after 1753 as* Essays and Treatises on Several Subjects) *he presented in a more literary and popular form the arguments of that first work, modifying some of the ideas and elaborating others. His speculative writings were completed by 1757 and thereafter he turned to the writing of history.*

In 1747 he had been a member of a military mission to Vienna and Turin, acting as secretary to General St. Clair. But most of his experience in the conduct of international affairs came in the later period of his life after his literary and philosophical reputation had been established. During 1763–66 he lived in Paris, serving as secretary to Lord Hertford, the British ambassador there, and later as secretary to the embassy. Received in Parisian literary society with great enthusiasm, he became a friend of d'Alembert, Diderot, and Turgot, and brought Rousseau to London with him, although a few months later the two philosophers quarreled. In the following year he became Under-Secretary of State to General Conway at the British Foreign Office, and in 1769 he retired to Edinburgh.

The dominant philosophers of Hume's day held that men based their value judgments, and thus their motives to action, on reason. Hume denied this and asserted that men acted only at the dictates of their passions. Subordinate to the passions, reason merely suggested possible objects of passion and selected means for their attainment. "Reason is,

The editions used are A *Treatise of Human Nature*, 3 vols. London, John Noon, 1739–40; *Philosophical Essays on Morals, Literature, and Politics*, 2 vols. Georgetown, D.C., W. Duffy, 1817.

and ought only to be the slave of the passions, and can never pretend to any other office than to serve and obey them." [1]

Hume did not deny the existence of general laws of social and political conduct which all men should obey. These rules, however, were not a natural law discerned by reason but certain behavior which men had found by experience to be productive of the most satisfaction. The study of political morals—that is, of salutary political habits—must therefore proceed by observation.

Hume believed "that it is utterly impossible for men to remain any considerable time in that savage condition which precedes society; but that his very first state and situation may justly be esteemed social." [2] Disagreeing with those philosophers who believed that the state of nature had really existed, Hume declared it to be "a mere philosophical fiction, which never had, and never could have any reality." [3] The simplest state in which man finds himself, then, is a society without civil government. This simple society is very closely analogous to international relations. In this state men voluntarily observe rules of justice which they have arrived at by convention out of self-interest.

. . . in order to form society, it is requisite not only that it be advantageous; but also that men be sensible of these advantages; and it is impossible, in their wild uncultivated state, that by study and reflection alone, they should ever be able to attain this knowledge. Most fortunately, therefore, there is conjoined to those necessities, whose remedies are remote and obscure, another necessity, which, having a present and more obvious remedy, may justly be regarded as the first and original principle of human society. This necessity is no other than that natural appetite betwixt the sexes, which unites them together, and preserves their union till a new tie takes place in their concern for their common offspring. This new concern becomes also a principle of union betwixt the parents and offspring, and forms a more numerous society; where the parents govern by the advantage of their superior strength and wisdom, and at the same time are restrained in the exercise of their authority by that natural affection, which they bear their children. In a little time, custom and habit operating on the tender minds of the children, makes them sensible of the advantages, which they may reap

1. *A Treatise of Human Nature*, 2, 248.
2. *Ibid.*, 3, 64–5.
3. *Ibid.*

from society, as well as fashions them by degrees for it, by rubbing off those rough corners and untoward affections, which prevent their coalition.

For it must be confessed, that however the circumstances of human nature may render a union necessary, and however those passions of lust and natural affection may seem to render it unavoidable; yet there are other particulars in our *natural temper,* and in our *outward circumstances,* which are very incommodious, and are even contrary to the requisite conjunction. Among the former, we may justly esteem our *selfishness* to be the most considerable. I am sensible, that, generally speaking, the representations of this quality have been carried much too far; and that the descriptions, which certain philosophers delight so much to form of mankind in this particular, are as wide of nature as any accounts of monsters, which we meet with in fables and romances. So far from thinking, that men have no affection for anything beyond themselves, I am of opinion, that though it be rare to meet with one who loves any single person better than himself; yet it is as rare to meet with one in whom all the kind affections, taken together, do not overbalance all the selfish. . . .

But though this generosity must be acknowledged to the honour of human nature, we may at the same time remark, that so noble an affection, instead of fitting men for large societies, is almost as contrary to them, as the most narrow selfishness. For while each person loves himself better than any other single person, and in his love to others bears the greatest affection to his relations and acquaintance, this must necessarily produce an opposition of passions, and a consequent opposition of actions; which cannot but be dangerous to the new-established union.

It is, however worth while to remark, that this contrariety of passions would be attended with but small danger, did it not concur with a peculiarity in our *outward circumstances* which affords it an opportunity of exerting itself. There are three different species of goods, which we are possessed of: the internal satisfaction of our minds, the external advantages of our body, and the enjoyment of such possessions as we have acquired by our industry and good fortune. We are perfectly secure in the enjoyment of the first. The second may be ravished from us, but can be of no advantage to him who deprives us of them. The last only are both exposed to the violence of others, and may be transferred without suffering any loss or alteration; while at the same time, there is not a sufficient quantity of them to supply every one's desires and necessities. As the improvement, therefore, of these goods is the chief advantage of society, so the *instability* of their possession, along with their scarcity, is the chief impediment. . . . .

The remedy . . . is not derived from nature, but from *artifice;* or more properly speaking, nature provides a remedy in the judgment and understanding, for what is irregular and incommodious in the affections. For when men, from their early education in society, have become sensible of the infinite advantages that result from it, and have besides acquired a new affection to company and conversation; and when they have observed, that the principal disturbance in society arises from those goods, which we call external, and from their looseness and easy transition from one person to another; they must seek for a remedy, by putting these goods, as far as possible, on the same footing with the fixed and constant advantages of the mind and body. This can be done after no other manner, than by a convention entered into by all the members of the society to bestow stability on the possession of those external goods, and leave every one in the peaceable enjoyment of what he may acquire by his fortune and industry. By this means, every one knows what he may safely possess; and the passions are restrained in their partial and contradictory motions. Nor is such a restraint contrary to these passions; for if so, it could never be entered into, nor maintained; but it is only contrary to their heedless and impetuous movement. Instead of departing from our own interest, or from that of our nearest friends, by abstaining from the possessions of others, we cannot better consult both these interests, than by such a convention; because it is by that means we maintain society, which is so necessary to their well-being and subsistence, as well as to our own.

This convention is not of the nature of a *promise:* for even promises themselves . . . arise from human conventions. It is only a general sense of common interest; which sense all the members of the society express to one another, and which induces them to regulate their conduct by certain rules. . . . .

No one can doubt, that the convention for the distinction of property, and for the stability of possession, is of all circumstances the most necessary to the establishment of human society, and that after the agreement for the fixing and observing of this rule, there remains little or nothing to be done towards settling a perfect harmony and concord. All the other passions, beside this of interest, are either easily restrained or are not of such pernicious consequence when indulged.[4]

4. *Ibid.* 52–63.

All men are sensible of the necessity of justice to maintain peace and order; and all men are sensible of the necessity of peace and order for the maintenance of society. Yet, notwithstanding this strong and obvious necessity, such is the frailty or perverseness of our nature! it is impossible to keep men, faithfully and unerringly, in the paths of justice. Some extraordinary circumstances may happen, in which a man finds his interests to be more promoted by fraud or rapine, than hurt by the breach which his injustice makes in the social union. But much more frequently, he is seduced from his great and important, but distant interests, by the allurement of present, though often very frivolous temptations. This great weakness is incurable in human nature.

Men must, therefore, endeavour to palliate what they cannot cure. They must institute some persons, under the appellation of magistrates, whose peculiar office it is, to point out the decrees of equity, to punish transgressors, to correct fraud and violence, and to oblige men, however reluctant, to consult their own real and permanent interests. In a word *obedience* is a new duty which must be invented to support that of *justice;* and the ties of equity must be corroborated by those of allegiance.[5]

A civil government, once organized, can render more positive services than the mere prevention of injustice between its subjects. One of its most important functions is to organize defense against other societies. Hume thought that the urgent need for such defense was probably the first and strongest motive for forming a government.

. . . so far am I from thinking with some philosophers, that men are utterly incapable of society without government, that I assert the first rudiments of government to arise from quarrels, not among men of the same society, but among those of different societies. A less degree of riches will suffice to this latter effect, than is requisite for the former. Men fear nothing from public war and violence but the resistance they meet with, which, because they share it in common, seems less terrible; and because it comes from strangers, seems less pernicious in its consequences, than when they are exposed singly against one whose commerce is advantageous to them, and without whose society it is impossible they can subsist. Now foreign war to a society without government necessarily produces civil war. Throw any considerable goods among men, they instantly fall a quarrelling, while each strives to get possession of what pleases him, without regard to the consequences. In

5. "Of the Origin of Government," *Essays, 1,* 63–4.

a foreign war the most considerable of all goods, life and limbs, are at stake; and as every one shuns dangerous ports, seizes the best arms, seeks excuse for the slightest wounds, the laws, which may be well enough observed while men were calm, can now no longer take place, when they are in such a commotion.

This we find verified in the *American* tribes, where men live in concord and amity among themselves without any established government; and never pay submission to any of their fellows, except in time of war, when their captain enjoys a shadow of authority, which he loses after their return from the field, and the establishment of peace with the neighbouring tribes. This authority, however, instructs them in the advantages of government, and teaches them to have recourse to it, when either by the pillage of war, by commerce, or by any fortuitous inventions, their riches and possessions have become so considerable as to make them forget, on every emergency, the interest they have in the preservation of peace and justice.[6]

Sovereign states stand in almost, but not quite, the same relationship to each other as that between individuals who recognize laws of justice but lack civil government. The difference arises from the fact that the intercourse of states is not so constant, so intimate, and so essential to human welfare as that of individuals. For this reason the laws of justice between nations are not so rigid or so binding as those between individuals. Hume did not think it possible to define international morality in precise terms but he thought that all men had an implicit notion of it.

If a state considers the laws of international justice no longer serve its interests, it can have recourse to war. War is the suspension of the rules of justice, and since those laws derive their value from reciprocal observance, a belligerent can observe no more restraint against an opponent than the enemy himself observes.

When civil government has been established over the greatest part of mankind, and different societies have been formed contiguous to each other, there arises a new set of duties among the neighbouring states, suitable to the nature of that commerce, which they carry on with each other. Political writers tell us, that in every kind of intercourse, a body politic is to be considered as one person; and indeed this assertion is so far just, that different nations, as well as private persons, require mutual assistance; at the same time that their selfishness and

6. *Treatise, 3,* 142–4.

ambition are perpetual sources of war and discord. But though nations in this particular resemble individuals, yet as they are very different in other respects, no wonder they regulate themselves by different maxims, and give rise to a new set of rules, which we call *the laws of nations.* Under this head we may comprise the sacredness of the persons of ambassadors, the declaration of war, the abstaining from poisoned arms, with other duties of that kind, which are evidently calculated for the commerce that is peculiar to different societies.

But though these rules be superadded to the laws of nature, the former do not entirely abolish the latter; and one may safely affirm, that the three fundamental rules of justice, the stability of possession, its transference by consent, and the performance of promises, are duties of princes as well as of subjects. The same interest produces the same effect in both cases. Where possession has no stability, there must be perpetual war. Where property is not transferred by consent, there can be no commerce. Where promises are not observed, there can be no leagues nor alliances. The advantages, therefore, of peace, commerce, and mutual succour, make us extend to different kingdoms the same notions of justice, which take place among individuals.

There is a maxim very current in the world, which few politicians are willing to avow, but which has been authorized by the practice of all ages, *that there is a system of morals calculated for princes, much more free than that which ought to govern private persons.* It is evident this is not to be understood of the lesser *extent* of public duties and obligations; nor will anyone be so extravagant as to assert, that the most solemn treaties ought to have no force among princes. For as princes do actually form treaties among themselves, they must propose some advantage from the execution of them; and the prospect of such advantage must engage them to perform their part, and must establish that law of nature. The meaning, therefore, of this political maxim is, that though the morality of princes has the same *extent,* yet it has not the same *force* as that of private persons, and may lawfully be transgressed from a more trivial motive. However shocking such a proposition may appear to certain philosophers, it will be easy to defend it upon those principles, by which we have accounted for the origin of justice and equity.

When men have found by experience, that it is impossible to subsist without society, and that it is impossible to maintain society, while they give free course to their appetites; so urgent an interest quickly restrains their actions, and imposes an obligation to observe those rules which we call *the laws of justice*. This obligation of interest rests not here; but by the necessary course of the passions and sentiments, gives rise to the moral obligation of duty; while we approve of such actions as tend to the peace of society, and disapprove of such as tend to its disturbance. The same *natural* obligation of interest takes place among independent kingdoms, and gives rise to the same *morality;* so that no one of ever so corrupt morals will approve of a prince, who voluntarily, and of his own accord, breaks his word, or violates any treaty. But here we may observe, that though the intercourse of different states be advantageous, and even sometimes necessary, yet it is not so necessary nor advantageous as that among individuals, without which it is utterly impossible for human nature ever to subsist. Since, therefore, the *natural* obligation to justice, among different states, is not so strong as among individuals, the *moral* obligation, which arises from it, must partake of its weakness; and we must necessarily give a greater indulgence to a prince or minister, who deceives another; than to a private gentleman, who breaks his word of honour.

Should it be asked, *what proportion these two species of morality bear to each other?* I would answer, that this is a question, to which we can never have any precise answer; nor is it possible to reduce to numbers the proportion, which we ought to fix betwixt them. One may safely affirm, that this proportion finds itself, without any art or study of men; as we may observe on many other occasions. The practice of the world goes further in teaching us the degrees of our duty, than the most subtle philosophy which was ever yet invented. And this may serve as a convincing proof, that all men have an implicit notion of the foundation of those moral rules concerning natural and civil justice, and are sensible, that they arise merely from human conventions, and from the interest, which we have in the preservation of peace and order. For otherwise the diminution of the interest would never produce a relaxation of the morality, and reconcile us more easily to any transgression of justice among princes and republics, than in the private commerce of one subject with another.[7]

The rage and violence of public war; what is it but a suspension of justice among the warring parties, who perceive, that this virtue is now no longer of any *use* or advantage to them? The laws of war, which then succeed to those of equity and justice, are rules calculated for the *advantage* and *utility* of that particular state, in which men are now

7. *Ibid.*, pp. 188–93.

placed. And were a civilized nation engaged with barbarians, who observed no rules even of war; the former must also suspend their observance of them, where they no longer serve to any purpose; and must render every action or encounter as bloody and pernicious as possible to the first aggressor.[8]

According to Hume international relations were generally conducted on the "maxim of preserving the balance of power." This system he characterized as one in which "every prevailing power was sure to meet with a confederacy against it, and that often composed of its former friends and allies." [9] *Hume thought this was an admirable means of promoting a general spirit of moderation and preserving the liberties of mankind. His description of the balance of power has become a classic. He deplored a British tendency to lose sight of the balance and enter wars so wholeheartedly as to lose sight of probable results. In particular he feared that this might provoke a reaction into isolationism, a policy as deplorable as headstrong adventurousness.*

It is a question, whether the *idea* of the balance of power be owing entirely to modern policy, or whether the *phrase* only has been invented in these latter ages? It is certain that Xenophon, in his Institution of Cyrus, represents the combination of the Asiatic powers to have arisen from a jealousy of the increasing force of the Medes and Persians; and though that elegant composition should be supposed altogether a romance, this sentiment, ascribed by the author to the eastern princes, is at least a proof of the prevailing notion of ancient times.

In all the politics of Greece, the anxiety, with regard to the balance of power, is apparent, and is expressly pointed out to us, even by the ancient historians. Thucydides represents the league, which was formed against Athens, and which produced the Peloponnesian war, as entirely owing to this principle. . . .

Whoever will read Demosthenes's oration for the Megalopolitans, may see the utmost refinements on this principle, that ever entered into the head of a Venetian or English speculatist. And upon the first rise of the Macedonian power, this orator immediately discovered the danger, sounded the alarm throughout all Greece, and at last assembled that confederacy under the banners of Athens which fought the great and decisive battle of Chaeronea. . . . .

The successors of Alexander showed great jealousy of the balance of

8. "Concerning Principles of Morals," *Essays, 2,* 215–16.
9. "Of the Balance of Power," *Essays, 1,* 350.

power; a jealousy founded on true politics and prudence, and which preserved distinct for several ages the partition made after the death of that famous conqueror. The fortune and ambition of Antigonus threatened them anew with a universal monarchy; but their combination, and their victory at Ipsus saved them. . . .

The reason, why it is supposed, that the ancients were entirely ignorant of the *balance of power,* seems to be drawn from the Roman history more than the Grecian; and as the transactions of the former are generally more familiar to us, we have thence formed all our conclusions. It must be owned, that the Romans never met with any such general combination or confederacy against them, as might naturally have been expected from the rapid conquests and declared ambition; but were allowed peaceably to subdue their neighbours, one after another, till they extended their dominion over the whole known world. . . . .

The only prince we meet with in the Roman history, who seems to have understood the balance of power, is Hiero king of Syracuse. Though the ally of Rome, he sent assistance to the Carthaginians, during the war of the auxiliaries; "Esteeming it requisite," says Polybius, "both in order to retain his dominions in Sicily, and to preserve the Roman friendship, that Carthage should be safe; lest by its fall the remaining power should be able, without contrast or opposition, to execute every purpose and undertaking. And here he acted with great wisdom and prudence. For that is never, on any account, to be overlooked; nor ought such a force ever to be thrown into one hand, as to incapacitate the neighbouring states from defending their rights against it." Here is the aim of modern politics pointed out in express terms.

In short, the maxim of preserving the balance of power is founded so much on common sense and obvious reasoning, that it is impossible it could altogether have escaped antiquity, where we find, in other particulars, so many marks of deep penetration and discernment. If it was not so generally known and acknowledged as at present, it had, at least, an influence on all the wiser and more experienced princes and politicians. And indeed, even at present, however generally known and acknowledged among speculative reasoners, it has not, in practice, an authority much more extensive among those who govern the world. . . . .

In the general wars, maintained against this ambitious power, Great Britain has stood foremost; and she still maintains her station. Beside her advantages of riches and situation, her people are animated with such a national spirit, and are so fully sensible of the blessings of their government, that we may hope their vigour never will languish in so necessary and so just a cause. On the contrary, if we may judge by the past, their passionate ardour seems rather to require some moderation; and they have oftener erred from a laudable excess than from a blameable deficiency.

In the *first* place, we seem to have been more possessed with the ancient Greek spirit of jealous emulation, than actuated by the prudent views of modern politics. Our wars with France have been begun with justice, and even, perhaps from necessity; but have always been too far pushed from obstinacy and passion. The same peace, which was afterwards made at Ryswick in 1697, was offered so early as the year ninety-two; that concluded at Utrecht in 1712 might have been finished on as good conditions at Gertruytenberg in the year eight; and we might have given at Frankfort, in 1723, the same terms, which we were glad to accept of at Aix-la-Chapelle in the year forty-eight. Here then we see, that above half of our wars with France, and all our public debts, are owing more to our own imprudent vehemence than to the ambition of our neighbours.

In the *second* place, we are so declared in our opposition to French power, and so alert in defence of our allies, that they always reckon upon our force as upon their own; and expecting to carry on war at our expence, refuse all reasonable terms of accommodation. . . . All the world knows, that the factious vote of the House of Commons, in the beginning of the last parliament, with the professed humour of the nation, made the queen of Hungary inflexible in her terms, and prevented that agreement with Prussia, which would immediately have restored the general tranquillity of Europe.

In the *third* place, we are such true combatants, that, when once engaged, we lose all concern for ourselves and our posterity, and consider only how we may best annoy the enemy. To mortgage our revenues at so deep a rate, in wars, where we were only accessories, was surely the most fatal delusion, that a nation, which had any pretension to politics and prudence, has ever yet been guilty of. That remedy of funding, if it be a remedy, and not rather a poison, ought, in all reason, to be reserved to the last extremity; and no evil, but the greatest and most urgent, should ever induce us to embrace so dangerous an expedient.

These excesses, to which we have been carried, are prejudicial; and may, perhaps, in time, become still more prejudicial another way, by begetting, as is usual, the opposite extreme, and rendering us totally careless and supine with regard to the fate of Europe. The Athenians, from the most bustling, intriguing, warlike people of Greece, finding their error in thrusting themselves into every quarrel, abandoned all attention to foreign affairs; and in no contest ever took part on either side, except by their flatteries and complaisance to the victor.[10]

The true basis of Britain's strength, thought Hume, lay in her wealth and in the contentment and vigor of her people. It was true that monarchies and republics alike had a love of conquest but this was a mistaken ambition. Empire does not bring strength. On the contrary it produces tyranny and disaffection at home and therefore weakness abroad. Small states have the most contented subjects. Similarly, wealth is best obtained by trade and not by conquest. Moreover Hume denied the mercantilist thesis that commerce should be regarded as a struggle; it is a process benefiting all parties. Thus both the wealth and the contentment that make a nation strong are best sought in a system of moderate-sized, independent, and freely trading states.

. . . extensive conquests, when pursued, must be the ruin of every free government; and of the more perfect governments sooner than of the imperfect; because of the very advantages which the former possess above the latter. And though such a state ought to establish a fundamental law against conquests; yet republics have ambition as well as individuals, and present interest makes men forgetful of their posterity.[11]

Enormous monarchies are, probably, destructive to human nature; in their progress, in their continuance, and even in their downfall, which never can be very distant from their establishment. The military genius, which aggrandized the monarchy, soon leaves the court, the capital, and the centre of such a government; while the wars are carried on at a great distance, and interest so small a part of the state. The ancient nobility, whose affections attach them to their sovereign, live all at court; and never will accept of military employments, which would carry them to remote and barbarous frontiers, where they are distant both from their pleasures and their fortune. The arms of the state, must, therefore, be entrusted to mercenary strangers, without zeal, without attachment, without honour; ready on every occasion to turn them against the prince, and join each desperate malcontent, who offers pay

10. *Ibid.*, pp. 349–56.
11. "Idea of a Perfect Commonwealth," *Essays, 1,* 521.

and plunder. This is the necessary progress of human affairs: Thus human nature checks itself in its airy elevation: Thus ambition blindly labours for the destruction of the conqueror, of his family, and of everything near and dear to him. The Bourbons, trusting to the support of their brave, faithful, and affectionate nobility, would push their advantage without reserve or limitation. These, while fired with glory and emulation, can bear the fatigues and dangers of war; but never would submit to languish in the garrisons of Hungary or Lithuania, forgot at court, and sacrificed to the intrigues of every minion or mistress, who approaches the prince. The troops are filled with Cravates and Tartars, Hussars and Cossacs; intermingled, perhaps, with a few soldiers of fortune from the better provinces: And the melancholy fate of the Roman emperors, from the same cause, is renewed over and over again, till the final dissolution of the monarchy.[12]

The greatness of a state, and the happiness of its subjects, how independent soever they may be supposed in some respects, are commonly allowed as inseparable with regard to commerce; and as private men receive greater security, in the possession of their trade and riches, from the power of public, so the public becomes powerful in proportion to the opulence and extensive commerce of private men. This maxim is true, in general; though I cannot forbear thinking, that it may possibly admit of exceptions, and that we often establish it with too little reserve and limitation. There may be some circumstances, where the commerce and riches and luxury of individuals, instead of adding strength to the public, will serve only to thin its armies and diminish its authority among the neighbouring nations. . . . .

[However in general there is advantage in] *foreign* commerce, in augmenting the power of the state, as well as the riches and happiness of the subjects. It increases the stock of labour in the nation; and the sovereign may convert what share of it he finds necessary to the service of the public . . . In short, a kingdom, that has a large import and export, must abound more with industry, and that employed upon delicacies and luxuries, than a kingdom which rests contented with its native commodities. It is, therefore, more powerful, as well as richer and happier.[13]

It is very usual, in nations ignorant of the nature of commerce, to prohibit the exportation of commodities, and to preserve among them-

12. "Of the Balance of Power," *Essays, 1,* 356–7.
13. "Of Commerce," *Essays, 1,* 269–82.

selves whatever they think valuable and useful. They do consider not, that, in this prohibition, they act directly contrary to their intention; and that the more is exported of any commodity, the more will be raised at home. . . . .

. . . there still prevails, even in nations well acquainted with commerce, a strong jealousy with regard to the balance of trade, and a fear, that all their gold and silver may be leaving them. This seems to me, almost in every case, a groundless apprehension . . .[14]

. . . Nothing is more usual, among states which have made some advances in commerce, than to look at the progress of their neighbours with a suspicious eye, to consider all trading states as their rivals, and to suppose that it is impossible for any of them to flourish, but at their expence. In opposition to this narrow and malignant opinion, I will venture to assert, that the increase of riches and commerce in any one nation, instead of hurting, commonly promotes the riches and commerce of all its neighbours; and that a state can scarcely carry its trade and industry very far, where all the surrounding states are buried in ignorance, sloth, and barbarism. . . . .

. . . I shall therefore venture to acknowledge, that, not only as a man, but as a British subject, I pray for the flourishing commerce of Germany, Spain, Italy, and even France itself. I am at least certain, that Great Britain, and all those nations, would flourish more, did their sovereigns and ministers adopt such enlarged and benevolent sentiments towards each other.[15]

. . . *nothing is more favourable to the rise of politeness and learning, than a number of neighbouring and independent states, connected together by commerce and policy.* The emulation, which naturally arises among those neighbouring states, is an obvious source of improvement: but what I would chiefly insist on is the stop, which such limited territories give both to *power* and to *authority*.

Extended governments, where a single person has great influence, soon become despotic; but small ones change naturally into commonwealths. A large government is accustomed by degrees to tyranny; because each act of violence is at first performed upon a part, which, being distant from the majority, is not taken notice of, nor excites any violent ferment. . . .

In a small government, any act of oppression is immediately known

14. "Of the Balance of Trade," *Essays, 1,* 325–6.
15. "Of the Jealousy of Trade," *Essays, 1,* 343–7.

throughout the whole: The murmurs and discontents proceeding from it, are easily communicated . . .

But the divisions into small states are favourable to learning, by stopping the progress of *authority* as well as that of *power*. Reputation is often as great a fascination upon men as sovereignty, and is equally destructive to the freedom of thought and imagination. But where a number of neighbouring states have a great intercourse of arts and commerce, their mutual jealousy keeps them from receiving too lightly the law from each other, in matters of taste and of reasoning, and makes them examine every work of art with the greatest care and accuracy. The contagion of popular opinion spreads not so easily from one place to another. It readily receives a check in some state or other, where it concurs not with the prevailing prejudices. And nothing but nature and reason, or, at least, what bears them a strong resemblance, can force its way through all obstacles, and unite the most rival nations into an esteem and admiration of it.[16]

16. "The Rise of Arts and Sciences," *Essays, 1,* 138–9.

7. ADAM SMITH

1723-1790

LIKE *his friend David Hume, Adam Smith participated in the ferment of thought that distinguished the Scottish universities in the eighteenth century. In 1751 he was made Professor of Logic at the University of Glasgow and in the following year became Professor of Moral Philosophy there. A few years later, in 1759, he published* The Theory of Moral Sentiments, *a philosophical essay that brought him immediate acclaim. With the conclusion of the Seven Years War in 1763 he resigned his professorship and traveled to France as tutor to the young Duke of Buccleuch. Welcomed in the salons of Paris as Hume had been a decade before, he came into personal contact with the leaders of the Enlightenment. After his return to Scotland he spent several years in retirement, completing* The Inquiry into the Nature and Causes of the Wealth of Nations *in 1776. Two years afterward he was made commissioner of customs at Edinburgh.*

According to Smith men have a capacity for sympathizing with their fellows and sharing their feelings. In this way men are capable of some impartiality, even on issues which involve their own interests. Moreover, men's desire for the sympathy and approbation of others encourages beneficent conduct even when benevolence fails. Thus when the members of a society lack any affection for each other, they may yet maintain some justice and refrain from positive injuries toward each other. This just behavior is the minimum of cooperation upon which the survival of a society depends.

If men begin to inflict injury on each other, the injured have a right of self-defense. Men naturally resent and seek to forestall or punish offenses against them. Such self-defense and retaliation are, Smith avers,

The editions used are *The Works of Adam Smith*, 5 vols. London, T. Cadell and W. Davies, 1812; *Lectures on Justice, Police, Revenue and Arms*, ed. Edwin Cannan, Oxford, Clarendon Press, 1896.

the only proper occasions for resentment and punishment. Prevention of an offense, he adds, is always preferable to retaliation.

The state is the best instrument which men have designed for the enforcement of justice. All men have a deep regard for the particular state which protects them. This affection commonly manifests itself in a violent jealousy of other states. Every state suspects that another may attack it. Sovereign states, being in a similar condition to men without government, must similarly stand ready to prevent and avenge injuries. For this reason every increase in the power of other nations is deeply resented and frequently provokes attack. In this atmosphere of constant suspicion the so-called laws of nations are violated on the slightest pretext.

Smith admitted that a state might be justified in viewing with misgiving the growth of a neighbor's military power, but he deprecated a tendency to regard any advance in a nation's welfare as an attack on the interests of its neighbors. The greatest advances of mankind depended on peaceful improvements. An enlightened patriotism would transform international rivalry into competition in the peaceful arts. Nations would be wise to cooperate in promoting each other's advancement. The progress of civilization might, indeed, be the means of reducing the frequency of wars. For although Smith placed little faith in the balance of power of his own day, he believed that the spread of knowledge might enable all nations to achieve sufficient power to deter attack.

The state or sovereignty in which we have been born and educated, and under the protection of which we continue to live, is, in ordinary cases, the greatest society upon whose happiness or misery, our good or bad conduct can have much influence. It is accordingly, by nature, most strongly recommended to us. Not only we ourselves, but all the objects of our kindest affections, our children, our parents, our relations, our friends, our benefactors, all those whom we naturally love and revere the most, are commonly comprehended within it; and their prosperity and safety depend in some measure upon its prosperity and safety. It is by nature, therefore, endeared to us, not only by all our selfish, but by all our private benevolent affections. Upon account of our own connection with it, its prosperity and glory seem to reflect some sort of honour upon ourselves. When we compare it with other societies of the same kind, we are proud of its superiority, and mortified in some degree, if it appears in any respect below them . . . The patriot who lays down his life for the safety, or even for the vain-glory of this society, appears to act with the most exact propriety. He appears to view himself in the light in which the impartial spectator naturally and necessarily views him, as but one of the multitude, in the eye of that equitable judge, of no more consequence than any other in it, but bound at all times to sacrifice and devote himself to the safety, to the service, and even to the glory of the greater number . . .

The love of our nation often disposes us to view, with the most malignant jealousy and envy, the prosperity and aggrandizement of any other neighbouring nation. Independent and neighbouring nations, having no common superior to decide their disputes, all live in continual dread and suspicion of one another. Each sovereign, expecting little justice from his neighbours, is disposed to treat them with as little as he expects from them. The regard for the laws of nations, or for those rules which independent states profess or pretend to think themselves bound to observe in their dealings with one another, is often very little more than mere pretence and profession. From the smallest interest, upon the slightest provocation, we see those rules every day, either evaded or directly violated, without shame or remorse. Each nation foresees, or imagines it foresees, its own subjugation in the increasing power and aggrandizement of any of its neighbours; and the mean principle of national prejudice is often founded upon the noble one of the love of our own country. The sentence with which the elder Cato is said to have concluded every speech which he made in the senate, whatever might be the subject, *"It is my opinion likewise that Carthage ought to be destroyed,"* was the natural expression of the savage patriotism of a strong but coarse mind, enraged almost to madness against a foreign nation from which his own had suffered so much. The more humane sentence with which Scipio Nasica is said to have concluded all his speeches, *"It is my opinion, likewise, that Carthage ought not to be destroyed,"* was the liberal expression of a more enlarged and enlightened mind, who felt no aversion to the prosperity even of an old enemy, when reduced to a state which could no longer be formidable to Rome. France and England may each of them have some reason to dread the increase of the naval and military power of the other; but for either of them to envy the internal happiness and prosperity of the other, the cultivation of its lands, the advancement of its manufactures, the increase of its commerce, the security and number of its ports and harbours, its proficiency in all the liberal arts and sciences, is surely beneath the dignity of two such great nations. These are all real improvements of the world we live in. Mankind are benefited, human nature is ennobled by them. In such improvements each nation ought, not only to endeavour itself to excel, but from the love of mankind, to promote, instead of obstructing the excellence of its neighbours. These are all proper objects of national emulation, not of national prejudice or envy.

The love of our own country seems not to be derived from the love of mankind. The former sentiment is altogether independent of the latter, and seems sometimes even to dispose us to act inconsistently with it. France may contain, perhaps, near three times the number of inhabitants which Great Britain contains. In the great society of mankind, therefore, the prosperity of France should appear to be an object of much greater importance than that of Great Britain. The British subject, however, who, upon that account, should prefer upon all occasion the prosperity of the former to that of the latter country, would not be thought a good citizen of Great Britain. We do not love our country merely as a part of the great society of mankind: we love it for its own sake, and independently of any such consideration. That wisdom which contrived the system of human affections, as well as that of every other part of nature, seems to have judged that the interest of the great society of mankind would be best promoted by directing the principal attention of each individual to that particular portion of it, which was most within the sphere both of his abilities and of his understanding.

National prejudices and hatreds seldom extend beyond neighbouring nations. We very weakly, and foolishly, perhaps, call the French our natural enemies; and they perhaps, as weakly and foolishly, consider us in the same manner. Neither they nor we bear any sort of envy to the prosperity of China or Japan. It very rarely happens, however, that our good-will towards such distant countries can be exerted with much effect.

The most extensive public benevolence which can commonly be exerted with any considerable effect, is that of the statesmen, who project and form alliances among neighbouring or not very distant nations, for the preservation either of, what is called, the balance of power, or of the general peace and tranquillity of the states within the circle of their negotiations. The statesmen, however, who plan and execute such treaties, have seldom any thing in view, but the interest of their respective countries.[1]

The discovery of America, and that of a passage to the East Indies by the Cape of Good Hope, are the two greatest and most important events recorded in the history of mankind. Their consequences have

1. "The Theory of Moral Sentiments," *Works, 1,* 399–404.

already been very great: but, in the short period of between two and three centuries which has elapsed since these discoveries were made, it is impossible that the whole extent of their consequences can have been seen. What benefits, or what misfortunes to mankind may hereafter result from those great events, no human wisdom can foresee. By uniting, in some measure, the most distant parts of the world, by enabling them to relieve one another's wants, to increase one another's enjoyments, and to encourage one another's industry, their general tendency would seem to be beneficial. To the natives, however, both of the East and West Indies, all the commercial benefits which can have resulted from those events have been sunk and lost in the dreadful misfortunes which they have occasioned. These misfortunes, however, seem to have arisen rather from accident than from anything in the nature of those events themselves. At the particular time when these discoveries were made, the superiority of force happened to be so great on the side of the Europeans, that they were enabled to commit with impunity every sort of injustice in those remote countries. Hereafter, perhaps, the natives of those countries may grow stronger, or those of Europe may grow weaker, and the inhabitants of all the different quarters of the world may arrive at that equality of courage and force which, by inspiring mutual fear, can alone overawe the injustice of independent nations into some sort of respect for the rights of one another. But nothing seems more likely to establish this equality of force than that mutual communication of knowledge and of all sorts of improvements which an extensive commerce from all countries to all countries naturally, or rather necessarily, carries along with it.[2]

Smith observed that the law of nations received scant respect whenever a dispute arose between nations. Nor were the laws of war much better observed when hostilities broke out. Despite this, Smith outlined some principles to define a just war and to regulate conduct during war. He admitted, however, that abstract principles might often be rightly overridden by necessity.

The propriety of our moral sentiments is never so apt to be corrupted, as when the indulgent and partial spectator is at hand, while the indifferent and impartial one is at a great distance.

Of the conduct of one independent nation towards another, neutral nations are the only indifferent and impartial spectators. But they are placed at so great a distance that they are almost quite out of sight.

2. "Wealth of Nations," *Works*, 3, 458–9.

When two nations are at variance, the citizen of each pays little regard to the sentiments which foreign nations may entertain concerning his conduct. His whole ambition is to obtain the approbation of his own fellow-citizens; and as they are all animated by the same hostile passions which animate himself, he can never please them so much as by enraging and offending their enemies. The partial spectator is at hand: the impartial one at a great distance. In war and negotiation, therefore, the laws of justice are very seldom observed. Truth and fair dealing are almost totally disregarded. Treaties are violated; and the violation, if some advantage is gained by it, sheds scarce any dishonour upon the violator. The ambassador who dupes the minister of a foreign nation, is admired and applauded. The just man who disdains either to take or to give any advantage, but who would think it less dishonourable to give than to take one; the man who, in all private transactions would be the most beloved and the most esteemed; in those public transactions is regarded as a fool and an idiot, who does not understand his business; and he incurs always the contempt, and sometimes even the detestation, of his fellow-citizens. In war, not only what are called the laws of nations are frequently violated, without bringing (among his own fellow-citizens, whose judgments he only regards) any considerable dishonour upon the violator; but those laws themselves are, the greater part of them, laid down with very little regard to the plainest and most obvious rules of justice.[3]

First, [when is war lawful?] In general whatever is the foundation of a proper law suit before a court of justice may be a just occasion of war. The foundation of a law suit is the violation of some perfect right whose performance may be extorted by force, and is so extorted in a rude society, but in modern times is decided by the magistrate, lest the society should be disturbed by every one taking justice at his own hands. When one nation encroaches on the property of another, or puts to death the subjects of another, imprisons them, or refuses them justice when injured, the sovereign is bound to demand satisfaction for the offence, as it is the intention of the government to protect its several members from foreign enemies, and if redress is refused, there is a foundation for war. In the same manner breach of contract, as when a debt is due by one nation to another, and payment refused, is a very just occasion of war. If, for example, the king of Prussia should refuse to pay the money advanced for him by the British nation in the time

3. "Moral Sentiments," *Works, 1,* 261–3.

of the last war, a declaration of war against him would be just and
reasonable. Every offence of the sovereign of one country against the
sovereign of another, or of the sovereign against the subject, or of the
subject of one country against the subject of another, without giving
reasonable satisfaction, may be the cause of a war.

Second, [what is lawful in war?] How far a nation may push the
resentment of an injury against the nation which has injured them, is not
easy to determine. The practice of ancient and modern nations differs
extremely. In general, when an injury is clearly and distinctly done, or
when it is plainly intended and satisfaction refused, resentment is necessary and just. There are a few cases in which it is lawful even without
satisfaction being demanded. If a robber was plainly intending to kill
you, it would be quite lawful in you to do all you could to prevent him.
The injury is plain. In the same manner, when one nation seems to be
conspiring against another, though it may have done no real injury, it
is necessary that it should be obliged to declare its intentions, and to
give security when this demand would not subject it to inconveniences.
Though this satisfaction be not demanded, when the King of Prussia
saw his dominions about to be overwhelmed by the Elector of Saxony
and the Queen of Hungary, it was quite right in him to be beforehand
with them, and to take possession of their territories, and nothing would
have been more absurd than for him to have told them that he was going
to attack them. On the other hand, if it be only a debt that is due, it
would be as unreasonable to go to war without demanding satisfaction,
and it is only upon the dilatory and evasive manner of giving satisfaction that a war in this case becomes lawful.

But to consider a little more particularly what is lawful in war, suppose a subject of any government is injured, they who have injured
him become natural objects of resentment, and also the government
which protects him if it refuse satisfaction, but the greater part of the
nation is perfectly innocent, and knows nothing about the affair. In the
late war with France, not one out of twenty, either of the French or us,
knew anything of the offences done. Upon what principle or foundation
of justice therefore do we take their goods from them, and distress them
in all possible ways? This can by no means be founded upon justice and
equity, properly so called, it must be upon necessity, which, indeed,
in this case, is a part of justice. . . . .

The real cause why the whole nation is thought a reasonable object
of resentment is that we do not feel for those at a distance as we do
for those near us. We have been injured by France, our resentment

rises against the whole nation instead of the government, and they, through a blind indiscriminating faculty natural to mankind, become the objects of an unreasonable resentment. . . . This is however quite contrary to the rules of justice, observed with regard to our own subjects. We would rather choose that ten guilty persons should escape than that one innocent person should suffer. Another cause is that it is often very difficult to get satisfaction from a subject or from a sovereign that may have offended. They are generally in the heart of the country and perfectly well secured. If we could get at them no doubt they would be the first objects of our resentment, but as this is impossible, we must make reprisals some other way. We have suffered unjustly on account of our connexions, let them also suffer unjustly on account of theirs. In war there must always be the greatest injustice, but it is inevitable.[4]

The frequent warfare which characterizes international relations makes it essential that a nation be prepared to defend itself. Citizens of a highly civilized country have less time to devote to military training than those of a primitive nation. Moreover, improvements in the art of war make it necessary for part of the population to devote themselves to supplying munitions. Yet an "industrious, and upon that account a wealthy nation, is of all nations the most likely to be attacked."[5] It therefore becomes the duty of government to provide an efficient professional defense force. This should not be carried to such lengths that the bulk of the population loses all interest in military affairs, for the basic strength of a nation will still depend upon the courage of its inhabitants.

The art of war . . . as it is certainly the noblest of all arts, so in the progress of improvement it necessarily becomes one of the most complicated among them. The state of the mechanical, as well as of some other arts, with which it is necessarily connected, determines the degree of perfection to which it is capable of being carried at any particular time. But in order to carry it to this degree of perfection, it is necessary that it should become the sole or principal occupation of a particular class of citizens, and the division of labour is as necessary for the improvement of this, as of every other art. Into other arts the division of labour is naturally introduced by the prudence of individuals, who find that they promote their private interest better by confining themselves

4. *Lectures on Justice, Police, Revenue and Arms,* pp. 266–70.
5. "Wealth of Nations," *Works,* 2, 192.

to a particular trade than by exercising a great number. But it is the wisdom of the state only which can render the trade of a soldier a particular trade separate and distinct from all others. A private citizen who, in time of profound peace, and without any particular encouragement from the public, should spend the greater part of his time in military exercises, might, no doubt, both improve himself very much in them, and amuse himself very well; but he certainly would not promote his own interest. It is the wisdom of the state only which can render it for his interest to give up the greater part of his time to this peculiar occupation: and states have not always had this wisdom, even when their circumstances had become such that the preservation of their existence required that they should have it.[6]

That in the progress of improvement the practice of military exercises, unless government takes proper pains to support it, goes gradually to decay, and, together with it, the martial spirit of the great body of the people, the example of modern Europe sufficiently demonstrates. But the security of every society must always depend, more or less, upon the martial spirit of the great body of the people. In the present times, indeed, that martial spirit alone, and unsupported by a well-disciplined standing army, would not, perhaps, be sufficient for the defence and security of any society. But where every citizen had the spirit of a soldier, a smaller standing army would surely be requisite. That spirit, besides, would necessarily diminish very much the dangers to liberty, whether real or imaginary, which are commonly apprehended from a standing army. As it would very much facilitiate the operations of that army against a foreign invader, so it would obstruct them as much if unfortunately they should ever be directed against the constitution of the state.

. . . Even though the martial spirit of the people were of no use towards the defence of the society, yet to prevent that sort of mental mutilation, deformity, and wretchedness, which cowardice necessarily involves in it, from spreading themselves through the great body of the people, would still deserve the most serious attention of government; in the same manner as it would deserve its most serious attention to prevent a leprosy, or any other loathsome and offensive disease, though neither mortal nor dangerous, from spreading itself among them; though, perhaps, no other public good might result from such attention besides the prevention of so great a public evil.[7]

6. *Ibid.*, *4*, 53–4.
7. *Ibid.*, pp. 189–91.

An important element in the strength of a nation is its economic prosperity. Smith's greatest contribution to political and economic thought was, of course, his analysis of national wealth. His studies of the division of labor and of international trade laid the foundations for the system of free trade which England adopted in the nineteenth century. Smith discredited the mercantilist theories of international commerce. He particularly derided the belief that the prosperity of other nations conflicted with England's welfare. Every nation, he declared, benefited from the advancement of every other nation. For these reasons Smith advocated the adoption of free trade. Protectionism benefited only special interest groups at the expense of the nation at large. Smith made an exception in the case of strategic industries. It might be advisable to accept the losses involved in protecting such industries in the interest of national security.

To give the monopoly of the home-market to the produce of domestic industry, in any particular art or manufacture, is in some measure to direct private people in what manner they ought to employ their capitals, and must, in almost all cases, be either a useless or a hurtful regulation. If the produce of domestic can be brought there as cheap as that of foreign industry, the regulation is evidently useless. If it cannot, it must generally be hurtful. It is the maxim of every prudent master of a family, never to attempt to make at home what it will cost him more to make than to buy. . . .

What is prudence in the conduct of every private family, can scarce be folly in that of a great kingdom. If a foreign country can supply us with a commodity cheaper than we ourselves can make it, better buy it of them with some part of the produce of our own industry, employed in a way in which we have some advantage. The general industry of the country, being always in proportion to the capital which employs it, will not thereby be diminished, . . . but only left to find out the way in which it can be employed with the greatest advantage. It is certainly not employed to the greatest advantage, when it is thus directed towards an object which it can buy cheaper than it can make.[8]

. . . Nations have been taught that their interest consisted in beggaring all their neighbours. Each nation has been made to look with an invidious eye upon the prosperity of all the nations with which it trades, and to consider their gain as its own loss. Commerce, which ought naturally to be, among nations, as among individuals, a bond of union and friendship, has become the most fertile source of discord

8. *Ibid.*, 3, 182–3.

and animosity. The capricious ambition of kings and ministers has not, during the present and the preceding century, been more fatal to the repose of Europe, than the impertinent jealousy of merchants and manufacturers. The violence and injustice of the rulers of mankind is an ancient evil, for which, I am afraid, the nature of human affairs can scarce admit of a remedy. But the mean rapacity, the monopolizing spirit of merchants and manufacturers, who neither are, nor ought to be, the rulers of mankind, though it cannot perhaps be corrected, may very easily be prevented from disturbing the tranquillity of any body but themselves.

That it was the spirit of monopoly which originally both invented and propagated this doctrine, cannot be doubted; and they who first taught it were by no means such fools as they who believed it. In every country it always is and must be the interest of the great body of the people to buy whatever they want of those who sell it cheapest. The proposition is so very manifest, that it seems ridiculous to take any pains to prove it; nor could it ever have been called in question, had not the interested sophistry of merchants and manufacturers confounded the common sense of mankind. Their interest is, in this respect, directly opposite to that of the great body of the people. . . .

The wealth of a neighbouring nation, however, though dangerous in war and politics, is certainly advantageous in trade. In a state of hostility it may enable our enemies to maintain fleets and armies superior to our own; but in a state of peace and commerce it must likewise enable them to exchange with us to a greater value, and to afford a better market, either for the immediate produce of our own industry, or for whatever is purchased with that produce. As a rich man is likely to be a better customer to the industrious people in his neighbourhood, than a poor, so is likewise a rich nation. A rich man, indeed, who is himself a manufacturer, is a very dangerous neighbour to all those who deal in the same way. All the rest of the neighbourhood, however, by far the greatest number, profit by the good market which his expence affords them. They even profit by his underselling the poorer workmen who deal in the same way with him. The manufacturers of a rich nation, in the same manner, may no doubt be very dangerous rivals to those of their neighbours. This very competition, however, is advantageous to the great body of the people, who profit greatly besides by the good market which the great expence of such a nation affords them in every other way. Private people who want to make a fortune, never think of retiring to the remote and poor provinces of the country, but resort either to the capital, or to some of the great commercial towns. They know, that, where little wealth circulates, there is little to be got, but that where a great deal is in motion, some share of it may fall to them. The same maxims which would in this manner direct the common sense of one, or ten, or twenty individuals, should regulate the judgment of one, or ten, or twenty millions, and should make a whole nation regard the riches of its neighbours, as a probable cause and occasion for itself to acquire riches. A nation that would enrich itself by foreign trade, is certainly most likely to do so when its neighbours are all rich, industrious, and commercial nations. . . . The modern maxims of foreign commerce, by aiming at the impoverishment of all our neighbours, so far as they are capable of producing their intended effect, tend to render that very commerce insignificant and contemptible. . . . .

. . . the very same circumstances which would have rendered an open and free commerce between the two countries so advantageous to both, have occasioned the principal obstructions to that commerce. Being neighbours, they are necessarily enemies, and the wealth and power of each becomes, upon that account, more formidable to the other; and what would increase the advantage of national friendship, serves only to inflame the violence of national animosity. They are both rich and industrious nations; and the merchants and manufacturers of each, dread the competition of the skill and activity of those of the other. Mercantile jealousy is excited, and both inflames, and is itself inflamed, by the violence of national animosity: And the traders of both countries have announced, with all the passionate confidence of interested falsehood, the certain ruin of each, in consequence of that unfavourable balance of trade, which, they pretend, would be the infallible effect of an unrestrained commerce with the other.[9]

There seem, however, to be two cases in which it will generally be advantageous to lay some burden upon foreign, for the encouragement of domestic industry.

The first is, when some particular sort of industry is necessary for the defence of the country. The defence of Great Britain, for example, depends very much upon the number of its sailors and shipping. The act of navigation, therefore, very properly endeavours to give the sailors and shipping of Great Britain the monopoly of the trade of their own country, in some cases, by absolute prohibitions, and in others by heavy burdens upon the shipping of foreign countries. . . . .

9. *Ibid.,* pp. 243-9.

When the act of navigation was made, though England and Holland were not actually at war, the most violent animosity subsisted between the two nations. It had begun during the government of the Long Parliament, which first framed this act, and it broke out soon after in the Dutch wars during that of the Protector and of Charles the Second. It is not impossible, therefore, that some of the regulations of this famous act may have proceeded from national animosity. They are as wise, however, as if they had all been dictated by the most deliberate wisdom. National animosity at that particular time aimed at the very same object which the most deliberate wisdom would have recommended, the diminution of the naval power of Holland, the only naval power which could endanger the security of England.

The act of navigation is not favourable to foreign commerce, or to the growth of that opulence which can arise from it. . . . As defence, however, is of much more importance than opulence, the act of navigation is, perhaps, the wisest of all the commercial regulations of England.[10]

Smith's theories of international trade led him to condemn the mercantile structure of the British Empire. He did not deny that Britain benefited from its colonial trade, but he asserted that trade would be even more advantageous if the monopoly system were abandoned. Exclusive trading privileges worked only to the profit of a narrow class of trader. If Britain were to throw open the colonial trade and relax the bonds of empire, it not only would benefit economically but also, in Smith's opinion, would gain politically by earning the gratitude of the colonies.

We must carefully distinguish between the effects of the colony trade and those of the monopoly of that trade. The former are always and necessarily beneficial; the latter always and necessarily hurtful. But the former are so beneficial, that the colony trade, though subject to a monopoly, and notwithstanding the hurtful effects of that monopoly, is still upon the whole beneficial, and greatly beneficial; though a good deal less so than it otherwise would be.

The effect of the colony trade in its natural and free state, is to open a great, though distant market for such parts of the produce of British industry as may exceed the demand of the markets nearer home, of those of Europe, and of the countries which lie round the Mediterranean sea. In its natural and free state, the colony trade, without draw-

10. *Ibid.*, pp. 192–5.

ing from those markets any part of the produce which had ever been sent to them, encourages Great Britain to increase the surplus continually, by continually presenting new equivalents to be exchanged for it. . . .

The monopoly of the colony trade, on the contrary, by excluding the competition of other nations, and thereby raising the rate of profit both in the new market and in the new employment, draws produce from the old market and capital from the old employment. To augment our share of the colony trade beyond what it otherwise would be, is the avowed purpose of the monopoly. If our share of that trade were to be no greater with, than it would have been without the monopoly, there could have been no reason for establishing the monopoly. . . . But whatever forces into a branch of trade of which the returns are slower and more distant than those of the greater part of other trades, a greater proportion of the capital of any country, than what of its own accord would go to that branch, necessarily renders the whole quantity of productive labour annually maintained there, the whole annual produce of the land and labour of that country, less than they otherwise would be. . . .

The natural good effects of the colony trade, however, more than counterbalance to Great Britain the bad effects of the monopoly, so that, monopoly and all together, that trade, even as it is carried on at present, is not only advantageous, but greatly advantageous. The new market and the new employment which are opened by the colony trade, are of much greater extent than that portion of the old market and of the old employment which is lost by the monopoly. . . . If the colony trade, however, even as it is carried on at present, is advantageous to Great Britain, it is not by means of the monopoly, but in spite of the monopoly.[11]

. . . The expence of the ordinary peace establishment of the colonies amounted, before the commencement of the present disturbances, to the pay of twenty regiments of foot; to the expence of the artillery, stores, and extraordinary provisions with which it was necessary to supply them; and to the expence of a very considerable naval force which was constantly kept up, in order to guard, from the smuggling vessels of other nations, the immense coast of North America, and that of our West Indian islands. The whole expence of this peace establish-

11. *Ibid.*, pp. 429–31.

ment was a charge upon the revenue of Great Britain, and was, at the same time, the smallest part of what the dominion of the colonies has cost the mother country. If we would know the amount of the whole, we must add to the annual expence of this peace establishment the interest of the sums which, in consequence of her considering her colonies as provinces subject to her dominion, Great Britain has upon different occasions laid out upon their defence. We must add to it, in particular, the whole expence of the late war, and a great part of that of the war which preceded it. . . .

Under the present system of management, therefore, Great Britain derives nothing but loss from the dominion which she assumes over her colonies.

To propose that Great Britain should voluntarily give up all authority over her colonies, and leave them to elect their own magistrates, to enact their own laws, and to make peace and war as they might think proper, would be to propose such a measure as never was, and never will be adopted, by any nation in the world. No nation ever voluntarily gave up the dominion of any province, how troublesome soever it might be to govern it, and how small soever the revenue which it afforded might be in proportion to the expence which it occasioned. Such sacrifices, though they might frequently be agreeable to the interest, are always mortifying to the pride of every nation, and what is perhaps of still greater consequence, they are always contrary to the private interest of the governing part of it, who would thereby be deprived of the disposal of many places of trust and profit, of many opportunities of acquiring wealth and distinction, which the possession of the most turbulent, and, to the great body of the people, the most unprofitable province seldom fails to afford. The most visionary enthusiast would scarce be capable of proposing such a measure, with any serious hopes at least of its ever being adopted. If it was adopted, however, Great Britain would not only be immediately freed from the whole annual expence of the peace establishment of the colonies, but might settle with them such a treaty of commerce as would effectually secure to her a free trade, more advantageous to the great body of the people, though less so to the merchants, than the monopoly which she at present enjoys. By thus parting good friends, the natural affection of the colonies to the mother country, which, perhaps, our late dissensions have well nigh extinguished, would quickly revive. It might dispose them not only to respect, for whole centuries together, that treaty of commerce which they had concluded with us at parting, but to favour us in war as well as in trade, and, instead of turbulent and factious subjects, to become our most faithful, affectionate, and generous allies; and the same sort of parental affection on the one side, and filial respect on the other, might revive between Great Britain and her colonies, which used to subsist between those of ancient Greece and the mother city from which they descended.[12]

12. *Ibid.*, pp. 442–4.

8. ADAM FERGUSON

1723-1816

ADAM FERGUSON *was educated to be a clergyman and served as deputy chaplain with the Black Watch Highland Regiment during the War of the Austrian Succession. Abandoning the clergy, he succeeded David Hume to a librarianship in Edinburgh, later was employed as a tutor in the family of Lord Bute, and in 1759 joined the faculty of the University of Edinburgh. While professor of moral philosophy there he published* An Essay on the History of Civil Society *and* Institutes of Moral Philosophy, *and wrote a* History of the Progress and Termination of the Roman Republic. *For two years (1774–76) he traveled on the continent. In 1778 he came to Philadelphia as a member of a conciliation commission which made an unsuccessful attempt to negotiate an early peace with the colonies. He retired from the university in 1785 and published his* Principles of Moral and Political Science *in 1792.*

Ferguson contended that any fruitful study of human affairs must begin with an examination of man himself. Concerned as he was with the moral improvement of man and acutely aware of the differences between "the actual state [and] the improvable capacity of man," Ferguson held it "evident, that, the subjects being connected, we cannot proceed in the second, but upon the foundations which are laid in the first." [1] *He therefore set out to examine the existing state of mankind. Ferguson paid special attention to relations between nations, believing that international politics, though based on the same human nature as all politics, were sufficiently distinct to merit separate consideration.*

In those philosophies which defined a pristine and anarchistic state of

1. *Principles*, 1, 5.

The editions used are *An Essay on the History of Civil Society*, 6th ed. London, T. Cadell, and Edinburgh, W. Creech, and Bell and Bradfute, 1793; *Institutes of Moral Philosophy*, 2d ed. Edinburgh, A. Kincaid and W. Creech, and J. Bell, 1773; *Principles of Moral and Political Science*, 2 vols. London, A. Strahan and T. Cadell, and Edinburgh, W. Creech, 1793.

nature, thereby implying that contemporary societies were somehow unnatural, Ferguson saw only misunderstanding. He insisted that, far from being unnatural, organized society was an inevitable consequence of human nature. Biological and geographical necessity threw mankind into groups. Men are thus inescapably in societies. But although Ferguson disagreed with those who identified a state of nature which was either "a state of war, or of amity," [2] *he conceded the importance of deciding whether "in a mixed scene of benevolence and malice . . . man is, by his nature, limited to one or to the other."* [3] *Declaring that history shows men "are to one another mutual objects both of fear and of love,"* [4] *Ferguson concluded that both characteristics were present together.*

Man's love of rivalry tends to divide him from his fellows but his sociability urges him to form groups. As a result of these tendencies men have gathered themselves into nations and will probably continue to do so. These nations are commonly the objects of fervent affection and loyalty. They are "led by their situations to admire particular qualities, as the military and pacific virtues," [5] *and thus they acquire distinctive national characters and purposes.*

Mere estrangement approaches to jealousy; and men do not desire to associate with persons entirely unknown. Hence the species is never observed to act in one, but in manifold troops and companies; and, although without any physical bar to prevent their union, are still observed, under the notion of independence and freedom, to affect separation.

Hence the multiplicity of hordes in barbarous ages: But, in human nature, separation itself has an effect in straitening the bands of society; for the members of each separate nation feel their connection the more, that the name of fellow-countryman stands in contradistinction to that of an alien. . . . what seems to divide the species tends also to unite them in leagues more extensive than they would otherwise form. Hence the coalition of families, tribes, and extensive tracts of country, into nations, under political establishments, that combine the strength and the resources of many for common protection and safety.

The love of company is gratified in the resorts of a few; and predilec-

2. *Essay*, p. 26.
3. *Principles*, *1*, 26.
4. *Essay*, p. 26.
5. *Institutes*, p. 107.

tion ever implies acquaintance and esteem: But national establishments far exceed these bounds; and comprehend, in the same state or
community, persons far removed from one another, and mutually unknown.

Nations are formed upon a principle of expediency, and to obtain
security against foreign enemies, or domestic disorders: But, notwithstanding this origin, the name of a country ever carries an object of the
warmest affection; hence the ardent enthusiasm, with which the good
citizen sacrifices, to a public cause, every personal consideration of
ease, profit, or safety.[6]

Amidst the varieties of political character, nations differ also in respect
to the objects on which they are chiefly intent: One nation is intent
upon commerce, or busied with the arts of subsistence and accommodation: another has its existence to contend for at the edge of the
sword, is therefore intent upon the arts of war, and the advantages to
be gained or lost in the contest with its neighbours. In either case, the
fitness of men to promote the prosperity, or to watch over the safety of
their country, is an essential circumstance in estimating the political
value of their numbers.

Commercial nations have not any interest in the increase of population, except in so far the people are industrious, or possessed of some
profitable art. The idle, the profligate and the prodigal become, in
proportion to their numbers, a source of public distress and calamity.

Warlike hordes, on the contrary, would multiply warriors, not traders
or pacific inhabitants. The Romans, in the first state of their principality
or republic, hastened their population by the indiscriminate admission
of strangers to a participation of all their political rights. They had no
occasion to make any selection of those, they were to admit on the rolls
of their people; for all the hordes in their neighbourhood from which
their numbers could be supplied were warriors like themselves, and
every accession to their number from the nations around them, was an
addition to their military lists.[7]

*The same competition for its own sake or for scarce values which
gives rise to struggles between individuals also promotes conflict between nations. In the "divided state of the world incompatible interests
are formed, or, at least, apprehended; and the members of different
societies are engaged on opposite sides." Consequently, "separate so-*

6. *Principles, 1,* 30–5.
7. *Ibid.,* 2, 417–19.

cieties are, for the most part, rivals or enemies." [8] *There being no common judge over nations to settle these conflicts, their "arbitrament" must be by war.*

"War may originate in rapacity, emulation, *or* malice, *in* error *or* misapprehension of right."* [9] *The supposed conflict of interest is aggravated by mere fondness for dissension. Some even seek war for its own sake or prolong and intensify existing wars for love of fighting.*

Ferguson did not wholly deplore these international conflicts, for he believed that such struggles play a useful role in human affairs. Wars bind each state more firmly together. They provide men with an outlet for their energies; the warlike may engage in fighting, the peaceable, in conciliation. Moreover the existence of many independent nations makes possible a variety to suit tastes and opinions.

In the intercourse of separate nations there being no government or common magistrate to whom they are subject, their case is, or may be nearly the same with that which was supposed in a preceding section under the relation of parties *strangers* and *unconnected*. They are subject to the law of nature alone, however it may be modified by special conventions, and the law of nature for this reason is also termed the law of nations. In their differences or disagreements they may appeal to the judgment of neutral powers; but if a difference is not otherwise removed, they may have recourse to *war* and the decision of *arms*.

The law of nations, which proceeds upon the supposition of peace when there is no existing offence, proceeds upon the supposition of war when differences arise that cannot be otherwise reconciled; and is therefore, relatively to such occasions, termed also the law of peace and of war.[10]

. . . Mankind not only find in their condition the sources of variance and dissension; they appear to have in their minds the seeds of animosity, and to embrace the occasions of mutual opposition, with alacrity and pleasure. In the most pacific situation, there are few who have not their enemies, as well as their friends; and who are not pleased with opposing the proceedings of one, as much as with favouring the designs of another. . . .

. . . We love individuals on account of personal qualities; but we love our country, as it is a party in the divisions of mankind; and our

8. *Ibid., 1*, 33.
9. *Ibid., 2*, 296.
10. *Ibid., 2*, 294.

zeal for its interest, is a predilection in behalf of the side we maintain. . . . .

Societies, as well as individuals, being charged with the care of their
own preservation, and having separate interests, which give rise to
jealousies and competitions, we cannot be surprized to find hostilities
arise from this source. But were there no angry passions of a different
sort, the animosities which attend an opposition of interest, should bear
a proportion to the supposed value of the subject. "The Hottentot nations," says Kolben, "trespass on each other by thefts of cattle and of
women; but such injuries are seldom committed, except with a view
to exasperate their neighbours, and bring them to a war." Such depreda-
tions, then, are not the foundation of a war, but the effects of a hostile
intention already conceived. . . . What is it that stirs in the breasts
of ordinary men when the enemies of their country are named? Whence
are the prejudices that subsist between different provinces, cantons,
and villages, of the same empire and territory? What is it that excites
one half of the nations of Europe against the other? The statesman may
explain his conduct on motives of national jealousy and caution, but the
people have dislikes and antipathies, for which they cannot account. . . .

These observations seem to arraign our species, and to give an unfavourable picture of mankind; and yet the particulars we have mentioned are consistent with the most amiable qualities of our nature,
and often furnish a scene for the exercise of our greatest abilities. They
are sentiments of generosity and self-denial that animate the warrior
in defence of his country; and they are dispositions most favourable
to mankind, that become the principles of apparent hostility to men. . . .

Without the rivalship of nations, and the practice of war, civil society
itself could scarcely have found an object, or a form. Mankind might
have traded without any formal convention, but they cannot be safe
without a national concert. The necessity of a public defence, has given
rise to many departments of state, and the intellectual talents of men
have found their busiest scene in wielding their national forces. To
overawe, or intimidate, or, when we cannot persuade with reason, to
resist with fortitude, are the occupations which give its most animating
exercise, and its greatest triumphs, to a vigorous mind; and he who have
never struggled with his fellow-creatures, is a stranger to half the sentiments of mankind.

The quarrels of individuals, indeed, are frequently the operations of
unhappy and detestable passions; malice, hatred, and rage. If such pas-

sions alone possess the breast, the scene of dissension becomes an object of horror; but a common opposition maintained by numbers, is always allayed by passions of another sort. Sentiments of affection and friendship mix with animosity; the active and strenuous become the guardians of their society; and violence itself is, in their case, an exertion of generosity, as well as of courage.

. . . we may hope, in some instances, to disarm the angry passions of jealousy and envy; we may hope to instil into the breasts of private men sentiments of candour towards their fellow-creatures, and a disposition to humanity and justice. But it is vain to expect that we can give to the multitude of a people a sense of union among themselves, without admitting hostility to those who oppose them. Could we at once, in the case of any nation, extinguish the emulation which is excited from abroad, we should probably break or weaken the bands of society at home, and close the busiest scenes of national occupations and virtues.[11]

We should owe little to that statesman who were to contrive a defence that might supersede the external uses of virtue. It is wisely ordered for man, as a rational being, that the employment of reason is necessary to his preservation; it is fortunate for him, in the pursuit of distinction, that his personal consideration depends on his character; and it is fortunate for nations, that, in order to be powerful and safe, they must strive to maintain the courage, and cultivate the virtues, of their people. By the use of such means, they at once gain their external ends, and are happy.

Peace and unanimity are commonly considered as the principal foundations of public felicity; yet the rivalship of separate communities, and the agitations of a free people, are the principles of political life, and the school of men. How shall we reconcile these jarring and opposite tenets? It is, perhaps, not necessary to reconcile them. The pacific may do what they can to allay the animosities, and to reconcile the opinions, of men; and it will be happy if they can succeed in repressing their crimes, and in calming the worst of their passions. Nothing, in the meantime, but corruption or slavery can suppress the debates that subsist among men of integrity, who bear an equal part in the administration of state.

A perfect agreement in matters of opinion is not to be obtained in the most select company; and if it were, what would become of society? . . .

11. *Essay*, pp. 33–41.

Forms of government are supposed to decide of the happiness or misery of mankind. But forms of government must be varied, in order to suit the extent, the way of subsistence, the character, and the manners of different nations. . . . How is it possible, therefore, to find any single form of government that would suit mankind in every condition? [12]

Nations, like individuals, have a right to defend themselves if attacked. For defense nations must rely on their own exertions and "no nation . . . however wise in its measures, is entitled to think itself exempted from the common lot of mankind; or to suppose that its rights are safe without the precautions that are necessary to secure them." [13]

The right of self-defense exists only in the case of unprovoked attacks, but it is rarely possible to apportion responsibility accurately. Sometimes it may be justifiable to anticipate attack or to curb the dangerous growth of another state. In practice Ferguson thought "we may wave the question of justice, in the cause of a war, as depending on the actual circumstances of the particular case, and consider nations, acting without guilt or premeditated malice of either side, as entitled to the privileges of a fair defence." [14] *This right of defense should be exercised with moderation. The aggrieved nation should not act with more severity than is sufficient to correct the injury. On occasion it may be wiser to forego completely the right of retaliation.*

As national councils are composed of members differing in their opinions and dispositions; and often fluctuating in their resolutions, according to the influence of contending parties, communities cannot be known to one another, as individuals are known, under any permanent character of tried affection and fidelity. Nations are, therefore, almost in every instance, mutual objects of jealousy and distrust; and must think themselves safe so far only, as they are severally in condition to maintain their respective rights. They must keep a watchful eye on the powers by which they may be annoyed from abroad, no less than attend to the means of defence with which they are furnished at home. Their independence must cease to exist, the moment it is held at the discretion of any foreign power: what a neighbour, therefore, is about to gain, may be to them no less a subject of alarm, than what they themselves are about to lose; and a war may be justly undertaken, by one state, to check the dangerous progress of another; as well as to make any other provision necessary to its own preservation.

12. *Ibid.*, pp. 101–3.
13. *Principles*, 2, 410.
14. *Ibid.*, p. 302.

This may render the question of right and wrong between nations extremely complicated, and suspend or perplex the decisions of justice respecting the cause of a war.[15]

We may conclude, therefore, that the use of force, which is admissible in the case of defence, whether immediate or remote, is also limited to such cases; and that although men are bound, under every other sanction of duty, to avoid being authors of harm, yet, that they are, in this duty of abstaining from harm, peculiarly repressible by force also . . .

In treating of this subject, accordingly, we are not so much to consider the obligation under which every person lies to be innocent, as to consider the right which every person has to defend himself, and his fellow creature, by every effectual means in his power.

The right amounts to a permission of whatever may be necessary to safety, but does not contain any positive injunction to do all that be wanted for this purpose. A person attacked in his person may kill the aggressor; but is not required to do so much. . . . .

According to the law of defence a *right* may be maintained by any means which are *effectual* and *necessary* for this purpose.

It were irrational to employ means ineffectual, and it might be cruel in some instances to employ severities that might have been spared.

If means are supposed to be necessary, it is implied that the end cannot be obtained without them; and to suppose that a defence is allowed, and yet that the necessary means are prohibited would be to suppose, that the law of nature is inconsistent with itself; proposes the end, and yet forbids the pursuit.

It is true, that in some cases the necessary means may be so severe, and even so destructive to the party against whom they are employed, that humanity revolts against the use of them; and persons of a certain mild disposition may submit to harm, rather than employ, for defence, measures of any cruel effect to which the aggressor may have exposed himself.

In the contest of parties even the aggressor does not immediately forfeit every right; and there are accordingly limits to the very means of defence that may be employed against him; but the forbearance of any necessary means of defence however severe, is a voluntary effort of goodness in the person wronged, not such a concession as the aggressor may claim as a right due to himself.

As the law of defence, therefore, permits the use of any means which are necessary, so it allows to the person against whom they are employed,

15. *Ibid.*, pp. 300–1.

an exception in the want of necessity, when means destructive or harmful are unnecessarily employed against him.[16]

Ferguson believed there are various means a nation might employ in its defense and that each of these has its special properties. In a dispute a nation should aim at bringing its opponents to concede its demands. The character of the opponent is therefore highly relevant to the selection of means. A nation should choose means calculated to achieve the desired result with the least injury to its enemy. Violence is a means requiring particularly careful management because it rapidly leads to the abandonment of all moderation. Ferguson admitted, however, that in actual warfare these humane and prudent considerations are usually ignored, either out of unscrupulousness or because of fear that the enemy, for his part, will observe no restraint.

As soon as one nation yields, its opponent should grant a peace. Continuance of the war can only be wasteful for both belligerents. Unlike other agreements procured under duress, treaties of peace are morally binding. Otherwise wars could never end short of the annihilation of one side.

The circumstances under which a right is exposed or invaded, may direct us to the means of defence which may be respectively proper or sufficient on such occasions. In one set of circumstances, or on one occasion, *persuasion* may be sufficient; in another it may be required to employ *deception* or *stratagem;* and in a third it may be necessary to employ *force,* at any hazard of suffering to the injurious party. The means of defence, therefore, may be enumerated under the titles of *persuasion, deception,* and *force.* The first may take place among friends; the two last are lawful only upon the supposition of enmity, and are termed hostilities. . . . .

. . . although persons who consult the reputation of bravery may think that open force is preferable to deception or disguise of any sort; yet, upon the general principle, that rights are to be defended by means the least hurtful to the persons against whom they are employed, deception and artifice is in general to be preferred to the use of actual force.

The use of *force,* it is true, may not always be more severe or destructive in its effects than the use of deception; but, as force repelled by force is likely to proceed to the highest extremities, it is justly placed as the last resort of the injured in defending their rights, and not to be employed where it is safe to rely on persuasion or stratagem.

16. *Ibid.,* pp. 182–9.

Under this title of *force* may be included not only the use of arms and actual violence, forcible restraint, and the infliction of punishment, but even threats, or the denunciation of violence, which may operate on the fears of those against whom they are employed.

Such being the gradation of means, that may be employed in defence of a right, the law of nature is modified, in particular circumstances, by a regard to the choice which is to be made of such means, according to the degree in which they are severally effectual or necessary.[17]

The means of defence were, in a former section, referred to three separate titles, *persuasion, stratagem,* and *force.*

The first, it was said, may be employed among friends, and in obtaining a favour, as well as in repelling an injury. In cases where it may be used with success, or where it may be safe to warn an enemy of a claim, that may be supported by force against him, it is no doubt required, that proper representations should be made, as the least hurtful means that can be employed in urging a claim of right. . . . .

Stratagem, implying some species of deception, is more the resort of an enemy than of a friend. It may be employed in misleading the injurious from his aim, or in obtaining from him concessions which he might not otherwise be willing to make.

. . . the injurious can [not] take any just exception to the use of *stratagem,* or complain that he is *deceived* when the effect is merely to counteract the wrong he commits. There is, however, one form in which deception is reprobated by mankind in general, even in the midst of hostilities, and under the utmost animosity of a national contest.

Although it be allowed to mislead an enemy by false apearances, and even by false informations, it is not allowed to enter into illusive treaties, or to stipulate articles for the sake of an advantage to be gained by a subsequent breach of faith.

It is allowed that hostilities cancel the obligation of preceding conventions, but not the obligation of treaties that may be entered into after commencement of a war. . . .

In all these instances, the faith plighted, though even to an enemy, and under the operation of force, is held, by the general consent of all civilized nations, to be sacred in the highest degree. The obligation, though possibly not founded in the principle of strict law, certainly rests on a principle of humanity, absolutely necessary to the welfare of mankind, as without it, the calamities of war, once begun, could scarcely ever be brought to an end. Peace itself rests upon the faith of a treaty

17. *Ibid.,* pp. 258–61.

concluded, while nations were yet at war; and, if it were admitted that such treaties could be entered into, and concluded merely to deceive an enemy, and draw him into a snare, it is evident, that the only means left to mankind, by which to stop the issues of blood, without the final extermination of an enemy, would be cut off, and two nations at war would be obliged to persist in hostilities to the utter destruction of one or the other.

On this ground, breach of faith, even during war, is reprobated among civilized nations; and indeed, the advantage that might be derived from it, in any particular instance, would be more than counterbalanced by the general distrust which the faithless would incur, in cases where it might be their interest to have credit given to their declarations or professions.

Force is the ordinary and ultimate resort of nations who cannot settle their differences upon amicable terms. But, even in this last resort, the law of nature, we have observed, directs a choice to be made of such means, as being effectual, are least hurtful to the parties against whom they are employed. The effect to be aimed at is the redress of a wrong; and any harm done, even to an enemy, beyond what is necessary to this effect, we have observed, is itself a wrong, and by the law of nature forbidden. . . . .

Whatever may have been the subject in contest, the immediate object of hostilities employed by either party, is to reduce an antagonist to a state of concession, so that he may no longer resist what is claimed as a right. This is the situation into which one party is reduced by a defeat; and the advantage gained by it accrues to the other, by having vanquished his enemy.

The first or immediate object of military operations, then, being to obtain the victory, a second is, to employ the advantage gained, so as to preserve, secure, or recover the right which was originally in question. And the state of war between nations may be divided into two periods; the first, that which precedes; the second, that which comes after the victory. In the first period, parties are still contending; in the second, one or other is in condition to enforce his demands, or both, tired of the contest, wish for an accommodation.

With respect to the first period, or during the contest of parties, it is evident, that as hostilities are lawful only in preserving a right, or in obtaining reparation of a wrong; so, in the choice of hostilities, such only are to be deemed lawful as are necessary to obtain the victory.

This maxim in speculation is abundantly clear, but in practice it is often difficult to apply it; for, while one party resists or presses with all his force, and takes every opportunity to strengthen himself and to weaken his antagonist, the other party will think himself justified in employing every means in his power to counteract operations, of which he knows not the precise extent.

Contending nations, for the most part, thus urged by an apprehension of what an enemy may be devising against them, proceed at once to extremities; use weapons and engines the most destructive, and employ means the most likely to reduce their enemy to submission, without any scrupulous enquiry into the degree in which such means may be necessary, provided they are likely to be effectual for obtaining the purpose to which they are employed. . . . .

During the period of contest, to whatever extremity an enemy that resists may be urged, it is evident, from the general principle which limits the operations of war to such means as are necessary to obtain the victory, that an enemy who submits or yields, is thereby entitled to quarter. The end of the war, with respect to him, is already obtained; and to refuse quarter, is justly considered amongst civilized nations as an object of detestation and horror.[18]

Ferguson asserted that the welfare of humanity would best be preserved in a world composed of several independent states approximately equal in power. Although he conceded the occasional necessity of permanently subordinating an aggressive or troublesome nation, he insisted that there could be no general right of conquest apart from such defensive cases. He admitted, however, that this principle did not enjoy universal acceptance and that a love of conquest exercised great influence on national policies. In particular he noted that a successful defensive war easily became one for conquest. Given the technological advances of the eighteenth century he feared that it might be possible for some nation to establish an empire greater than that of Rome. Fortunately the same century also saw the balance of power more jealously guarded than ever before. This, Ferguson thought, was the proper policy to preserve the integrity of independent nations.

The emulation of nations proceeds from their division. A cluster of states, like a company of men, find the exercise of their reason, and the test of their virtues, in the affairs they transact, upon a foot of equality, and separate interest. The measures taken for safety, including great

18. *Ibid.*, pp. 302–10.

part of the national policy, are relative in every state to what is apprehended from abroad. . . . .

When we reason in behalf of our species, therefore, although we may lament the abuses which sometimes arise from independence, and opposition of interest; yet whilst any degrees of virtue remain with mankind, we cannot wish to crowd, under one establishment, numbers of men who may serve to constitute several; or to commit affairs to the conduct of one senate; one legislative or executive power, which, upon a distinct and separate footing, might furnish an exercise of ability, and a theatre of glory to many.

This may be a subject upon which no determinate rule can be given; but the admiration of boundless dominion is a ruinous error; and in no instance, perhaps, is the real interest of mankind more entirely mistaken.

The measure of enlargement to be wished for in any particular state, is often to be taken from the condition of its neighbours. Where a number of states are contiguous, they should be near an equality, in order that they may be mutually objects of respect and consideration, and in order that they may possess that independence in which the political life of a nation consists.

When the kingdoms of Spain were united, when the great fiefs in France were annexed to the crown, it was no longer expedient for the nations of Great Britain to continue disjoined.

The small republics of Greece, indeed, by their subdivisions, and the balance of their power, found almost in every village the object of nations. Every little district was a nursery of excellent men, and what is now the wretched corner of a great empire, was the field on which mankind have reaped their principal honours. But in modern Europe, republics of a similar extent are like shrubs, under the shade of a taller wood, choked by the neighbourhood of more powerful states. . . .

Independent communities . . . however weak, are averse to a coalition, not only where it comes with an air of imposition, or unequal treaty, but even where it implies no more than the admission of new members to an equal share of consideration with the old. The citizen has no interest in the annexation of kingdoms; he must find his importance diminished, as the state is enlarged: But ambitious men, under the enlargement of territory, find a more plentiful harvest of power, and of wealth, while government itself is an easier task. Hence the ruinous progress of empire; and hence free nations, under the shew of acquiring dominion, suffer themselves, in the end, to be yoked with the slaves they had conquered.

Our desire to augment the force of a nation is the only pretext for enlarging its territory; but this measure, when pursued to extremes, seldom fails to frustrate itself.[19]

Injustice or wrong has reference to a person injured or wronged, who may defend himself; and to a person committing an injury, or doing a wrong, who, instead of reaping benefit from his wrong, exposes himself to suffer whatever may be necessary to obtain reparation of the harm he may have done.

This negative proposition were too obvious to need being formally stated, if it were not necessary to correct a common solecism in language, by which we are told of the *right of conquest*, arising from a successful application of mere force, without regard to the justice or injustice of the cause in which that force was employed.

Where conquest is matter of right, there must be supposed a previous title to the subject conquered; and, if such title be verified, the conquest amounts to no more than a just possession obtained by force.[20]

The maxims of conquest are not always to be distinguished from those of self-defence. If a neighbouring state be dangerous, if it be frequently troublesome, it is a maxim founded in the consideration of safety, as well as of conquest, That it ought to be weakened or disarmed: If, being once reduced, it be disposed to renew the contest, it must from thenceforward be governed in form. . . . .

It is vain to affirm, that the genius of any nation is adverse to conquest. Its real interests indeed most commonly are so; but every state, which is prepared to defend itself, and to obtain victories, is likewise in hazard of being tempted to conquer. . . . .

The Romans, with inferior arts of communication both by sea and land, maintained their dominion in a considerable part of Europe, Asia, and Africa, over fierce and intractable nations: What may not the fleets and armies of Europe, with the access they have by commerce to every part of the world, and the facility of their conveyance, effect, if that ruinous maxim should prevail, That the grandeur of a nation is to be estimated from the extent of its territory; or, That the interest of any particular people consists in reducing their neighbours to servitude? [21]

Even where we pretend to found our opinions on reason, and to justify our preference of one nation to another, we frequently bestow our

19. *Essay,* pp. 98–100.
20. *Principles,* 2, 200–1.
21. *Essay,* pp. 254–7.

esteem on circumstances which do not relate to national character, and which have little tendency to promote the welfare of mankind. Conquest, or great extent of territory, however peopled, and great wealth, however distributed or employed, are titles upon which we indulge our own, and the vanity of other nations, as we do that of private men on the score of their fortunes and honours. We even sometimes contend, whose capital is the most overgrown; whose king has the most absolute powers; and at whose court the bread of the subject is consumed in the most senseless riot. These indeed are the notions of vulgar minds; but it is impossible to determine, how far the notions of vulgar minds may lead mankind.[22]

Where a happy system of nations is formed, they do not rely for the continuance of their separate names, and for that of their political independence, on the barriers erected by nature. Mutual jealousies lead to the maintenance of a balance of power; and this principle, more than the Rhine and the Ocean, than the Alps and the Pyrenees in modern Europe; more than the straits of Thermopylae, the mountains of Thrace, or the bays of Salamine and Corinth in ancient Greece, tended to prolong the separation, to which the inhabitants of these happy climates have owed their felicity as nations, the lustre of their fame, and their civil accomplishments.[23]

Separate principalities were, like the parts of an engine, ready to be joined, and, like the wrought materials of a building, ready to be erected. They were in the result of their struggles put together, or taken asunder with facility. The independence of weak states was preserved only by the mutual jealousies of the strong, or by the general attention of all to maintain a balance of power.

The happy system of policy on which European states have proceeded in preserving this balance; the degree of moderation which is, in adjusting their treaties, become habitual even to victorious and powerful monarchies, does honour to mankind, and may give hopes of a lasting felicity, to be derived from a prepossession, never, perhaps, equally strong in any former period, or among any number of nations, that the first conquering people will ruin themselves, as well as their rivals.[24]

22. *Ibid.*, p. 343.
23. *Ibid.*, pp. 201–2.
24. *Ibid.*, pp. 222–3.

9. EDMUND BURKE

1729-1797

EDMUND BURKE *devoted his life to an active participation in British politics. He began to write political pamphlets in the late 1750's, and in 1766 he entered the House of Commons, where he was to sit until 1794. He was an eager reformer of abuses but a zealous opponent of revolution. His career of advocating cautious adjustment to altered circumstances ended in a passionate resistance to the radical changes proposed by the French Revolution and its sympathizers.*

Burke's political philosophy is to be found in his speeches and pamphlets on contemporary events. There, in masterly English prose, are the fruits of his deep reflections upon affairs. He was wary of laying down rules. He taught a way of thinking rather than a body of thought. He admitted there were general principles of politics, but these were few and simple, and could be quickly grasped by any man of sense. The important and difficult task was to meet each problem with a wise application of these principles. Of American affairs he declared, in typical vein, "All the reasonings about it, that are likely to be at all solid, must be drawn from its actual circumstances." [1] *Sometimes circumstances may make it impossible to pursue the course which seems to be clearly demanded by theory; nevertheless a statesman must have a policy: "the question is not, whether their spirit deserves praise or blame—what, in the name of God, shall we do with it?"* [2] *It is best to put legalism on one side and to act cautiously on the merits of each case. In this way men*

1. "Observations on a Late Publication, Intituled, 'The Present State of the Nation,'" *Works*, 1, 395.
2. "Speech on Moving Resolutions for Conciliation with America," *Works*, 2, 127.

The editions used are *The Works of the Right Honorable Edmund Burke*, rev. ed. 12 vols. Boston, Little, Brown and Company, 1865–67; *Correspondence of the Right Honourable Edmund Burke*, ed. Charles William, Earl Fitzwilliam, and Sir Richard Bourke, 4 vols. London, Francis and John Rivington, 1844; *The Parliamentary History of England*, London, T. C. Hansard, 1817.

may act well enough in affairs which they cannot reduce to rules and theories. "No lines can be laid down for civil or political wisdom. They are a matter incapable of exact definition. But, though no man can draw a stroke between the confines of day and night, yet light and darkness are upon the whole tolerably distinguishable." [3] *To act thus is to be prudent, and prudence is "not only the first in rank of the virtues political and moral, but . . . the director, the regulator, the standard of them all."* [4]

In the last phase of his career Burke's attention concentrated on international relations. Previously he had been concerned with domestic reform and, above all, imperial affairs. The French Revolution, however, seemed to him to threaten all he held dear. In speeches and pamphlets on the Revolution he discussed many aspects of foreign policy. Perhaps the most striking feature of these thoughts was the quickness with which Burke realized that the Revolution was something new in international affairs, demanding new policies and a fresh approach.

The basic unit in Burke's discussion of foreign affairs was the nation. For Burke the nation was the instrument of human happiness and held a meaning transcending the interests of its members at any one time. In Burke's eyes the *"nature of man is intricate; the objects of society are of the greatest possible complexity."* [5] The existing state system had developed into a mechanism highly suitable for satisfying that nature and pursuing those objects. It should therefore be handled with the greatest respect.

A man's own nation must always be the center of his interest and affection, but there also exists a *"genuine communion of mankind,"* [6] and *"we have obligations to mankind at large . . . they arise from the relation of man to man, and the relation of man to God."* [7] There is a particular community among the nations of Europe which have developed a similarity of habits and standards beyond anything achieved elsewhere. These conformities do much more than any formal agreements to prevent strife and moderate its consequences.

. . . a nation is not an idea only of local extent and individual momentary aggregation, but it is an idea of continuity which extends in

---

3. "Thoughts on the Cause of the Present Discontents," *Works, 1,* 477.
4. "An Appeal from the New to the Old Whigs," *Works, 4,* 81.
5. "Reflections on the Revolution in France," *Works, 3,* 212.
6. *Correspondence, 3,* 108.
7. "Appeal to the Old Whigs," *Works, 4,* 166.

time as well as in numbers and in space. And this is a choice not of one day or one set of people, not a tumultuary and giddy choice; it is a deliberate election of ages and of generations; it is a constitution made by what is ten thousand times better than choice; it is made by the peculiar circumstances, occasions, tempers, dispositions, and moral, civil, and social habitudes of the people, which disclose themselves only in a long spread of time.[8]

Our political system is placed in a just correspondence and symmetry with the order of the world, and with the mode of existence decreed to a permanent body composed of transitory parts—wherein, by the disposition of a stupendous wisdom, molding together the great mysterious incorporation of the human race, the whole, at one time, is never old or middle-aged or young, but, in a condition of unchangeable constancy, moves on through the varied tenor of perpetual decay, fall, renovation, and progression. Thus, by preserving the method of Nature in the conduct of the state, in what we improve we are never wholly new, in what we retain we are never wholly obsolete.[9]

 . . . In the intercourse between nations, we are apt to rely too much on the instrumental part. We lay too much weight upon the formality of treaties and compacts. We do not act much more wisely, when we trust to the interests of men as guarantees of their engagements. The interests frequently tear to pieces the engagements, and the passions trample upon both. Entirely to trust to either is to disregard our own safety, or not to know mankind. Men are not tied to one another by papers and seals. They are led to associate by resemblances, by conformities, by sympathies. It is with nations as with individuals. Nothing is so strong a tie of amity between nation and nation as correspondence in laws, customs, manners, and habits of life. They have more than the force of treaties in themselves. They are obligations written in the heart. They approximate men to men without their knowledge, and sometimes against their intentions. The secret, unseen, but irrefragable bond of habitual intercourse holds them together, even when their perverse and litigious nature sets them to equivocate, scuffle, and fight about the terms of their written obligations.
 . . . The conformity and analogy of which I speak, incapable, like everything else, of preserving perfect trust and tranquillity among men, has a strong tendency to facilitate accommodation, and to produce a

8. "Speech on the Representation of Commons in Parliament," *Works,* 7, 95.
9. "Reflections," *Works,* 3, 275.

generous oblivion of the rancor of their quarrels. With this similitude, peace is more of peace, and war is less of war. I will go further. There have been periods of time in which communities apparently in peace with each other have been more perfectly separated than in later times many nations in Europe have been in the course of long and bloody wars. The cause must be sought in the similitude throughout Europe of religion, laws, and manners. At bottom, these are all the same. The writers on public law have often called this *aggregate* of nations a commonwealth. They had reason. It is virtually one great state, having the same basis of general law, with some diversity of provincial customs and local establishments.[10]

Men cannot act without affecting the lives of others. The same is true of nations, and nations, like men, are bound by the duties of neighborhood to do nothing which infringes the rights of others. Because nations have no common judge to enforce this obligation, they must enforce it themselves. If nations wish to enjoy the protection of this discipline, they must play their part in enforcing it. For example, "if England shows herself indifferent and unconcerned, when these powers are combined against the enterprises of France, she is to look with certainty for the same indifference on the part of these powers, when she may be at war with that nation." [11] *This does not mean that a nation should actively resent every injustice without regard to its own welfare. It should act only when its own particular interest is clearly affected by the threat to the general interest. "Nations . . . were not to sit like judges, to act with perfect impartiality, to the exclusion of all ideas of self. Their first duty was, to take care of themselves . . ."* [12]

The whole body of this new [French] scheme of manners, in support of the new scheme of politics, I consider as a strong and decisive proof of determined ambition and systematic hostility. I defy the most refining ingenuity to invent any other cause for the total departure of the Jacobin Republic from every one of the ideas and usages, religious, legal, moral, or social, of this civilized world, and for her tearing herself from its communion with such studied violence, but from a formed resolution of keeping no terms with that world. It has not been as has been falsely and insidiously represented, that these miscreants had only

10. "Three Letters to a Member of Parliament on Proposals for Peace with the Regicide Directory of France," *Works,* 5, 317–18.

11. "Heads for Consideration on the Present State of Affairs," *Works,* 4, 398.

12. *Parliamentary History,* 30, 433.

broke with their old government. They made a schism with the whole universe, and the schism extended to almost everything, great and small. For one, I wish, since it is gone thus far, that the breach had been so complete as to make all intercourse impracticable: but, partly by accident, partly by design, partly from the resistance of the matter, enough is left to preserve intercourse, whilst amity is destroyed or corrupted in its principle.

This violent breach of the community of Europe we must conclude to have been made (even if they had not expressly declared it over and over again) either to force mankind into an adoption of their system or to live in perpetual enmity with a community the most potent we have ever known. Can any person imagine, that, in offering to mankind this desperate alternative, there is no indication of a hostile mind, because men in possession of the ruling authority are supposed to have a right to act without coercion in their own territories? As to the right of men to act anywhere according to their pleasure, without any moral tie, no such right exists. Men are never in a state of *total* independence of each other. It is not the condition of our nature: nor is it conceivable how any man can pursue a considerable course of action without its having some effect upon others, or, of course, without producing some degree of responsibility for his conduct. The *situations* in which men relatively stand produce the rules and principles of that responsibility, and afford directions to prudence in exacting it.

. . . There is a *law of neighborhood* which does not leave a man perfect master on his own ground. When a neighbor sees a *new erection*, in the nature of a nuisance, set up at his door, he has a right to represent it to the judge, who, on his part, has a right to order the work to be stayed, or, if established, to be removed. On this head the parent law is express and clear, and has made many wise provisions, which, without destroying, regulate and restrain the right of *ownership* by the right of *vicinage*. No *innovation* is permitted that may redound, even secondarily, to the prejudice of a neighbor. . . .

Such is the law of civil vicinity. Now where there is no constituted judge, as between independent states there is not, the vicinage itself is the natural judge. It is, preventively, the assertor of its own rights, or, remedially, their avenger. Neighbors are presumed to take cognizance of each other's acts. *"Vicini vicinorum facta proesumuntur scire."* This principle, which, like the rest, is as true of nations as of individual men, has bestowed on the grand vicinage of Europe a duty to know and a right to prevent any capital innovation which may amount to the erection of a dangerous nuisance. Of the importance of that innovation, and the mischief of that nuisance, they are, to be sure, bound to judge not litigiously: but it is in their competence to judge. They have uniformly acted on this right. What in civil society is a ground of action in politic society is a ground of war. But the exercise of that competent jurisdiction is a matter of moral prudence. As suits in civil society, so war in the political, must ever be a matter of great deliberation. It is not this or that particular proceeding, picked out here and there, as a subject of quarrel, that will do. There must be an aggregate of mischief. There must be marks of deliberation; there must be traces of design; there must be indications of malice; there must be tokens of ambition. There must be force in the body where they exist; there must be energy in the mind. When all these circumstances combine, or the important parts of them, the duty of the vicinity calls for the exercise of its competence: and the rules of prudence do not restrain, but demand it.[13]

Thus the right of neighborly interference extends to the internal affairs of other nations. Burke believed the Jacobin revolution should be suppressed by foreign intervention because it was inimical to the interests of the French people and dangerous to other states. The danger to other states was particularly acute in view of the peculiarly subversive nature of the Jacobins, who sought to destroy other states, not by "making a direct conquest of them, but, by disturbing them through a propagation of their principles . . ." [14] *The enemy was not France but Jacobinism. Such a movement must be vigorously attacked. Against a power which is "not so truly dangerous in its fortresses nor in its territories as in its spirit and its principles. . . . there can be no security in any defensive plan . . ."* [15]

The government of that [French] kingdom is fundamentally monarchical. The public law of Europe has never recognised in it any other form of government. The potentates of Europe have, by that law, a right, an interest, and a duty to know with what government they are to treat, and what they are to admit into the federative society—or, in other words, into the diplomatic republic of Europe. This right is clear and indisputable.

What other and further interference they have a right to in the in-

13. "Regicide Peace," *Works*, 5, 320–4.
14. "Thoughts on French Affairs," *Works*, 4, 345.
15. "Regicide Peace," *Works*, 5, 347.

terior of the concerns of another people is a matter on which, as on every political subject, no very definite or positive rule can well be laid down. Our neighbors are men; and who will attempt to dictate the laws under which it is allowable or forbidden to take a part in the concerns of men, whether they are considered individually or in a collective capacity, whenever charity to them, or a care of my own safety, calls forth my activity? Circumstances perpetually variable, directing a moral prudence and discretion, the *general* principles of which never vary, must alone prescribe a conduct fitting on such occasions. The latest casuists of public law are rather of a republican cast, and, in my mind, by no means so averse as they ought to be to a right in the people (a word which, ill defined, is of the most dangerous use) to make changes at their pleasure in the fundamental laws of their country. These writers, however, when a country is divided, leave abundant liberty for a neighbor to support any of the parties according to his choice. This interference must, indeed, always be a right, whilst the privilege of doing good to others, and of averting from them every sort of evil, is a right: circumstances may render that right a duty. It depends wholly on this, whether it be a *bonâ fide* charity to a party, and a prudent precaution with regard to yourself, or whether, under the pretence of aiding one of the parties in a nation, you act in such a manner as to aggravate its calamities and accomplish its final destruction. In truth, it is not the interfering or keeping aloof, but iniquitous intermeddling or treacherous inaction, which is praised or blamed by the decision of an equitable judge.[16]

. . . the present evil of our time, though in a great measure an evil of ambition, is not one of common political ambition, but in many respects entirely different. It is not the cause of nation as against nation; but, as you will observe, the cause of mankind against those who have projected the subversion of that order of things, under which our part of the world has so long flourished, and indeed, been in a progressive state of improvement; the limits of which, if it had not been thus rudely stopped, it would not have been easy for the imagination to fix. If I conceive rightly of the spirit of the present combination, it is not at war with France, but with Jacobinism. They cannot think it right that a second kingdom should be struck out of the system of Europe, either by destroying its independence, or by suffering it to have such a *form*

16. "Remarks on the Policy of the Allies," *Works, 4,* 433–5.

in its independence, as to keep it, as a perpetual fund of revolutions, in the very centre of Europe, in that region which alone touches almost every other, and must influence, even where she does not come in contact. As long as Jacobinism subsists there, in any form, or under any modification, it is not, in my opinion, the gaining a fortified place or two, more or less, or the annexing to the dominion of the allied powers this or that territorial district, that can save Europe, or any of its members. We are at war with a *principle*, and with an example, which there is no shutting out by fortresses, or excluding by territorial limits. No lines of demarcation can bound the Jacobin empire. It must be extirpated in the place of its origin, or it will not be confined to that place. In the whole circle of military arrangements and of political expedients, I fear that there cannot be found any sort of *merely defensive* plan of the least force, against the effect of the *example* which has been given in France. That *example* has shown, for the first time in the history of the world, that it is very possible to subvert the whole frame and order of the best constructed states, by corrupting the common people with the spoil of the superior classes. It is by that instrument that the French orators have accomplished their purpose, to the ruin of France; and it is by that instrument that, if they can establish themselves in France (however broken or curtailed by themselves or others), sooner or later, they will subvert every government in Europe. The effect of *erroneous doctrines* may be soon done away; but example of *successful pillage* is of a nature more permanent, more applicable to use, and a thing which speaks more forcibly to the interests and passions of the corrupt and unthinking part of mankind, than a thousand theories. Nothing can weaken the lesson contained in that example, but to make a strong example on the other side. . . . If any government should be settled in France, upon any other idea than that of the faithful restitution of all property of all descriptions, and that of the rigorous and exemplary punishment of the principal authors and contrivers of its ruin, I am convinced to a certainty, that property, and along with property, government, must fall in every other state in Europe . . . [17]

Small states may buy their existence with a servile submission to greater powers, but great nations can only remain great by being strong enough to command respect. No nation should allow its power to fall below that of its neighbors to such an extent that it is "reduced to a servile dependence on their mercy,—acquiescing in assurances of friend-

17. *Correspondence*, 4, 138–41.

ship which she does not trust,—complaining of hostilities which she dares not resent . . ." [18]

A wise nation will base its policy on an estimate of the resistance it may meet; "enemies . . . can only cease to be truly formidable by our entertaining a due respect for their power. Our danger will not be lessened by shutting our eyes to it . . ." [19] *The strength of a nation depends upon the enthusiasm with which it pursues its aims and the resources which it is willing to expend. There is a great advantage in taking the offensive. "For it is in the nature of all defensive measures to be sharp and vigorous under the impressions of the first alarm, and to relax by degrees, until at length the danger, by not operating instantly, comes to appear as a false alarm,—so much so that the next menacing appearance will look less formidable, and will be less provided against."* [20]

The rules and definitions of prudence can rarely be exact, never universal. I do not deny, that, in small, truckling states, a timely compromise with power has often been the means, and the only means, of drawling out their puny existence; but a great state is too much envied, too much dreaded, to find safety in humiliation. To be secure, it must be respected. Power and eminence and consideration are things not to be begged; they must be commanded: and they who supplicate for mercy from others can never hope for justice through themselves. . . .

. . . where the essential public force (of which money is but a part) is in any degree upon a par in a conflict between nations, that state which is resolved to hazard its existence rather than to abandon its objects must have an infinite advantage over that which is resolved to yield rather than to carry its resistance beyond a certain point. Humanly speaking, that people which bounds its efforts only with its being must give the law to that nation which will not push its opposition beyond its convenience.[21]

The British state is, without question, that which pursues the greatest variety of ends, and is the least disposed to sacrifice any one of them to another or to the whole. It aims at taking in the entire circle of human desires, and securing for them their fair enjoyment. Our legislature has been ever closely connected, in its most efficient part, with individual feeling and individual interest. Personal liberty, the most lively of these

18. "Letter to the Sheriffs of Bristol," *Works, 2, 203.*
19. "Two Letters to Gentlemen in the City of Bristol," *Works, 2, 251.*
20. "French Affairs," *Works, 4, 355.*
21. "Regicide Peace," *Works, 5, 241-3.*

feelings and the most important of these interests, which in other European countries has rather arisen from the system of manners and the habitudes of life than from the laws of the state, (in which it flourished more from neglect than attention,) in England has been a direct object of government.

On this principle, England would be the weakest power in the whole system. Fortunately, however, the great riches of this kingdom, arising from a variety of causes, and the disposition of the people, which is as great to spend as to accumulate, has easily afforded a disposable surplus that gives a mighty momentum to the state.[22]

France differs essentially from all those governments which are formed without system, which exist by habit, and which are confused with the multitude and with the complexity of their pursuits. What now stands as government in France is struck out at a heat. The design is wicked, immoral, impious, oppressive: but it is spirited and daring; it is systematic; it is simple in its principle; it has unity and consistency in perfection. In that country, entirely to cut off a branch of commerce, to extinguish a manufacture, to destroy the circulation of money, to violate credit, to suspend the course of agriculture, even to burn a city or to lay waste a province of their own, does not cost them a moment's anxiety. To them the will, the wish, the liberty, the toil, the blood of individuals, is as nothing. Individuality is left out of their scheme of government. The state is all in all. Everything is referred to the production of force; afterwards, everything is trusted to the use of it. It is military in its principle, in its maxims, in its spirit, and in all its movements. The state has dominion and conquest for its sole objects,—dominion over minds by proselytism, over bodies of arms.

Thus constituted, with an immense body of natural means which are lessened in their amount only to be increased in their effect, France has, since the accomplishment of the Revolution, a complete unity in its direction. It has destroyed every resource of the state which depends upon opinion and the good will of individuals. The riches of convention disappear. The advantages of Nature in some measures remain; even these, I admit, are astonishingly lessened; the command over what remains is complete and absolute. We go about asking when assignats will expire, and we laugh at the last price of them. But what signifies the fate of those tickets of despotism? The despotism will find despotic means of supply. . . . Were France but half of what it is in population, in com-

22. *Ibid.*, p. 374.

pactness, in applicability of its force, situated as it is, and being what it is, it would be too strong for most of the states of Europe, constituted as they are, and proceeding as they proceed. Would it be wise to estimate what the world of Europe, as well as the world of Asia, had to dread from Genghiz Khân, upon a contemplation of the resources of the cold and barren spot in the remotest Tartary, from whence first issued that scourge of the human race? . . .

Material resources never have supplied, nor ever can supply, the want of unity in design and constancy in pursuit. But unity in design and perseverance and boldness in pursuit have never wanted resources, and never will. We have not considered as we ought the dreadful energy of a state in which the property has nothing to do with the government.[23]

War, in Burke's view, is a "means of wrong and violence," but it is also "the sole means of justice amongst nations. Nothing can banish it from the world." [24] *It is as a means of justice that it should be used. The lives and rights of men are worth defending by war. It should be used for no lesser purpose.*

It is always desirable to bring war to a conclusion. But peace should not be made without due regard for circumstances. It may be a grave error to surrender in the face of misfortune. Burke scorned "a false, reptile prudence, the result, not of caution, but of fear." [25] *Once the weaker power disarms, it has lost everything; so long as it continues to fight, there is hope that the tide may turn. Nevertheless, peace implies reconciliation and it may be the true part of wisdom to make concessions to obtain it.*

. . . War never leaves where it found a nation. It is never to be entered into without a mature deliberation,—not a deliberation lengthened out into a perplexing indecision, but a deliberation leading to a sure and fixed judgment. When so taken up, it is not to be abandoned without reason as valid, as fully and as extensively considered. Peace may be made as unadvisedly as war. Nothing is so rash as fear; and the counsels of pusillanimity very rarely put off, whilst they are always sure to aggravate, the evils from which they would fly.

In that great war carried on against Louis the Fourteenth for near eighteen years, government spared no pains to satisfy the nation, that, though they were to be animated by a desire of glory, glory was not

23. *Ibid.*, pp. 375–7.
24. *Ibid.*, p. 318.
25. *Ibid.*, p. 241.

their ultimate object; but that everything dear to them, in religion, in law, in liberty, everything which as freemen, as Englishmen, and as citizens of the great commonwealth of Christendom, they had at heart, was then at stake. This was to know the true art of gaining the affections and confidence of an high-minded people; this was to understand human nature. A danger to avert a danger, a present inconvenience and suffering to prevent a foreseen future and a worse calamity,—these are the motives that belong to an animal who in his constitution is at once adventurous and provident, circumspect and daring,—whom his Creator has made, as the poet says, "of large discourse, looking before and after." But never can a vehement and sustained spirit of fortitude be kindled in a people by a war of calculation. It has nothing that can keep the mind erect under the gusts of adversity. . . . The calculation of profit in all such wars is false. On balancing the account of such wars, ten thousand hogsheads of sugar are purchased at ten thousand times their price. The blood of man should never be shed but to redeem the blood of man. It is well shed for our family, for our friends, for our God, for our country, for our kind. The rest is vanity; the rest is crime.[26]

There is always an augury to be taken of what a peace is likely to be from the preliminary steps that are made to bring it about. We may gather something from the time in which the first overtures are made, from the quarter whence they come, from the manner in which they are received. These discover the temper of the parties. If your enemy offers peace in the moment of success, it indicates that he is satisfied with something. It shows that there are limits to his ambition or his resentment. If he offers nothing under misfortune, it is probable that it is more painful to him to abandon the prospect of advantage than to endure calamity. If he rejects solicitation, and will not give even a nod to the suppliants for peace, until a change in the fortune of the war threatens him with ruin, then I think it evident that he wishes nothing more than to disarm his adversary to gain time. Afterwards a question arises, which of the parties is likely to obtain the greater advantages by continuing disarmed and by the use of time?

. . . peace too eagerly sought is not always the sooner obtained. The discovery of vehement wishes generally frustrates their attainment, and your adversary has gained a great advantage over you when he finds you impatient to conclude a treaty. There is in reserve not only something of dignity, but a great deal of prudence too. A sort of courage

26. *Ibid.*, pp. 303–5.

belongs to negotiation, as well as to operations of the field. A negotiator must often seem willing to hazard the whole issue of his treaty, if he wishes to secure any one material point.[27]

. . . Peace implies reconciliation; and where there has been a material dispute, reconciliation does in a manner always imply concession on the one part or on the other. In this state of things I make no difficulty in affirming that the proposal ought to originate from us. Great and acknowledged force is not impaired, either in effect or in opinion, by an unwillingness to exert itself. The superior power may offer peace with honor and with safety. Such an offer from such a power will be attributed to magnanimity. But the concessions of the weak are the concessions of fear. When such a one is disarmed, he is wholly at the mercy of his superior; and he loses forever that time and those chances which, as they happen to all men, are the strength and resources of all inferior power.[28]

The need to preserve that balance of power which characterizes the European system provides one of the most compelling reasons for a victor to offer a moderate peace. It is necessary to restrain one's own ambition as well as that of others. Burke admitted that, in practice, the only states which consistently sought to preserve the existing balance were "those whose state of weakness or mediocrity is such as to give them greater cause of apprehension from what may destroy them than of hope from anything by which they may be aggrandized." [29] *Sooner or later, however, immoderate ambition provokes opposition. "Nothing is so fatal to a nation as an extreme of self-partiality, and the total want of consideration of what others will naturally hope or fear."* [30] *It was in conformity with this view that Burke, who urged the annihilation of the French Republic, nevertheless insisted on the preservation of a powerful France as essential weight in the balance of power.*

As to the power of France as a state, and in its exterior relations, I confess my fears are on the part of its extreme reduction. There is undoubtedly something in the vicinity of France, which makes it naturally and properly an object of our watchfulness and jealousy, whatever form its government may take. But the difference is great between a plan for our own security and a scheme for the utter destruction of

27. *Ibid.*, pp. 251–3.
28. "Conciliation with America," *Works*, 2, 108.
29. "French Affairs," *Works*, 4, 330–1.
30. "Policy of the Allies," *Works*, 4, 447.

France. If there were no other countries in the political map but these two, I admit that policy might justify a wish to lower our neighbor to a standard which would even render her in some measure, if not wholly, our dependent. But the system of Europe is extensive and extremely complex. However formidable to us, as taken in this one relation, France is not equally dreadful to all other states. On the contrary, my clear opinion is, that the liberties of Europe cannot possibly be preserved but by her remaining a very great and preponderating power. The design at present evidently pursued by the combined potentates, or of the two who lead, is totally to destroy her as such a power. For Great Britain resolves that she shall have no colonies, no commerce, and no marine. Austria means to take away the whole frontier, from the borders of Switzerland to Dunkirk. It is their plan also to render the interior government lax and feeble, by prescribing, by force of the arms of rival and jealous nations, and without consulting the natural interests of the kingdom, such arrangements as, in the actual state of Jacobinism in France, and the unsettled state in which property must remain for a long time, will inevitably produce such distraction and debility in government as to reduce it to nothing, or to throw it back into its old confusion. One cannot conceive so frightful a state of a nation. A maritime country without a marine and without commerce; a continental country without a frontier, and for a thousand miles surrounded with powerful, warlike, and ambitious neighbors! It is possible that she might submit to lose her commerce and her colonies: her security she never can abandon. If, contrary to all expectations, under such a disgraced and impotent government, any energy should remain in that country, she will make every effort to recover her security, which will involve Europe for a century in war and blood. . . .

Take it the other way, and let us suppose that France so broken in spirit as to be content to remain naked and defenceless by sea and by land. Is such a country no prey? Have other nations no prey? Have other nations no views? Is Poland the only country of which it is worth while to make a partition? We cannot be so childish as to imagine that ambition is local, and that no others can be infected with it but those who rule within certain parallels of latitude and longitude. In this way I hold war equally certain. But I can conceive that both these principles may operate: ambition on the part of Austria to cut more and more from France; and French impatience under her degraded and unsafe condition. . . .

. . . Among precautions against ambition, it may not be amiss to take one precaution against our *own*. I must fairly say, I dread our *own* power and our *own* ambition; I dread our being too much dreaded. It is ridiculous to say we are not men, and that, as men, we shall never wish to aggrandize ourselves in some way or other. Can we say that even at this very hour we are not invidiously aggrandized? We are already in possession of almost all the commerce of the world. Our empire in India is an awful thing. If we should come to be in a condition not only to have all this ascendant in commerce, but to be absolutely able, without the least control, to hold the commerce of all other nations totally dependent upon our good pleasure, we may say that we shall not abuse this astonishing and hitherto unheard-of-power. But every other nation will think we shall abuse it. It is impossible but that, sooner or later, this state of things must produce a combination against us which may end in our ruin. . . . .

So far is France from being formidable to its neighbors for its domestic strength, that I conceive it will be as much as all its neighbors can do, by a steady guarantee, to keep that monarchy at all upon its basis. It will be their business to nurse France, not to exhaust it.[31]

Burke spent a great part of his life discussing the affairs of India and America. All the rights of the mother country could, he thought, be reconciled with the happiness of the colonies. The downtrodden masses of India and the English freemen of America were very different materials on which to work, but Burke insisted that respect for the rights of the subject was the key to sound imperial policy in both cases. He was well aware, however, that no one form of government could suit the affairs of India and America: "government was a practical thing, made for the happiness of mankind, and not to furnish out a spectacle of uniformity to gratify the schemes of visionary politicians."[32] The contentment of the subject was the strongest bond of empire.

For the English colonists Burke advocated a generous measure of control over their own affairs. The Empire must be the guardian of their liberties. "English colonies must be had on these terms or not had at all."[33] Burke also sought to guarantee the people of India their rights as humans but he saw that they could not maintain them for themselves.

31. *Ibid.*, pp. 454–8.
32. "Letter to the Sheriffs of Bristol," *Works*, 2, 227.
33. *Ibid.*, p. 233.

The natives should have as much liberty as they are capable of enjoying. As their capacities develop, so should their liberties.

. . . My hold of the colonies is in the close affection which grows from common names, from kindred blood, from similar privileges, and equal protection. These are ties which, though light as air, are as strong as links of iron. Let the colonies always keep the idea of their civil rights associated with your government,—they will cling and grapple to you, and no force under heaven will be of power to tear them from their allegiance. But let it be once understood that your government may be one thing and their privileges another, and these two things may exist without any mutual relation,—the cement is gone, the cohesion is loosened, and everything hastens to decay and dissolution. As long as you have the wisdom to keep the sovereign authority of this country as the sanctuary of liberty, the sacred temple consecrated to our common faith, wherever the chosen race and sons of England worship freedom, they will turn their faces towards you. The more they multiply, the more friends you will have; the more ardently they love liberty, the more perfect will be their obedience. Slavery they can have anywhere. It is a weed that grows in every soil. They may have it from Spain, they may have it from Prussia. But until you become lost to all feeling of your true interest and your natural dignity, freedom they can have from none but you. This is the commodity of price, of which you have the monopoly. This is the true Act of Navigation, which binds to you the commerce of the colonies, and through them secures to you the wealth of the world. Deny them this participation of freedom, and you break that sole bond which originally made, and must still preserve, the unity of the empire. . . . .

. . . Magnanimity in politics is not seldom the truest wisdom; and a great empire and little minds go ill together. If we are conscious of our situation, and glow with zeal to fill our place as becomes our station and ourselves, we ought to auspicate all our public proceedings on America with the old warning of the Church, *Sursum corda!* We ought to elevate our minds to the greatness of that trust to which the order of Providence has called us.[34]

. . . I must beg leave to observe, that, if we are not able to contrive some method of governing India *well*, which will not of necessity become the means of governing Great Britain *ill*, a ground is laid for their eternal separation, but none for sacrificing the people of that country

34. "Conciliation with America," *Works*, 2, 179–81.

to our Constitution. I am, however, far from being persuaded that any such incompatibility of interest does at all exist. On the contrary, I am certain that every means effectual to preserve India from oppression is a guard to preserve the British constitution from its worst corruption. . . . .

. . . Our own authority is, indeed, as much a trust originally as the [East India] Company's authority is a trust derivatively; and it is the use we make of the resumed power that must justify or condemn us . . . By that test we stand or fall; and by that test I trust that it will be found, in the issue, that we are going to supersede a charter abused to the full extent of all the powers which it could abuse, and exercised in the plenitude of despotism, tyranny, and corruption,—and that in one and the same plan we provide a real chartered security for *the rights of men*, cruelly violated under that charter.

This bill, and those connected with it, are intended to form the *Magna Charta* of Hindostan. Whatever the Treaty of Westphalia is to to the liberty of the princes and free cities of the Empire, and to the three religions there professed;—whatever the Great Charter, the Statute of Tallage, the Petition of Right, and the Declaration of Right are to Great Britain, these bills are to the people of India. Of this benefit I am certain their condition is capable: and when I know that they are capable of more, my vote shall most assuredly be for our giving to the full extent of their capacity of receiving; and no charter of dominion shall stand as a bar in my way to their charter of safety and protection.[35]

35. "Speech on Mr. Fox's East India Bill," *Works*, 2, 436–41.

10. THOMAS PAINE

1737-1809

BORN *a British subject, Thomas Paine became a citizen of America, of France and, so he claimed, of the world. In 1774, when he was thirty-seven, Paine met Benjamin Franklin in London and impressed him with his active and original mind. With an introduction from Franklin Paine came to America. By 1775 he was editing* The Pennsylvania Magazine *and agitating for American independence. In January 1776 he published* Common Sense, *the widely read pamphlet which so aroused anti-imperial sentiment that it ranks as one of the most powerful impulses to the Declaration of Independence.*

Paine joined the Revolutionary army and while on service composed a series of pamphlets known as The Crisis. *In 1777 Congress appointed him Secretary of the Committee of Foreign Affairs, a post he held for two years. Later he returned to England, where he wrote* The Rights of Man *as a reply to Burke's* Reflections on the French Revolution. The Rights of Man *prompted the nervous British government to charge Paine with sedition and he escaped to France just before he was outlawed. In Paris he associated with the Girondins and cooperated with Condorcet in drafting the constitution of 1793. The coming of the Terror disillusioned Paine and he was himself imprisoned for ten months. Released by the efforts of James Monroe, the American minister, Paine remained in France until 1802 and then returned to America, where he died poverty stricken in 1809.*

Paine believed that "the moral duty of man consists in imitating the moral goodness and beneficence of God manifested in the creation toward all his creatures" [1] *and that men have a conscience that makes them wish to be benevolent. He thought that if every man pursued his own interest intelligently, the interests of all would prove to be com-*

1. "Age of Reason," *Writings*, 4, 83.

The edition used is *The Writings of Thomas Paine*, ed. Moncure Daniel Conway, 4 vols. New York, G. P. Putnam's Sons, 1894–96.

*plementary and not mutually exclusive. "Reason and discussion will
soon bring things right, however wrong they begin." At first Paine was
inclined to attribute all political strife to ill-designed institutions which
obscured men's interests and thwarted their benevolence. Later he
noticed that the reforms carried out by the American and French Revolutions did not bring harmony to those nations, and he concluded that
his earlier diagnosis had been incomplete. A deep and universal change
of mind, if not of heart, was necessary, as well as the reform of institutions. It was to this problem that Paine addressed himself in his
last great work,* The Age of Reason.

*Paine's observation of the world led him to conclude that whereas
individuals had become civilized and ordered, nations retained "all
the original rudeness of nature." International relations were characterized by wars and deceit. Most of these wars originated in hope for glory
or material reward. Paine considered this hope illusory. The so-called
glory of war was based on mistaken values: there could be no glory in
anything as cruel and unreasonable as war. Even more ridiculous was
the expectation of profit. Nations always emerged poorer from wars
whether they won or lost, particularly because the states of Europe
would never allow any one nation to gain any significant ascendancy.*

*Paine explained the survival of a practice so pernicious as war in
terms of public ignorance and the vested interest of officials and government contractors. Although the nation suffered, many individuals
profited from war. The monarchical system was the chief culprit, for no
other type of government accumulated so many officeholders, indulged
in so many extravagances, placed so much value on military pomp, or
had such a need of distracting the people from the real condition of
the state.*

There is such an idea existing in the world, as that of *national honour,* and this, falsely understood, is oftentimes the cause of war. In
a Christian and philosophical sense, mankind seems to have stood
still at individual civilization, and to retain as nations all the original
rudeness of nature. Peace by treaty is only a cessation of violence for a
reformation of sentiment. It is a substitute for a principle that is wanting and ever will be wanting till the idea of *national honour* be rightly
understood. As individuals we profess ourselves Christians; but as nations we are heathens, Romans, and what not. I remember the late
Admiral Saunders declaring in the House of Commons, and that in the

time of peace, "That the city of Madrid laid in ashes was not a sufficient atonement for the Spaniards taking off the rudder of an English sloop of war." I do not ask whether this is Christianity or morality, I ask whether it is decency? whether it is proper language for a nation to use? In private life we call it by the plain name of bullying, and the elevation of rank cannot alter its character. It is, I think, exceedingly easy to define what ought to be understood by national honour; for that which is the best character for an individual is the best character for a nation; and wherever the latter exceeds or falls beneath the former, there is a departure from the line of true greatness.[2]

What has been the event of all the wars of England, but an amazing accumulation of debt, and an unparalleled burden of taxes? Sometimes the pretence has been to support one outlandish cause, and sometimes another. At one time Austria, at another time Prussia, another to oppose Russia, and so on; but the consequence has always been TAXES. A few men have enriched themselves by jobs and contracts, and the groaning multitude bore the burthen. What has England gained by war since the year 1738, only fifty years ago, to recompence her for TWO HUNDRED MILLIONS sterling, incurred as a debt within that time, and under the annual interest of which, besides what was incurred before, she is now groaning? Nothing at all.

The glare of fancied glory has often been held up, and the shadowy recompence imposed itself upon the senses. Wars that might have been prevented have been madly gone into, and the end has been debt and discontent. A sort of something which man cannot account for is mixed in his composition, and renders him the subject of deception by the very means he takes not to be deceived.

That jealousy which individuals of every nation feel at the supposed design of foreign powers, fits them to be the prey of Ministers, and of those among themselves whose trade is war, or whose livelihood is jobs and contracts. . . .

When we consider, for the feelings of Nature cannot be dismissed, the calamities of war and the miseries it inflicts upon the human species, the thousands and tens of thousands of every age and sex who are rendered wretched by the event, surely there is something in the heart of man that calls upon him to think! Surely there is some tender chord tuned by the hand of its Creator, that struggles to emit in the hearing

2. "The American Crisis," *Writings*, 1, 279.

of the soul a note of sorrowing sympathy. Let it then be heard, and let man learn to feel, that the true greatness of a nation is founded on the principles of humanity; and that to avoid a war when our own existence is wantonly sacrificed, is a higher principle of true honour than madly to engage in it.[3]

In Paine's world the system of international politics which he described and so roundly condemned was the European system. "Europe," wrote Paine, "is too thickly planted with kingdoms to be long at peace." [4] *Any state which could cut itself off from European politics would be well advised to do so. Paine suggested that Britain should renounce entangling alliances with continental powers.*

Perhaps there is not a greater instance of the folly of calculating upon events than are to be found in the treaties of alliance. As soon as they have answered the immediate purpose of either of the parties they are but little regarded. Pretences afterwards are never wanting to explain them away, nor reasons to render them abortive. And if half the money which nations lavish on speculative alliances were reserved for their own immediate purpose, whenever the occasion shall arrive, it would be more productively and advantageously employed.

Monarchs and Ministers, from ambition or resentment, often contemplate to themselves schemes of future greatness, and set out with what appears to them the fairest prospect: In the meanwhile, the great wheel of time and fate revolves unobserved, and something never dreamed of turns up and blasts the whole. A few fancied or unprofitable laurels supply the absence of success, and the exhausted nation is HUZZA'D INTO NEW TAXES.

The politics and interests of European Courts are so frequently varying with regard to each other, that there is no fixing even the probability of their future conduct. But the great principle of alliancing seems to be but little understood, or little cultivated in Courts, perhaps the least of all, in that of England.—No alliance can be operative that does not embrace within itself, not only the attachment of the Sovereigns, but the real interest of the nations. . . . .

In short, this alliance of national interest is the only one that can be trusted, and the only one that can be operative. All other alliances formed on the mere will and caprice of Sovereigns, of family connec-

3. "Prospects on the Rubicon," *Writings*, 2, 194–5.
4. "Common Sense," *Writings*, 1, 89.

tions, uncombined with national interests, are but the quagmire of politics, and never fail to become a loss to that nation who wastes its present substance on the expectancy of distant returns.[5]

The most able English Statesmen and Politicians have always held it as a principle, that foreign connections served only to embarrass and exhaust England. That, surrounded by the ocean, she could not be invaded, as countries are on the Continent of Europe, and that her insular situation dictated to her a different system of politics to what those countries required, and that to be enleagued with them was sacrificing the advantages of situation to a capricious system of politics. That tho' she might serve them they could not much serve her, and that as the service must all times be paid for, it could always be procured when it was wanted; and that it would be better to take it up in this line than to embarrass herself with speculative alliances that served rather to draw her into a Continental war on their account, than extricate her from a war undertaken on her own account.[6]

Turning to the American colonies Paine urged them to take advantage of their geographical situation and isolate themselves politically. He made this possibility of cutting America off from European wars a powerful argument for independence. This harmonized with Paine's other reasons for condemning the imperial connection. He believed that no such remote government could ever be a good one. Moreover, he was convinced that the mercantile pattern of trade was harmful to all and particularly to the colonies. But despite the zeal with which he advanced these arguments Paine laid most stress on the possibility of avoiding European wars. In this way he became a founding father of the American tradition of isolationism.

I challenge the warmest advocate for reconciliation to show a single advantage that this continent can reap by being connected with Great Britain. I repeat the challenge; not a single advantage is derived. Our corn will fetch its price in any market in Europe, and our imported goods must be paid for by them where we will.

But the injuries and disadvantages which we sustain by that connection, are without number; and our duty to mankind at large, as well as to ourselves, instruct us to renounce the alliance: because, any submission to, or dependance on, Great Britain, tends directly to in-

5. "Prospects," *Writings*, 2, 196–7.
6. *Ibid.*, p. 203.

volve this Continent in European wars and quarrels, and set us at variance with nations who would otherwise seek our friendship, and against
whom we have neither anger nor complaint. As Europe is our market
for trade, we ought to form no partial connection with any part of it. It
is the true interest of America to steer clear of European contentions,
which she never can do, while, by her dependance on Britain, she is
made the makeweight in the scale of British politics.

Europe is too thickly planted with Kingdoms to be long at peace, and
whenever a war breaks out between England and any foreign power,
the trade of America goes to ruin, *because of her connection with Britain.* The next war may not turn out like the last, and should it not, the
advocates for reconciliation now will be wishing for separation then,
because neutrality in that case would be a safer convoy than a man of
war.[7]

. . . That America hath flourished *at the time* she was under the government of Britain, is true; but there is every natural reason to believe,
that had she been an independent country from the first settlement
thereof, uncontrolled by any foreign power, free to make her own laws,
regulate and encourage her own commerce, she had by this time been
of much greater worth than now. . . . . .

But what weigh most with all men of serious reflection are, the *moral
advantages* arising from independence; war and desolation have become
the trade of the old world; and America neither could nor can be under
the government of Britain without becoming a sharer of her guilt, and
a partner in all the dismal commerce of death. The spirit of duelling,
extended on a national scale, is a proper character for European wars.
They have seldom any other motive than pride, or any other object
than fame. The conquerors and the conquered are generally ruined
alike, and the chief difference at last is, that the one marches home
with his honors, and the other without them. 'Tis the natural temper
of the English to fight for a feather, if they suppose that feather to be
an affront; and America, without the right of asking why, must have
abetted in every quarrel, and abided by its fate. It is a shocking situation to live in, that one country must be brought into all the wars of
another, whether the measure be right or wrong, or whether she will
or not; yet this, in the fullest extent, was, and ever would be, the unavoidable consequence of the connection.[8]

7. "Common Sense," *Writings, 1,* 88–9.
8. "American Crisis," *Writings, 1,* 202–6.

As to government matters, 'tis not in the power of Britain to do this continent justice: the business of it will soon be too weighty and intricate to be managed with any tolerable degree of convenience, by a power so distant from us and so very ignorant of us; for if they cannot conquer us, they cannot govern us. To be always running three or four thousand miles with a tale of a petition, waiting four or five months for an answer, which, when obtained, requires five or six more to explain it in, will in a few years be looked upon as folly and childishness. There was a time when it was proper, and there is a proper time for it to cease.

Small islands not capable of protecting themselves are the proper objects of governments to take under their care; but there is something absurd, in supposing a Continent to be perpetually governed by an island. In no instance hath nature made the satellite larger than its primary planet; and as England and America, with respect to each other, reverse the common order of nature, it is evident that they belong to different systems. England to Europe: America to itself.[9]

Paine was too optimistic to believe that the bad European system of international politics was beyond hope of cure. The American and French revolutions and their accompaniment of political speculation led him to believe the world had made sufficient intellectual and economic progress to set on foot projects of international reform. Later developments of both revolutions caused him to revise his opinion and to argue in The Age of Reason *that progress must wait for a further freeing of the mind.*

At the time of the French revolution, however, he believed the new age of democracy had dawned. This age would be one of harmony, for men were not naturally enemies; they were merely set at odds by bad political systems. Paine was confident that the benefits of universal democracy would include international peace. Democracy would bring national policy into conformity with national interest, and this interest could never lie in aggressive war. Under this new dispensation he was even prepared to envisage a confederation of Europe.

There is a morning of reason rising upon man on the subject of government that has not appeared before. As the barbarism of the present old government expires, the moral conditions of nations with respect to each other will be changed. Man will not be brought up with the savage idea of considering his species as his enemy, because the accident of

9. *Ibid.*, pp. 92, 95.

birth gave the individuals existence in countries distinguished by different names; and as constitutions have always some relation to external as well as to domestic circumstances, the means of benefiting by every change, foreign or domestic, should be a part of every constitution. We already see an alteration in the national disposition of England and France towards each other, which, when we look back to only a few years, is itself a Revolution. Who could have foreseen, or who could have believed, that a French National Assembly would ever have been a popular toast in England, or that a friendly alliance of the two nations should become the wish of either? It shews, that man, were he not corrupted by governments, is naturally the friend of man, and that human nature is not of itself vicious. That spirit of jealousy and ferocity, which the governments of the two countries inspired, and which they rendered subservient to the purpose of taxation, is now yielding to the dictates of reason, interest, and humanity. The trade of courts is beginning to be understood, and the affection of mystery, with all the artificial sorcery by which they imposed upon mankind, is on the decline. . . . For what we can foresee, all Europe may form but one great Republic, and man be free of the whole.[10]

There is a greater fitness in mankind to extend and complete the civilization of nations with each other at this day, than there was to begin it with the unconnected individuals at first; in the same manner that it is somewhat easier to put together the materials of a machine after they are formed than it was to form them from original matter. The present condition of the world, differing so exceedingly from what it formerly was, has given a new cast to the mind of man, more than what he appears to be sensible of. The wants of the individual, which first produced the idea of society, are now augmented into the wants of the nation, and he is obliged to seek from another country what before he sought from the next person.

Letters, the tongue of the world, have in some measure brought all mankind acquainted, and by an extension of their uses are every day promoting some new friendship. Through them distant nations become capable of conversation, and losing by degrees the awkwardness of strangers, and the moroseness of suspicion, they learn to know and understand each other. Science, the partisan of no country, but the beneficent patroness of all, has liberally opened a temple where all may meet. Her influence on the mind, like the sun on the chilled earth

10. "The Rights of Man," *Writings*, 2, 453.

has long been preparing it for higher cultivation and further improvement. . . . .

There are many things which in themselves are neither morally good
nor bad, but they are productive of consequences, which are strongly
marked with one or other of these characters. Thus commerce, though
in itself a moral nullity, has had a considerable influence in tempering
the human mind. . . .

. . . the introduction of commerce furnished the world with objects, which, in their extent, reach every man, and give him something
to think about and something to do; by these his attention is me-
chanically drawn from the pursuits which a state of indolence and an
unemployed mind occasioned, and he trades with the same countries,
which in former ages, tempted by their productions, and too indolent
to purchase them, he would have gone to war with.

Thus, as I have already observed, the condition of the world being
materially changed by the influence of science and commerce, it is put
into a fitness not only to admit of, but to desire, an extension of civilization. The principal and almost only remaining enemy, it now has to
encounter, is *prejudice;* for it is evidently the interest of mankind to
agree and make the best of life. . . . In short, the objects for war are
exceedingly diminished, and there is now left scarcely any thing to
quarrel about, but what arises from that demon of society, prejudice,
and the consequent sullenness and untractableness of the temper. . . . .

Perhaps no two events ever united so intimately and forcibly to com-
bat and expel prejudice, as the revolution of America and the alliance with France. Their effects are felt, and their influence already
extends as well to the old world as the new. Our style and manner of
thinking have undergone a revolution, more extraordinary than the
political revolution of the country. We see with other eyes; we hear
with other ears; and think with other thoughts, than those we formerly
used. We can look back on our own prejudices, as if they had been
the prejudices of other people. We now see and know they were prejudices and nothing else; and relieved from their shackles, enjoy a freedom of mind, we felt not before.[11]

. . . Monarchical sovereignty, the enemy of mankind, and the source
of misery, is abolished; and the sovereignty itself is restored to its natural
and original place, the Nation. Were this the case throughout Europe,
the cause of wars would be taken away.

11. "Letter to the Abbe Raynal," *Writings,* 2, 102–5.

It is attributed to Henry the Fourth of France, a man of enlarged and benevolent heart, that he proposed, about the year 1610, a plan for abolishing war in Europe. The plan consisted in constituting an European Congress, or as the French authors stile it, a Pacific Republic; by appointing delegates from the several Nations who were to act as a Court of arbitration in any disputes that might arise between nation and nation.

Had such a plan been adopted at the time it was proposed, the taxes of England and France, as two of the parties, would have been at least ten millions sterling annually to each Nation less than they were at the commencement of the French Revolution.

To conceive a cause why such a plan has not been adopted (and that instead of a Congress for the purpose of *preventing* war, it has been called only to *terminate* a war, after a fruitless expence of several years) it will be necessary to consider the interest of Governments as a distinct interest to that of Nations.

Whatever is the cause of taxes to a Nation, becomes also the means of revenue to Government. Every war terminates with an addition of taxes, and consequently with an addition of revenue; and in any event of war, in the manner they are now commenced and concluded, the power and interest of Governments are increased. War, therefore, from its productiveness, as it easily furnishes the pretence of necessity for taxes and appointments to places and offices, becomes a principal part of the system of old Governments; and to establish any mode to abolish war, however advantageous it might be to Nations, would be to take from such Government the most lucrative of its branches. The frivolous matters upon which war is made, shew the disposition and avidity of Governments to uphold the system of war, and betray the motives upon which they act.

Why are not Republics plunged into war, but because the nature of their Government does not admit of an interest distinct from that of the Nation? . . .

As war is the system of Government on the old construction, the animosity which Nations reciprocally entertain, is nothing more than what the policy of their Governments excites to keep up the spirit of the system. Each Government accuses the other of perfidy, intrigue and ambition, as a means of heating the imagination of their respective Nations, and incensing them to hostilities. Man is not the enemy of man, but through the medium of a false system of Government. Instead, therefore, of exclaiming against the ambition of Kings, the exclamation should be directed against the principle of such Governments; and instead of seeking to reform the individual, the wisdom of a nation should apply itself to reform the system. . . . .

From what we now see, nothing of reform in the political world ought to be held improbable. It is an age of Revolutions, in which everything may be looked for. The intrigue of Courts, by which the system of war is kept up, may provoke a confederation of Nations to abolish it: and an European Congress to patronise the progress of free Government, and promote the civilisation of Nations with each other, is an event nearer in probability, than once were the revolutions and alliance of France and America.[12]

Paine had so much faith in international cooperation that he was willing to modify his insistence on American isolation in order that the United States might participate in international organization. He suggested that an alliance of democratic great powers might impose beneficial changes on the world. Such a concert might institute a limitation of naval armaments, serving at the same time the causes of both peace and economy. The alliance might also liberate colonial areas and extend the range of free commerce.

These schemes were not mere theorizing but were intended for immediate application. Paine's favorite proposal for international organization was a league of neutrals, and in this case he arrived at the point of circulating a draft treaty. The most striking feature of the scheme was its use of economic and financial sanctions as a coercive instrument. Paine believed such sanctions would be effective against belligerents without imposing a great burden on the members of the league. Thus he believed his league demanded no more of its members than the coordination of actions that their self-interest would in any case prompt them to take singly.

In the preceding part of this work, I have spoken of an alliance between England, France, and America, for purposes that were to be afterwards mentioned. Though I have no direct authority on the part of America, I have good reason to conclude, that she is disposed to enter into a consideration of such a measure, provided, that the governments with which she might ally, acted as national governments and not as courts enveloped in intrigue and mystery. That France as a nation, and a national government, would prefer an alliance with England, is a matter of certainty. Nations, like individuals, who have

12. "Rights of Man," *Writings,* 2, 387–9.

long been enemies, without knowing each other, or knowing why, become the better friends when they discover the errors and impositions under which they had acted.

Admitting, therefore, the probability of such a connection, I will state some matters by which such an alliance, together with that of Holland, might render service, not only to the parties immediately concerned, but to all Europe.

It is, I think, certain, that if the fleets of England, France, and Holland were confederated, they could propose, with effect, a limitation to, and a general dismantling of, all the navies in Europe, to a certain proportion to be agreed upon.

First, that no new ship of war shall be built by any power in Europe, themselves included.

Second, that all the navies now in existence shall be put back suppose to one-tenth of their present force. This will save to France and England, at least two millions sterling annually to each, and their relative force be in the same proportion as it is now. If men will permit themselves to think, as rational beings ought to think, nothing can appear more ridiculous and absurd, exclusive of all moral reflections, than to be at the expence of building navies, filling them with men, and then hauling them into the ocean, to try which can sink each other fastest. Peace, which costs nothing, is attended with infinitely more advantage, than any victory with all its expence. But this, though it best answers the purpose of nations, does not that of court governments, whose habited policy is pretence for taxation, places, and offices.

It is, I think, also certain, that the above confederated powers, together with that of the United States of America, can propose with effect, to Spain, the independence of South America, and the opening those countries of immense extent and wealth to the general commerce of the world, as North America now is.[13]

During the American war, the plan of the armed neutrality was formed and put in execution: but it was inconvenient, expensive, and ineffectual. This being the case, the problem is, does not commerce contain within itself, the means of its own protection? It certainly does, if the neutral nations will employ that means properly.

Instead then of an *armed neutrality,* the plan would be directly the contrary. It should be an *unarmed neutrality.* In the first place the rights of neutral nations are easily defined. They are such as are exercised by

13. *Ibid.,* pp. 510–11.

nations in their intercourse with each other in time of peace, and which ought not, and cannot of right, be interrupted in consequence of war breaking out between any two or more of them.

Taking this as a principle, the next thing is to give it effect. The plan of the armed neutrality was to effect it by threatening war; but an unarmed neutrality can effect it by much easier and more powerful means.

Were the neutral nations to associate, under the honourable injunction of fidelity to each other, and publicly declare to the world, that if any belligerent power shall seize or molest any ship or vessel belonging to the citizens or subjects of any of the powers composing that Association, that the whole Association will shut its ports against the flag of the offending nation, and will not permit any goods, wares, or merchandise, produced or manufactured in the offending nation, or appertaining thereto, to be imported into any of the ports included in the Association, until reparation be made to the injured party,—the reparation to be three times the value of the vessel and cargo,—and moreover that all remittances on money, goods, and bills of exchange, do cease to be made to the offending nation, until the said reparation be made: were the neutral nations only to do this, which it is their direct interest to do, England, as a nation, depending on the commerce of neutral nations in time of war, dare not molest them, and France would not. But whilst, from the want of a common system, they individually permit England to do it, because individually they cannot resist it, they put France under the necessity of doing the same thing. The supreme of all laws, in all cases, is that of self-preservation.[14]

14. "The Eighteenth Fructidor," *Writings*, 3, 366–7.

11. ALEXANDER HAMILTON

1757-1804

ALEXANDER HAMILTON *played a major part in the formative years of the United States. At the beginning of the revolutionary upheaval Hamilton was inclined to favor the established order but serious reflection, and perhaps ambition, led him to take up the colonial cause. He fought in the Revolutionary Army and became* aide-de-camp *to Washington.*

After the war Hamilton was alarmed by the looseness of the Confederation. He was active in the Constitutional Convention, where he advocated an extremely strong central government, including a lifetime president with power to appoint the state governors. Although the new Constitution fell short of Hamilton's ideals it contained many of his ideas and he campaigned energetically for its ratification. At this time he collaborated with Madison and Jay in writing The Federalist. *Once the Constitution was established, Hamilton, as Secretary of the Treasury, became the first vigorous exponent of the theory of implied powers. Until his death in a duel with Aaron Burr, he worked constantly to strengthen the Union and lay the foundations of its commercial and fiscal policy.*

In his political writings Hamilton asserted that society and government had emerged by contract from a state of nature. This state was not one of anarchy, for it was governed by a system of moral law established by God. Man's reason was capable of perceiving this moral law upon which all human laws must rest. The moral law endowed all men with equal rights. These rights could only be safeguarded in a political state where the whole society shared in making the laws. All authority must stem from the people. This conviction did not prevent Hamilton from placing the highest value upon order in government. He believed

---

The editions used are *The Works of Alexander Hamilton*, ed. Henry Cabot Lodge, 12 vols. London and New York, G. P. Putnam's Sons, 1885–86; *The Federalist*, New York, the Modern Library, 1937.

that "the passions of men will not conform to the dictates of reason and justice, without constraint." [1] It was on the basis of this theory that Hamilton made his political and constitutional recommendations, but he was never a man to be rigidly bound by theory. Taking experience as his guide, he discussed each problem on its merits. Nearly all Hamilton's writings were closely related to current affairs.

A discussion in The Federalist of the fate of the thirteen colonies should they fail to unite contains the clearest exposition of Hamilton's view of international relations. He believed that men were "ambitious, vindictive, and rapacious." Sovereign states shared these characteristics of the individual, exaggerated by the lack of a collective conscience. It was therefore impossible for sovereign nations to exist side by side in peace and harmony. There would be constant disputes which, in the absence of any power to enforce a peaceful settlement, could only be decided by war.

Hamilton distinguished many causes of war. Some wars arose from a nation's craving for power. Others were caused by one nation's fear of its neighbor's intentions; for "safety from external danger is the most powerful director of national conduct." [2] In the past the desire for territory had been the foremost objective in war. Now commercial advantage was the prime motive. Hamilton was thus far from sharing the optimistic popular opinion of his day which held that commerce made for peaceful relations between nations.

Nor did he accept the opinion that war was the fruit of certain systems of government. The argument that war was a sport of kings which popular government would renounce found no favor with him. He believed that history proved republics as warlike as monarchies. Whatever the system, Hamilton observed that government was conducted by men and that they were subject to error and emotions which blinded them to their true interests and frequently impelled them to fight. "Wars oftener proceed from angry and perverse passions, than from cool calculations of interest." [3]

. . . To look for a continuation of harmony between a number of independent, unconnected sovereignties in the same neighborhood, would be to disregard the uniform course of human events, and to set at defiance the accumulated experience of ages.

1. *Federalist*, No. 15, p. 92.
2. *Federalist*, No. 8, p. 42.
3. *Works*, 4, 285.

The causes of hostility among nations are innumerable. There are some which have a general and almost constant operation upon the collective bodies of society. Of this description are the love of power or the desire of preeminence and dominion—the jealousy of power, or the desire of equality and safety. There are others which have a more circumscribed though an equally operative influence within their spheres. Such are the rivalships and competitions of commerce between commercial nations. And there are others, not less numerous than either of the former, which take their origin entirely in private passions; in the attachments, enmities, interests, hopes, and fears of leading individuals in the communities of which they are members. Men of this class, whether the favorites of a king or of a people, have in too many instances abused the confidence they possessed; and assuming the pretext of some public motive, have not scrupled to sacrifice the national tranquillity to personal advantage or personal gratification. . . . .

But notwithstanding the concurring testimony of experience, in this particular, there are still to be found visionary or designing men, who stand ready to advocate the paradox of perpetual peace between the States, though dismembered and alienated from each other. The genius of republics (say they) is pacific; the spirit of commerce has a tendency to soften the manners of men, and to extinguish those inflammable humors which have so often kindled into wars. Commercial republics, like ours, will never be disposed to waste themselves in ruinous contentions with each other. They will be governed by mutual interest, and will cultivate a spirit of mutual amity and concord.

Is it not (we may ask these projectors in politics) the true interest of all nations to cultivate the same benevolent and philosophic spirit? If this be their true interest, have they in fact pursued it? Has it not, on the contrary, invariably been found that momentary passions, and immediate interests, have a more active and imperious control over human conduct than general or remote considerations of policy, utility, or justice? Have republics in practice been less addicted to war than monarchies? Are not the former administered by *men* as well as the latter? Are there not aversions, predilections, rivalships, and desires of unjust acquisitions that affect nations as well as kings? Are not popular assemblies frequently subject to the impulses of rage, resentment, jealousy, avarice, and of other irregular and violent propensities? Is it not well known that their determinations are often governed by a few individuals in whom they place confidence, and are, of course, liable to be tinctured by the passions and views of those individuals? Has commerce hitherto done any thing more than change the objects of war? Is not the love of wealth as domineering and enterprising a passion as that of power or glory? Have there not been as many wars founded upon commercial motives since that has become the prevailing system of nations, as were before occasioned by the cupidity of territory or dominion? Has not the spirit of commerce, in many instances, administered new incentives to the appetite, both for the one and for the other? Let experience, the least fallible guide of human opinions, be appealed to for an answer to these inquiries. . . . .

In the government of Britain the representatives of the people compose one branch of the national legislature. Commerce has been for ages the predominant pursuit of that country. Few nations, nevertheless, have been more frequently engaged in war; and the wars in which that kingdom has been engaged have in numerous instances, proceeded from the people.

There have been, if I may so express it, almost as many popular as royal wars. The cries of the nation and the importunities of their representatives have, upon various occasions, dragged their monarchs into war, or continued them in it, contrary to their inclinations, and sometimes contrary to the real interests of the state. . . . .

So far is the general sense of mankind from corresponding with the tenets of those who endeavor to lull asleep our apprehensions of discord and hostility between the States, in the event of disunion, that it has from long observation of the progress of society become a sort of axiom in politics, that vicinity, or nearness of situation, constitutes nations natural enemies. An intelligent writer expresses himself on this subject to this effect: "NEIGHBORING NATIONS (says he) are naturally enemies of each other, unless their common weakness forces them to league in a CONFEDERATIVE REPUBLIC, and their constitution prevents the differences that neighborhood occasions, extinguishing that secret jealousy which disposes all states to aggrandize themselves at the expense of their neighbors." This passage, at the same time, points out the EVIL and suggests the REMEDY.[4]

Hamilton asserted that war was necessarily the only means of deciding international disputes which could not be amicably compromised. All law and order rested on some form of coercion. In disputes between communities where there was no common authority established to decide the issue, it could only be settled by military contest between the parties.

4. *Federalist*, No. 6, pp. 27–33.

Government implies the power of making laws. It is essential to the idea of a law, that it be attended with a sanction; or, in other words, a penalty or punishment for disobedience. If there be no penalty annexed to disobedience, the resolutions or commands which pretend to be laws will, in fact, amount to nothing more than advice or recommendation. This penalty, whatever it may be, can only be inflicted in two ways: by the agency of the courts and ministers of justice, or by military force; by the COERCION of the magistracy, or by the COERCION of arms. The first kind can evidently apply only to men; the last kind must of necessity, be employed against bodies politic, or communities, or States. It is evident that there is no process of a court by which the observance of the laws can, in the last resort, be enforced. Sentences may be denounced against them for violations of their duty; but these sentences can only be carried into execution by the sword. In an association where the general authority is confined to the collective bodies of the communities that compose it, every breach of the laws must involve a state of war; and military execution must become the only instrument of civil obedience. . . .

. . . Why has government been instituted at all? Because the passions of men will not conform to the dictates of reason and justice, without constraint. Has it been found that bodies of men act with more rectitude or greater disinterestedness than individuals? The contrary of this has been inferred by all accurate observers of the conduct of mankind; and the inference is founded upon obvious reasons. Regard to reputation has a less active influence, when the infamy of a bad action is to be divided among a number, than when it is to fall singly upon one. A spirit of faction, which is apt to mingle its poison in the deliberations of all bodies of men, will often hurry the persons of whom they are composed into improprieties and excesses, for which they would blush in a private capacity.[5]

In the system of international politics which Hamilton describes every nation will seize any opportunity to increase its power. This inclination may extend to efforts to establish a universal dominion. Because "self-preservation is the first duty of a nation," [6] *nations have a right to oppose the aggrandizement of any other state. This right extends so far as to justify preventive war. The right is not, however, a duty. A nation should enlist against a growing power only when convinced that its own vital interests are ultimately at stake.*

5. *Federalist*, No. 15, pp. 91–3.
6. "Pacificus," *Works, 4,* 159.

The conduct of France, from the commencement of her successes, has, by gradual developments, betrayed a spirit of universal domination; an opinion that she had a right to be the legislatrix of nations; that they are all bound to submit to her mandates, to take from her their moral, political, and religious creeds; that her plastic and regenerating hand is to mould them into whatever shape she thinks fit; and that her interest is to be the sole measure of the rights of the rest of the world. The specious pretence of enlightening mankind, and reforming their civil institutions, is the varnish to the real design of subjugating them. The vast projects of a Louis XIV dwindle into insignificance compared with the more gigantic schemes of his republican successors.

Men, well informed and unprejudiced, early discovered the symptoms of this spirit. Reasoning from human nature, they foresaw its growth with success; that from the love of dominion, inherent in the heart of man, the rulers of the most powerful nation in the world, whether a Committee of Safety or a Directory, will forever aim at an undue empire over other nations; and that this disposition, inflamed as it was by enthusiasm, if encouraged by a continuation of success, would be apt to exhibit itself, during the course of the French Revolution, in excesses of which there has been no example since the days of Roman greatness.

Every day confirms the justice of that anticipation. It is now indispensable that the disagreeable and menacing truth should be exposed in full day to the people of America; that they should contemplate it seriously, and prepare their minds for extremities, which nothing short of abject submission may be able to avert. This will serve them as an armour against the machinations of traitorous men, who may wish to make them instruments of the ambition of a foreign power, to persuade them to concur in forging chains for mankind, and to accept, as their award, the despicable privilege of wearing them a day later than others.[7]

The formal and definitive annexation to France of the territories over which her arms had temporarily prevailed, is another violation of just and moderate principles, into which the convention was betrayed by an intemperate zeal, if not by a culpable ambition; and of a nature to justify the jealousy and ill-will of every neighboring state.

The laws of nations give to a Power at war nothing more than a usufructuary or possessory right to the territories which it acquires;

7. "The Warning," Works, 5, 367–8.

suspending the absolute property and dominion till a treaty of peace, or something equivalent, shall have ceded or relinquished the conquered territory to the conqueror. This rule is one of primary importance to the tranquillity and security of nations—facilitating an adjustment of their quarrels and the preservation of ancient limits.

But France, by incorporating with herself in several instances the territories she had acquired, violated that rule, and multiplied infinitely the obstacles to peace and accommodation. The doctrine that a nation cannot consent to its own dismemberment but in a case of extreme necessity, immediately attached itself to all the conquered territories; while the progressive augmentation of the dominions of the most powerful empire in Europe, on a principle not of temporary possession but of permanent acquisition, threatened the independence of all other countries, and gave to neighboring neutral Powers the justest cause of discontent and apprehension. It is a principle well agreed, and founded on substantial reasons, that whenever a particular state adopts maxims of conduct contrary to those generally established among nations, calculated to interrupt their tranquillity and to expose their safety, they may justifiably make common cause to resist and control the state which manifests a disposition so suspicious and exceptionable.[8]

Independent of the commands of honor the coolest calculations of interest forbid our becoming the instruments of the ambition of France, by associating with her in the war. The question is no longer the establishment of liberty on the basis of republican government. This point the enemies of France have ceased to dispute. The question now is whether she shall be aggrandized by new acquisitions, and her enemies reduced by dismemberments, to a degree which may render her the mistress of Europe, and consequently, in a great measure, of America. This is truly the remaining subject of contention.

They who understand the real strength and resources of France before the present war, knew that she was intrinsically the most powerful nation of Europe. The incidents of the war have displayed this fact in a manner which is the astonishment of the world. If France can finally realize her present plan of aggrandizement, she will attain to a degree of greatness and power which, if not counteracted by internal disorder, will tend to make her the terror and the scourge of nations. The spirit of moderation in a state of overbearing power is a phenomenon which has not yet appeared, and which no wise man will expect ever to see.

8. "Pacificus," *Works, 4,* 155–6.

It is certain that a very different spirit has hitherto marked the career of the new republic; and it is due to truth to add, that the ardent, impetuous, and military genius of the French affords perhaps less prospect of such a spirit in them than in any other people.

It were therefore contrary to our true interest to assist in building up this colossus to the enormous size at which she aims. It were a policy as shortsighted as mean to seek safety in a subserviency to her views as the price of her clemency. This at best would be but a temporary respite from the rod; if indeed that can be called a respite, which is of itself the sacrifice of a real to a nominal independence.[9]

. . . There is no rule of public law better established, or on better grounds, than that when one nation unequivocally avows maxims of conduct dangerous to the security and tranquillity of others, they have a right to attack her and to endeavor to disable her from carrying her schemes into effect. They are not bound to wait till inimical designs are matured for action, when it may be too late to defeat them.

How far it may have been wise in a particular government to have taken up the gauntlet, or if, in its option, to have left France to the fermentations of the pernicious principles by which its leaders were actuated, is a question of mere expediency, distinct from the right. It is also a complicated and difficult question, one which able and upright men might decide different ways. But the right is still indisputable.[10]

The guiding principle of Hamilton's foreign policy recommendations was that of self-interest. He did not deny that there were moral standards to be observed, but he believed that they had only a limited application to international relations.

A nation could rely on its rights only if it was capable of enforcing them. "A nation, despicable by its weakness, forfeits even the privilege of being neutral." [11] A nation could never be obliged to act in a manner calculated to endanger its own security and existence. Thus there is plenty of room for discretion within the bounds of international morality. Hamilton insisted that this discretion should always be exercised in the self-interest of the nation.

He added two reservations to his principle of self-interest. In the first place he reminded his readers that a nation's true interest might not

9. "The Warning," *Works*, 5, 369–70.
10. "The Stand," *Works*, 5, 405–6.
11. *Federalist*, No. 11, p. 65.

lie in the most immediately selfish policy. There was, for example, value
in a good reputation—both at home and abroad—which might best be
secured by conceding the advantage in certain cases. Secondly Hamilton
pointed out that although it was clearly a statesman's duty to act in the
national interest, it was far from certain that he would in fact do so.
Statesmen were men and liable to error and emotion.

. . . it may not be without use to indulge some reflections on this
very favorite topic of gratitude to France, since it is at this shrine that
we are continually invited to sacrifice the true interests of the country;
as if "all for love, and the world well lost," were a fundamental maxim
in politics.

Faith and justice between nations are virtues of a nature the most
necessary and sacred. They cannot be too strongly inculcated, nor too
highly respected. Their obligations are absolute, their utility unques-
tionable; they relate to objects which, with probity and sincerity, generally admit of being brought within clear and intelligible rules.

But the same cannot be said of gratitude. It is not very often that
between nations it can be pronounced with certainty that there exists
a solid foundation for the sentiment; and how far it can justifiably be
permitted to operate, is always a question of still greater difficulty.

The basis of gratitude is a benefit received or intended, which there
was no right to claim, originating in a regard to the interest or advantage of the party on whom the benefit is, or is meant to be, conferred. If a service is rendered from views relative to the immediate interest of the party who performs it, and is productive of reciprocal advantages, there seems scarcely, in such a case, to be an adequate basis
for a sentiment like that of gratitude.

The effect at least would be wholly disproportioned to the cause, if
such a service ought to beget more than a disposition to render in turn
a correspondent good office, founded on mutual interest and reciprocal
advantage. But gratitude would require much more than this: it would
exact to a certain extent even a sacrifice of the interest of the party
obliged to the service or benefit of the one by whom the obligation had
been conferred.

Between individuals, occasion is not unfrequently given for the
exercise of gratitude. Instances of conferring benefits from kind and
benevolent dispositions or feelings toward the person benefited, without any other interest on the part of the person who renders the service,
than the pleasure of doing a good action, occur every day among in-

dividuals. But among nations they perhaps never occur. It may be affirmed as a general principle, that the predominant motive of good offices from one nation to another, is the interest or advantage of the nation which performs them.

Indeed, the rule of morality in this respect is not precisely the same between nations as between individuals. The duty of making its own welfare the guide of its actions, is much stronger upon the former than upon the latter; in proportion to the greater magnitude and importance of national compared with individual happiness, and to the greater permanency of the effects of national than of individual conduct. Existing millions, and for the most part future generations, are concerned in the present measures of a government; while the consequences of the private actions of an individual ordinarily terminate with himself, or are circumscribed within a narrow compass.

Whence it follows that an individual may, on numerous occasions, meritoriously indulge the emotions of generosity and benevolence, not only without an eye to, but even at the expense of, his own interest. But a government can rarely, if at all, be justifiable in pursuing a similar course; and, if it does so, ought to confine itself within much stricter bounds. Good offices which are indifferent to the interest of a nation performing them, or which are compensated by the existence or expectation of some reasonable equivalent, or which produce an essential good to the nation to which they are rendered, without real detriment to the affairs of the benefactors, prescribe perhaps the limits of national generosity or benevolence.

It is not here meant to recommend a policy absolutely selfish or interested in nations; but to show, that a policy regulated by their own interest, as far as justice and good faith permit, is, and ought to be, their prevailing one; and that either to ascribe to them a different principle of action, or to deduce, from the supposition of it, arguments for a self-denying and self-sacrificing gratitude on the part of a nation which may have received from another good offices, is to misrepresent or misconceive what usually are, and ought to be, the springs of national conduct.[12]

. . . in national controversies, it is of real importance to conciliate the good opinion of mankind; and it is even useful to preserve or gain that of our enemy. The latter facilitates accommodation and peace; the former attracts good offices, friendly interventions, sometimes direct

12. "Pacificus," *Works, 4,* 164–7.

support, from others. The exemplary conduct, in general, of our country, in our contest for independence, was probably not a little serviceable to us in this way; it secured to the intrinsic goodness of our cause every collateral advantage, and gave it a popularity among nations, unalloyed and unimpaired, which even stole into the cabinets of princes. A contrary policy tends to contrary consequences. Though nations, in the main, are governed by what they suppose their interest, he must be imperfectly versed in human nature who thinks it indifferent whether the maxims of a State tend to excite kind or unkind dispositions in others, or who does not know that these dispositions may insensibly mould or bias the views of self-interest. This were to suppose that rulers only reason—do not feel; in other words, are not men.[13]

There is nothing absurd or impracticable in the idea of a league or alliance between independent nations for certain defined purposes precisely stated in a treaty regulating all the details of time, place, circumstance, and quantity; leaving nothing to future discretion; and depending for its execution on the good faith of the parties. Compacts of this kind exist among all civilized nations, subject to the usual vicissitudes of peace and war, of observance and non-observance, as the interests or passions of the contracting powers dictate. In the early part of the present century there was an epidemical rage in Europe for this species of compacts, from which the politicians of the times fondly hoped for benefits which were never realized. With a view to establishing the equilibrium of power and the peace of that part of the world, all the resources of negotiations were exhausted, and triple and quadruple alliances were formed; but they were scarcely formed before they were broken, giving an instructive but afflicting lesson to mankind, how little dependence is to be placed on treaties which have no other sanction than the obligations of good faith, and which oppose general considerations of peace and justice to the impulse of any immediate interest or passion.[14]

In the actual conduct of foreign policy Hamilton advised vigilance and moderation. He insisted that a nation be ready to defend its vital interests with vigor, but he deprecated an irritable disposition and a hasty resort to the uncertain fortunes of war. Vital interests should not be mortgaged for minor issues. Except in the face of the most flagrant offenses, the first resort should be to negotiation.

13. "Camillus," *Works,* 5, 105–6.
14. *Federalist,* No. 15, p. 90.

True honor is a rational thing. It is as distinguishable from Quixotism as true courage from the spirit of the bravo. It is possible for one nation to commit so undisguised and unqualified an outrage upon another as to render a negotiation of the question dishonorable. But this seldom, if ever, happens. In most cases, it is consistent with honor to precede rupture by negotiation, and whenever it is, reason and humanity demand it. Honor cannot be wounded by consulting moderation. As a general rule, it is not till after it has become manifest that reasonable reparation for a clear premeditated wrong cannot be obtained by an amicable adjustment, that honor demands a resort to arms. In all the questions between us and Great Britain, honor permitted the moderate course; in those which regard the inexecution of the treaty of peace, there had undoubtedly been mutual faults. It was, therefore, a case for negotiation and mutual reparation. True honor, which can never be separated from justice, even requires reparation from us to Great Britain, as well as from her to us. The injuries we complain of in the present war, were also of a negotiable kind. The first was bottomed on a controverted point in the laws of nations. The second left open the question, whether the principal injury was a designed act of the government or a misconstruction of its courts. To have taken, therefore, the imperious ground which is recommended, in place of that which was taken, would have been not to follow the admonitions of honor, but to have submitted to the impulse of passion and phrensy.

So likewise, when it is asserted that war is preferable to the sacrifice of our rights and interests, this, to be true, to be rational, must be understood of such rights and interests as are certain, as are important, such as regard the honor, security, or prosperity of our country. It is not a right disputable, or of small consequence, it is not an interest temporary, partial, and inconsiderable, which will justify, in our situation, an appeal to arms.

Nations ought to calculate as well as individuals, to compare evils, and to prefer the lesser to the greater; to act otherwise, is to act unreasonably; those who counsel it are imposters or madmen.[15]

All ostensibly agree, that one more experiment of negotiation ought to precede actual war; but there is this serious difference in the practice. The sincere friends of peace and accommodation are for leaving things in a state which will enable Great Britain, without abandoning self-respect, to do us the justice we seek. The others are for placing things

15. "Camillus," *Works*, 4, 417–18.

upon a footing which would involve the disgrace or disrepute of having receded through intimidation.

This last scheme indubitably ends in war. The folly is too great to be seriously entertained by the discerning part of those who affect to believe the position—that Great Britain, fortified by the alliances of the greatest part of Europe, will submit to our demands, urged with the face of coercion, and preceded by acts of reprisal. She cannot do it without renouncing her pride and her dignity, without losing her consequence and weight in the scale of nations; and, consequently, it is morally certain that she will not do it. A proper estimate of the operation of the human passions, must satisfy us that she would be less disposed to receive the law from us than from any other nation—a people recently become a nation, not long since one of her dependencies, and as yet, if a Hercules, a Hercules in the cradle.

When one nation inflicts injuries upon another, which are causes of war, if this other means to negotiate before it goes to war, the usual and received course is to prepare for war, and proceed to negotiation, avoiding reprisals till the issue of the negotiation. This course is recommended by all enlightened writers on the laws of nations, as the course of moderation, propriety, and wisdom; and it is that commonly pursued, except where there is a disposition to go to war, or a commanding superiority of power.

Preparation for war, in such cases, contains in it nothing offensive. It is a mere precaution for self-defense, under circumstances which endanger the breaking out of war. It gives rise to no point of honor which can be a bar to equitable and amicable negotiation. But acts of reprisal speak a contrary effect—they change negotiation into peremptory demand, and they brandish a rod over the part on whom the demand is made. He must be humble indeed, if he comply with the demand to avoid the stripe. . . . .

. . . It is only to consult our own hearts to be convinced that nations, like individuals, revolt at the idea of being guided by external compulsion. They will, at least, only yield to that idea after resistance has been fruitlessly tried in all its forms.

It is as great an error for a nation to overrate us as to underrate itself. Presumption is as great a fault as timidity.

There are two ideas of immense consequence to us in the event of war: the disunion of our enemies; the perfect union of our own citizens. Justice and moderation, united with firmness, are the means to secure both these advantages; injustice or intemperance will lose both.

Unanimity among ourselves, which is the most important of the two ideas, can only be secured by its being manifest, if war ensues, that it was inevitable by another course of conduct. . . . .

Want of unanimity will naturally tend to render the operations of war feeble and heavy, to destroy both effort and perseverance. War, undertaken under such auspices, can scarcely end in any thing better than an inglorious and disadvantageous peace. What worse it may produce is beyond the reach of human foresight.[16]

Hamilton gave particular warning against setting too much store on which side in a dispute committed the first offense. Such questions were usually obscure. Without willingness to waive this issue and compromise, wars would become perennial and peace could never be made until one side was totally defeated.

Nations, no more than individuals, ought to persist in error, especially at the sacrifice of their peace and prosperity; besides, nothing is more common, in disputes between nations, than each side to charge the other with being the aggressor or delinquent. This mutual crimination, either from the nature of circumstances, or from the illusions of the passions, is sometimes sincere; at other times it is dictated by pride or policy. But . . . where one party is not powerful enough to dictate to the other and where there is a mutual disposition to avoid war, the natural retreat for both is in compromise, which waives the question of first aggression or delinquency. This is the salvo for national pride; the escape for mutual error; the bridge by which nations, arrayed against each other, are enabled to retire with honor, and without bloodshed, from the field of contest. In cases of mutual delinquency, the question of the first default is frequently attended with real difficulty and doubt. One side has an equal right with the other to have and maintain its opinion. What is to be done when the pride of neither will yield to the arguments of the other? War, or a waiver of the point, is the alternative. What sensible man, what humane man, will deny that a compromise, which secures substantially the objects of interest, is almost always preferable to war on so punctilious and unmanageable a point?

Reject the principle of compromise, and the feuds of nations must become much more deadly than they have hitherto been. There would scarcely ever be room for the adjustment of differences without an appeal to the sword; and, when drawn, it would seldom be sheathed but

16. *Works, 4,* 290–7.

with the destruction of one or the other party. The earth, now too often stained, would then continually stream with human gore.[17]

Hamilton had a clear idea of the place of the United States in the world. He advised his country to become self-sufficient economically so as to be independent in war. He warned against unnecessary entanglement in the "contests, broils, and wars of Europe." [18] *He hoped that his country might, by skilful diplomacy, keep the peace until better able to take part in the turmoil of world politics. Above all he urged his nation to make its own decisions and pursue a firmly American policy. But Hamilton, unlike many of his contemporaries, did not believe the United States could cut itself off from European politics and isolate the Western Hemisphere. He had the more modest ambition that the United States might come to dominate the Hemisphere and "become the arbiter of Europe in America."*

. . . A cloud has been for some time hanging over the European world. If it should break forth into a storm, who can insure us that in its progress a part of its fury would not be spent upon us? No reasonable man would hastily pronounce that we are entirely out of its reach. Or if the combustible materials that now seem to be collecting should be dissipated without coming to maturity, or if a flame should be kindled without extending to us, what security can we have that our tranquillity will long remain undisturbed from some other course or from some other quarter? Let us recollect that peace or war will not always be left to our option; that however moderate or unambitious we may be, we cannot count upon the moderation, or hope to extinguish the ambition of others.[19]

A further resource for influencing the conduct of European nations toward us, in this respect, would arise from the establishment of a federal navy. There can be no doubt that the continuance of the Union under an efficient government, would put it in our power, at a period not very distant, to create a navy which, if it could not vie with those of the great maritime powers, would at least be of respectable weight if thrown into the scale of either of two contending parties. This would be more peculiarly the case in relation to operations in the West Indies.

17. "Camillus," *Works,* 4, 394–5.
18. "Horatius," *Works,* 4, 367.
19. *Federalist,* No. 34, p. 206.

A few ships of the line, sent opportunely to the reinforcement of either side, would often be sufficient to decide the fate of a campaign, on the event of which interests of the greatest magnitude were suspended. Our position is, in this respect, a most commanding one. And if to this consideration we add that of the usefulness of supplies from this country, in the prosecution of military operations in the West Indies, it will readily be perceived that a situation so favorable would enable us to bargain with great advantage for commercial privileges. A price would be set not only upon our friendship, but upon our neutrality. By a steady adherence to the Union, we may hope, erelong, to become the arbiter of Europe in America, and to be able to incline the balance of European competitions in this part of the world as our interest may dictate.[20]

A very powerful state may frequently hazard a high and haughty tone with good policy; but a weak state can scarcely ever do it without imprudence. The last is yet our character; though we are the embryo of a great empire. It is, therefore, better suited to our situation to measure each step with the utmost caution; to hazard as little as possible, in the cases in which we are injured; to blend moderation with firmness; and to brandish the weapons of hostility only when it is apparent that the use of them is unavoidable.

It is not to be inferred from this, that we are to crouch to any power on earth, or tamely to suffer our rights to be violated. A nation which is capable of this meanness will quickly have no rights to protect, or honor to defend.

But the true inference is, that we ought not lightly to seek or provoke a resort to arms; that, in the differences between us and other nations, we ought carefully to avoid measures which tend to widen the breach; and that we should scrupulously abstain from whatever may be construed into reprisals, till after the employment of all amicable means has reduced it to a certainty that there is no alternative.

If we can avoid a war for ten or twelve years more, we shall then have acquired a maturity, which will make it no more than a common calamity, and will authorize us, in our national discussions, to take a higher and imposing tone.[21]

20. *Ibid.*, No. 11, pp. 64–5.
21. "Camillus," *Works, 4*, 387–8.

12. THOMAS JEFFERSON

1743-1826

THOMAS JEFFERSON *had fifty years to live after he had established his greatest single claim to fame by composing the Declaration of Independence. Within his long lifetime the American and French Revolutions remolded the world of politics, the age of reason gave way to the dawn of romanticism, and industrial technology outmoded the mercantile system.*

Jefferson's first important political act was the inspiration, in 1773, of committees of correspondence between the colonies to coordinate resistance to the British. He became a member of the Second Continental Congress in 1775, one year before he wrote the Declaration. From 1779 to 1781 he was Governor of Virginia. After a brief period in Congress, he was appointed American minister to France. With the establishment of the new constitution he returned to the United States to become the first secretary of state, an office he held three years. The year 1797 saw Jefferson return to active political life as vice-president of the United States. Four years later he became the nation's third president. At the end of his two terms he was eager to lay aside the burden of office, but he retained an energetic interest in the affairs of the nation and of his native Virginia. He was still on hand in 1823 to advise Monroe on the decisions that culminated in the famous doctrine.

As a political philosopher Jefferson's reputation is inextricably associated with the idea of democracy. He was not an original thinker. In all his political speculations he accepted the limitations he set himself in the Declaration of Independence, not "to say things which had never been said before; but to place before mankind the common sense of the subject." [1] His political thought was founded on the concept of natural

1. "Correspondence," *Writings*, 16, 118.

The edition used is *The Writings of Thomas Jefferson*, ed. Andrew A. Lipscomb and Albert Ellery Bergh, 20 vols. Washington, D.C., the Thomas Jefferson Memorial Association, 1903–04.

law so common in his day. He firmly believed in a moral order, but he did not admit that God had revealed that order through any one agent. Instead he relegated God to the status of first cause, a Creator who, having once made an orderly world, did not interfere in its workings. Every man could discover the Creator's intention by studying the creation. When his reason had discovered God's will, man's conscience would impel him to obey it.

Jefferson's own study of the world led him to conclude that all men had equal rights to equal opportunities. Flaws in men's consciences and errors in their reasoning made it necessary to institute governments to secure these rights. Government existed solely for the benefit of the governed and had no source of authority but the consent of the governed. All political power was dangerous and open to abuse. The most important task in politics was therefore to hedge authority with restrictions and safeguards. Jefferson at one time considered the Articles of Confederation an ideal government for America, and although he came to admit the need for a stronger system, it was he who hastened to add a Bill of Rights to preserve the freedom of the individual.

Jefferson believed that nations, not governments, were the truly responsible actors in international affairs. Nations, like individuals, had equal rights. Any group of men who wished to live as an independent nation had a right to "assume, among the powers of the earth, the separate and equal station, to which the laws of nature and of nature's God entitle them." [2] *These nations were under no common authority, but they were answerable to a system of morals. This moral code was identical with that which individuals should observe. Writing to refute Hamilton's assertion that America's obligations to France were annulled by the French Revolution, Jefferson declared; "I know but one code of morality for men whether acting singly or collectively. . . . If the morality of one man produces a just line of conduct in him, acting individually, why should not the morality of one hundred men produce a just line of conduct in them, acting together?"* [3]

Thus obligations between nations were as binding as between individuals. Jefferson conceded that a nation might be justified in breaking promises when fulfillment would be fatal to its existence. But he insisted

2. Quoted in Carl Becker, "What is Still Living in the Political Philosophy of Thomas Jefferson?" *Proceedings of the American Philosophical Society*, 87 (1943–44), 204.

3. "Correspondence," *Writings*, 7, 449–50.

that this dispensation could only be invoked in extreme cases, when the
danger was imminent and overwhelming.

I proceed in compliance with the requisition of the President to give
an opinion in writing on the general question, whether the United States
have a right to renounce their treaties with France, or to hold them suspended till the government of that country shall be established? . . . .

I consider the people who constitute a society or nation as the source
of all authority in that nation; as free to transact their common concerns
by any agents they think proper; to change these agents individually, or
the organisation of them in form or function whenever they please; that
all the acts done by those agents under the authority of the nation, are
the acts of the nation, are obligatory to them and ensure to their use, and
can in no wise be annulled or affected by any change in the form of the
government, or of the persons administering it, consequently the treaties
between the United States and France, were not treaties between the
United States and Louis Capet, but between the two nations of America
and France, and the nations remaining in existence, though both of
them have since changed their forms of government, the treaties are not
annulled by these changes. The Law of nations, by which this question
is to be determined, is composed of three branches. 1. The moral law of
our nature. 2. The usages of nations. 3. Their special conventions. The
first of these only concerns this question, that is to say the moral law to
which man has been subjected by his creator, and of which his feelings,
or Conscience as it is sometimes called, are the evidence with which his
creator has furnished him. The moral duties which exist between individual and individual in a state of nature, accompany them into a state
of society, and the aggregate of the duties of all the individuals composing the society constitutes the duties of that society towards any other;
so that between society and society the same moral duties exist as did
between the individuals composing them, while in an unassociated state
. . . their maker not having released them from those duties on their
forming themselves into a nation. Compacts then, between nation and
nation, are obligatory on them by the same moral law which obliges
individuals to observe their compacts. There are circumstances, however, which sometimes excuse the non-performance of contracts between
man and man; so are there also between nation and nation. When performance, for instance, becomes *impossible,* non-performance is not
immoral; so if performance becomes *self-destructive* to the party, the
law of self-preservation overrules the laws of obligation to others. For

the reality of these principles I appeal to the true fountains of evidence, the head and heart of every rational and honest man. It is there nature has written her moral laws, and where every man may read them for himself. He will never read there the permission to annul his obligations for a time, or forever, whenever they become dangerous, useless, or disagreeable; certainly not when merely useless or disagreeable . . . and though he may, under certain degrees of danger, yet the danger must be imminent, and the degree great. Of these, it is true, that nations are to be judges for themselves; since no one nation has a right to sit in judgment over another, but the tribunal of our consciences remains, and that also of the opinion of the world. These will revise the sentence we pass in our own case, and as we respect these, we must see that in judging ourselves we have honestly done the part of impartial and rigorous judges.[4]

Jefferson believed that true self-interest coincided with the demands of morality. A wise foreign policy should therefore be based on the conviction that "with nations, as with individuals, our interests soundly calculated, will ever be found inseparable from our moral duties; and history bears witness to the fact, that a just nation is taken on its word, when recourse is had to armaments and wars to bridle others." [5] *But even a nation pursuing a perfectly just foreign policy was not assured of peace. Such a nation was still vulnerable to the injustices of other states. A wise nation ought to stand ready to resent and punish injuries. Failure to retaliate when attacked would only invite further assaults.*

The justest dispositions possible in ourselves will not secure us against [injustice] . . . It would be necessary that all other nations were just also. Justice indeed, on our part, will save us from those wars which would have been produced by a contrary disposition. But how can we prevent those produced by the wrongs of other nations? By putting ourselves in a condition to punish them. Weakness provokes insult and injury, while a condition to punish, often prevents it. This reasoning leads to the necessity of some naval force; that being the only weapon by which we can reach an enemy. I think it to our interest to punish the first insult; because an insult unpunished is the parent of many others.[6]

4. "Official Papers," *Writings,* 3, 226–9.
5. "Inaugural Addresses and Messages," *Writings,* 3, 375–6.
6. "Correspondence," *Writings,* 5, 95.

. . . It has been peculiarly unfortunate for us, personally, that the portion in the history of mankind, at which we were called to take a share in the direction of their affairs, was such an one as history has never before presented. At any other period, the even-handed justice we have observed towards all nations, the efforts we have made to merit their esteem by every act which candor or liberality could exercise, would have preserved our peace, and secured the unqualified confidence of all other nations in our faith and probity. But the hurricane which is now blasting the world, physical and moral, has prostrated all the mounds of reason as well as right. All those calculations which, at any other period, would have been deemed honorable, of the existence of a moral sense in man, individually or associated, of the connection which the laws of nature have established betwen his duties and his interests, of a regard for honest fame and the esteem of our fellow men, have been a matter of reproach on us, as evidences of imbecility. As if it could be a folly for an honest man to suppose that others could be honest also, when it is their interest to be so.[7]

War, except in self-defense, could never serve the true interests of any nation. Even in defense war was a regrettable necessity. Unfortunately the political system of Europe involved its crowded nations in perpetual wars. Jefferson hoped that the geographical situation of America would provide her with an opportunity to stand aloof from these embroilments and pursue a new, more rational, and moral policy of peace.

You have not been mistaken in supposing my views and feelings to be in favor of the abolition of war. Of my disposition to maintain peace until its condition shall be made less tolerable than that of war itself, the world has had proofs, and more, perhaps, than it has approved. I hope it is practicable, by improving the mind and morals of society, to lessen the disposition to war; but of its abolition I despair. Still, on the axiom that a less degree of evil is preferable to a greater, no means should be neglected which may add weight to the better scale. The enrolment you propose, therefore, of my name in the records of your society cannot be unacceptable to me. It will be a true testimony of my principles and persuasion that the state of peace is that which most improves the manners and morals, the prosperity and happiness of mankind; and although I dare not promise myself that it can be perpetually

7. "Correspondence," *Writings*, 12, 357–8.

maintained, yet if, by the inculcations of reason or religion, the perversities of our nature can be so far corrected as sometimes to prevent the necessity, either supposed or real, of an appeal to the blinder scourges of war, murder, and devastation, the benevolent endeavors of the friends of peace will not be entirely without remuneration.[8]

We have seen with sincere concern the flames of war lighted up again in Europe, and nations with which we have the most friendly and useful relations engaged in mutual destruction. While we regret the miseries in which we see others involved, let us bow with gratitude to that kind Providence which, inspiring with wisdom and moderation our late legislative councils while placed under the urgency of the greatest wrongs, guarded us from hastily entering into the sanguinary contest, and left us only to look on and to pity its ravages. These will be heaviest on those immediately engaged. Yet the nations pursuing peace will not be exempt from all evil. In the course of this conflict, let it be our endeavor, as it is our interest and desire, to cultivate the friendship of the belligerent nations by every act of justice and of incessant kindness; to receive their armed vessels with hospitality from the distresses of the sea, but to administer the means of annoyance to none; to establish in our harbors such a police as may maintain law and order; to restrain our citizens from embarking individually in a war in which their country takes no part; to punish severely those persons, citizen or alien, who shall usurp the cover of our flag for vessels not entitled to it, infecting thereby with suspicion those of real Americans, and committing us into controversies for the redress of wrongs not our own; to exact from every nation the observance, toward our vessels and citizens, of those principles and practices which all civilized people acknowledge; to merit the character of a just nation, and maintain that of an independent one, preferring every consequence to insult and habitual wrong. . . . Separated by a wide ocean from the nations of Europe, and from the political interests which entangle them together, with productions and wants which render our commerce and friendship useful to them and theirs to us, it cannot be the interest of any to assail us, nor ours to disturb them. We should be most unwise, indeed, were we to cast away the singular blessings of the position in which nature has placed us, the opportunity she has endowed us with of pursuing, at a distance from foreign contentions, the paths of industry, peace, and happiness; of cultivating general friendship, and of bringing collisions of interest to the umpirage of rea-

8. "Private Papers," *Writings*, *18*, 298–9.

son rather than of force. How desirable then must it be, in a government like ours, to see its citizens adopt individually the views, the interest, and the conduct which their country should pursue, divesting themselves of those passions and partialities which tend to lessen useful friendships, and to embarrass and embroil us in the calamitous scenes of Europe.[9]

. . . Young as we are, and with such a country before us to fill with people and with happiness, we should point in that direction the whole generative force of nature, wasting none of it in efforts of mutual destruction. It should be our endeavor to cultivate the peace and friendship of every nation, even of that which has injured us most, when we shall have carried our point against her. Our interest will be to throw open the doors of commerce, and to knock off all its shackles, giving perfect freedom to all persons for the vent of whatever they may choose to bring into our ports, and asking the same in theirs. Never was so much false arithmetic employed on any subject, as that which has been employed to persuade nations that it is their interest to go to war. Were the money which it has cost to gain, at the close of a long war, a little town, or a little territory, the right to cut wood here, or to catch fish there, expended in improving what they already possess, in making roads, opening rivers, building ports, improving the arts, and finding employment for their idle poor, it would render them much stronger, much wealthier and happier. This I hope will be our wisdom. And, perhaps, to remove as much as possible the occasions of making war, it might be better for us to abandon the ocean altogether, that being the element whereon we shall be principally exposed to jostle with other nations; to leave to others to bring what we shall want, and to carry what we can spare. This would make us invulnerable to Europe, by offering none of our property to their prize, and would turn all our citizens to the cultivation of the earth; and, I repeat it again, cultivators of the earth are the most virtuous and independent citizens. It might be time enough to seek employment for them at sea, when the land no longer offers it.[10]

. . . And on the question . . . whether we can, in any form, take a bolder attitude than formerly in favor of liberty, I can give you but commonplace ideas. They will be but the widow's mite, and offered only because requested. The matter which now embroils Europe, the

9. "Inaugural Addresses and Messages," *Writings,* 3, 358–60.
10. "Notes on Virginia," *Writings,* 2, 240–41.

presumption of dictating to an independent nation the form of its government, is so arrogant, so atrocious, that indignation, as well as moral sentiment, enlists all our partialities and prayers in favor of one, and our equal execrations against the other. I do not know, indeed, whether all nations do not owe to one another a bold and open declaration of their sympathies with the one party, and their detestation of the conduct of the other. But farther than this we are not bound to go; and indeed, for the sake of the world, we ought not to increase the jealousies, or draw on ourselves the power of this formidable confederacy. I have ever deemed it fundamental for the United States, never to take active part in the quarrels of Europe. Their political interests are entirely distinct from ours. Their mutual jealousies, their balance of power, their complicated alliances, their forms and principles of government, are all foreign to us. They are nations of eternal war. All their energies are expended in the destruction of the labor, property and lives of their people. On our part, never had a people so favorable a chance of trying the opposite system, of peace and fraternity with mankind, and the direction of all our means and faculties to the purposes of improvement instead of destruction. With Europe we have few occasions of collision, and these, with a little prudence and forbearance, may be generally accommodated. Of the brethren of our own hemisphere, none are yet, or for an age to come will be, in a shape, condition, or disposition to war against us. And the foothold which the nations of Europe had in either America, is slipping from under them, so that we shall soon be rid of their neighborhood.[11]

In fact Jefferson went so far as to anticipate a day "when we may formally require a meridian of partition through the ocean which separates the two hemispheres, on the hither side of which no European gun shall ever be heard, nor an American on the other; and when, during the rage of the eternal wars of Europe, the lion and the lamb, within our regions, shall lie down together in peace." [12] *But while Jefferson urged America to remain as far as possible aloof from Europe's affairs, he recognized America's interest in the balance of power in Europe and between her neighbors in the New World. "We especially ought to pray,"* *he wrote, "that the powers of Europe may be so poised and counterpoised among themselves, that their own safety may require the presence of all their force at home, leaving the other quarters of the globe in*

11. "Correspondence," *Writings,* 15, 435–6.
12. *Ibid.,* p. 263.

undisturbed tranquility." [13] *At a time when it seemed that Britain might acquire Spain's possessions in America, Jefferson was concerned with the danger that, "instead of two neighbors balancing each other, we shall have one with more than the strength of both."* [14]

Surely none of us wish to see Bonaparte conquer Russia, and lay thus at his feet the whole continent of Europe. This done, England would be but a breakfast; and, although I am free from the visionary fears which the votaries of England have affected to entertain, because I believe he cannot effect the conquest of Europe; yet put all Europe into his hands, and he might spare such a force, to be sent in British ships, as I would as leave not have to encounter, when I see how much trouble a handful of British soldiers in Canada has given us. No. It cannot be to our interest that all Europe should be reduced to a single monarchy. . . . And were the consequences even to be the longer continuance of our war, I would rather meet them than see the whole force of Europe wielded by a single hand. [15]

While advocating a policy of aloofness and peace Jefferson admitted that the United States could not avoid all disputes with other nations. Americans were a trading people and their commerce would provide ample objects for the injuries of others. In such cases Jefferson hoped that adequate retaliation might be made by "those peaceable courses which are in the power of every nation," [16] *by which he meant cutting off economic relations. He conceded that in some cases it might be better to go to war than suffer continued injury. Even in war, however, Jefferson favored the use of means which kept hostilities as far away as possible.*

. . . Our people are decided in the opinion, that it is necessary for us to take a share in the occupation of the ocean, and their established habits induce them to require that the sea be kept open to them, and that that line of policy be pursued, which will render the use of that element to them as great as possible. I think it a duty in those entrusted with the administration of their affairs, to conform themselves to the decided choice of their constituents; and that therefore, we should, in every instance, preserve an equality of right to them in the transportation of

13. *Ibid., 13,* 119.
14. "Miscellaneous Papers," *Writings, 17,* 300.
15. "Correspondence," *Writings, 14,* 43–4.
16. *Ibid., 10,* 281–2.

commodities, in the right of fishing, and in the other uses of the sea. But what will be the consequence? Frequent wars without a doubt. Their property will be violated on the sea, and in foreign ports, their persons will be insulted, imprisoned, etc., for pretended debts, contracts, crimes, contraband, etc., etc. These insults must be resented, even if we had no feelings, yet to prevent their eternal repetition . . .[17]

The idea seems to gain credit that the naval powers combined against France, will prohibit supplies even of provisions, to that country. Should this be formally notified, I should suppose Congress would be called, because it is a justifiable cause of war, and as the Executive cannot decide the question of war on the affirmative side, neither ought it to do so on the negative side by preventing the competent body from deliberating on the question. But I should hope that war would not be their choice. I think it will furnish us a happy opportunity of setting another precious example to the world, by showing that nations may be brought to do justice by appeals to their interests as well as by appeals to arms. I should hope that Congress, instead of a denunciation of war, would instantly exclude from our ports all the manufactures, produce, vessels and subjects of the nations committing this aggression, during the continuance of the aggression, and till full satisfaction made for it. This would work well in many ways, safely in all, and introduce between nations another umpire than arms. It would relieve us, too, from the risks and the horrors of cutting throats.[18]

. . . So enviable a state in prospect for our country, induced me to temporize, and to bear with national wrongs which under no other prospect ought ever to have been unresented or unresisted. My hope was, that by giving time for reflection, and retraction of injury, a sound calculation of their own interests would induce the aggressing nations to redeem their own character by a return to the practice of right. But our lot happens to have been cast in an age when two nations to whom circumstances have given a temporary superiority over others, the one by land, the other by sea, throwing off all restraints of morality, all pride of national character, forgetting the mutability of fortune and the inevitable doom which the laws of nature pronounce against departure from justice, individual or national, have dared to treat her reclamations with derision, and to set up force instead of reason as the umpire of nations. Degrading themselves thus from the character of lawful so-

17. *Ibid.*, 5, 94.
18. *Ibid.*, 9, 33–4.

cieties into lawless bands of robbers and pirates, they are abusing their brief ascendency by desolating the world with blood and rapine. Against such a banditti, war had become less ruinous than peace, for then peace was a war on one side only. On the final and formal declarations of England, therefore, that she never would repeal her orders of council as to us, until those of France should be repealed as to other nations as well as us, and that no practicable arrangement against her impressment of our seamen could be proposed or devised, war was justly declared, and ought to have been declared.[19]

. . . Wars then must sometimes be our lot; and all the wise can do, will be to avoid that half of them which would be produced by our own follies and our own acts of injustice; and to make for the other half the best preparations we can. Of what nature should these be? A land army would be useless for offence, and not the best nor safest instrument of defence. For either of these purposes, the sea is the field on which we should meet an European enemy. On that element it is necessary we should possess some power. To aim at such a navy as the greatest nations of Europe possess, would be a foolish and wicked waste of the energies of our countrymen. It would be to pull on our own heads that load of military expense which makes the European laborer go supperless to bed, and moistens his bread with the sweat of his brows. It will be enough if we enable ourselves to prevent insults from those nations of Europe which are weak on the sea, because circumstances exist, which render even the stronger ones weak as to us. Providence has placed their richest and most defenceless possessions at our door; has obliged their most precious commerce to pass, as it were, in review before us. To protect this, or to assail, a small part only of their naval force will ever be risked across the Atlantic. The dangers to which the elements expose them here are too well known, and the greater dangers to which they would be exposed at home were any general calamity to involve their whole fleet. They can attack us by detachment only; and it will suffice to make ourselves equal to what they may detach. Even a smaller force than they may detach will be rendered equal or superior by the quickness with which any check may be repaired with us, while losses with them will be irreparable till too late. A small naval force then is sufficient for us, and a small one is necessary. What this should be, I will not undertake to say. I will only say, it should by no means be so great as we are able to make it.[20]

19. *Ibid.*, *13*, 355–6.
20. "Notes on Virginia," *Writings*, 2, 241–3.

13. WILLIAM GODWIN

1756-1836

GODWIN *was a prominent leader of English radical opinion at the end of the eighteenth century. He enjoyed a brief but resounding popularity during the years 1793–97 when enthusiasm for the ideas of the French Revolution had not yet been completely crushed by fear and reaction. Godwin's major work, an* Enquiry concerning Political Justice, *published in 1793, was one of the earliest expositions of anarchism. In addition to his political writings he published several successful novels.*

Godwin was an apostle of progress. He believed that men acted on the basis of their opinions and that, given proper education, they would always arrive at correct opinions. In this way men were "susceptible of perpetual improvement." Because men with proper opinions would always act justly, Godwin looked forward to the decay of governments which served only to suppress injustice. The demise of the state would result in a world of small autonomous parishes. Men could only be educated toward this end by rational argument. The gradual and peaceful influence of ideas was therefore the only true means to progress. So great was Godwin's dislike for organization of any kind that he condemned even unofficial cooperation to spread his teaching. "Everything," he wrote, "may be trusted to the tranquil and wholesome progress of knowledge." [1]

Godwin's distaste for the state pervaded his views on international relations. Believing as he did that individuals alone merited concern and that the state should decay, he could see no reason for disputes between nations. The issues of so-called national interest were not really important. They were a fiction by which privileged groups imposed

1. Pp. 361–2.

The edition used is *Enquiry concerning Political Justice and Its Influence on Morals and Happiness,* 3d ed., 2 vols. London, G. G. and J. Robinson, 1798. All of the following extracts are from volume 2 of this work.

sacrifices on the people at large. "War and conquest cannot be beneficial to the community. Their tendency is to elevate a few at the expense of the rest; and consequently they will never be undertaken, but where the many are the instruments of the few." [2] Trade rivalry, territorial ambition, and national honor were mere illusions. An enlightened democracy would perceive this and pursue a peaceful policy. The important relations were those between individuals. Informed men might fight for liberty, but on behalf of the men involved, not in the interests of any state.

. . . The only legitimate object of political institution is the advantage of individuals. All that cannot be brought home to them, national wealth, prosperity and glory, can be advantageous only to those self-interested imposters, who, from the earliest accounts of time, have confounded the understandings of mankind the more securely to sink them in debasement and misery.

The desire to gain a more extensive territory, to conquer or to hold in awe our neighbouring states, to surpass them in arts or arms, is a desire founded in prejudice and error. Usurped authority is a spurious and unsubstantial medium of happiness. Security and peace are more to be desired than a national splendour that should terrify the world. Mankind are brethren. We associate in a particular district or under a particular climate, because association is necessary to our internal tranquillity, or to defend us against the wanton attacks of a common enemy. But the rivalship of nations is a creature of the imagination. If riches be our object, riches can only be created by commerce; and the greater is our neighbours capacity to buy, the greater will be our opportunity to sell. The prosperity of all is the interest of all.

The more accurately we understand our own advantage, the less shall we be disposed to disturb the peace of our neighbour. The same principle is applicable to him in return. It becomes us therefore to desire that he may be wise. But wisdom is the growth of equality and independence, not of injury and oppression. If oppression had been the school of wisdom, the improvement of mankind would have been inestimable, for they have been in that school for many thousand years. We ought therefore to desire that our neighbour should be independent. We ought to desire that he should be free; for wars do not originate in the unbiassed propensities of nations, but in the cabals of government and the propensities that governments inspire into the people at large. If our

2. P. 143.

neighbour invade our territory all we should desire is to repel him from it; and for that purpose it is not necessary we should surpass him in prowess since upon our own ground his match is unequal. Not to say that to conceive a nation attacked by another, so long as its own conduct is sober, equitable and moderate, is an exceedingly improbable supposition.

Where nations are not brought into avowed hostility, all jealousy between them is an unintelligible chimera. I reside upon a certain spot, because that residence is most conducive to my happiness or usefulness. I am interested in the political justice and virtue of my species, because they are men, that is, creatures eminently capable of justice and virtue; and I have perhaps additional reason to interest myself for those who live under the same government as myself, because I am better qualified to understand their claims, and more capable of exerting myself in their behalf. But I can certainly have no interest in the infliction of pain upon others, unless so far as they are expressly engaged in acts of injustice. The object of sound policy and morality is to draw men nearer to each other, not to separate them; to unite their interests, not to oppose them.

Individuals ought, no doubt, to cultivate a more frequent and confidential intercourse with each other than at present subsists; but political societies of men, as such, have no interests to explain and adjust, except so far as error and violence may render explanation necessary. This consideration annihilates at once the principal objects of that mysterious and crooked policy which hitherto occupied the attention of governments. Before this principle officers of the army and the navy, ambassadors and negotiators, all the train of artifices that has been invented to hold other nations at bay, to penetrate their secrets, to traverse their machinations, to form alliances and counter alliances, sink into nothing. The expence of government is annihilated, and, together with its expence the means of subduing and undermining the virtues of its subjects.

Another of the great opprobriums of political science, is, at the same time, completely removed, that extent of territory subject to one head, respecting which philosophers and moralists have alternately disputed whether it be most unfit for a monarchy or for a democratical government. The appearance which mankind, in a future state of improvement, may be expected to assume, is a policy that, in different countries, will wear a similar form, because we have all the same faculties and the same wants; but a policy, the independent branches of which will extend their authority over a small territory, because neighbours are best informed of each other's concerns, and are perfectly equal to their adjustment. No recommendation can be imagined of an extensive rather than a limited territory, except that of external security.[3]

. . . Why should disingenuity and concealment be thought virtuous or beneficial on the part of nations, in cases where they would inevitably be discarded with contempt, by an upright individual? Where is there an ingenuous and enlightened man, who is not aware of the superior advantage that belongs to a proceeding, frank, explicit and direct? Who is there that sees not, that this inextricable labyrinth of reasons of state, was artfully invented, lest the people should understand their own affairs, and, understanding, become inclined to conduct them? With respect to treaties, it is to be suspected that they are, in all instances, superfluous. But, if public engagements ought to be entered into, what essential difference is there between the governments of two countries endeavouring to overreach each other, and the buyer and seller in any private transaction adopting a similar proceeding?

This whole system proceeds upon the idea of national grandeur and glory, as if, in reality, these words had any specific meaning. These contemptible objects, these airy names, have, from the earliest page of history, been made a colour for the most pernicious undertakings.[4]

The love of our country, has often been found to be a deceitful principle, as its direct tendency is to set the interests of one division of mankind in opposition to another, and to establish a preference built upon accidental relations and not upon reason. Much of what has been understood by the appellation, is excellent, but perhaps nothing that can be brought within the strict interpretation of the phrase. A wise and well informed man will not fail to be the votary of liberty and justice. He will be ready to exert himself in their defence, wherever they exist. It cannot be a matter of indifference to him, when his own liberty and that of other men with whose merits and capacities he has the best opportunity of being acquainted, are involved in the event of the struggle to be made. But his attachment will be to the cause, as the cause of man, and not to the country. Wherever there are individuals, who understand the value of political justice, and are prepared to assert it, that is his country. Wherever he can most contribute to the diffusion of these principles and the real happiness of mankind, that is his country. Nor does he desire, for any country, any other benefit than justice.[5]

3. Pp. 191–5.
4. P. 179.
5. Pp. 146–7.

Godwin's emphasis on the individual rather than the nation led him to place domestic affairs far above foreign affairs in the scale of importance. But he recognized that men had not yet attained to his ideal of enlightenment and justice. They had not discarded allegiance to their own state and jealousy of others. Thus international disputes arose and nations were tempted "to adjudge the controversies between them, not according to the dictates of reason and justice, but as either should prove most successful in devastation and murder." [6] *Even the best behaved state might find itself attacked. In such a case Godwin approved of armed defense. "I ought to take up arms against the despot by whom my country is invaded, because my capacity does not enable me by arguments to prevail on him to desist, and because my countrymen will not preserve their intellectual independence in the midst of oppression."* [7] *Nevertheless Godwin was not prepared to devote much of the nation's attention to defense. He believed that defense was easier than attack and that free men would fight better than oppressed men. Following this reasoning Godwin thought elaborate preparations for war unnecessary. Nor did he approve of treaties of alliance, for he did not believe that any ally would ever render assistance under treaty which would not be offered under mere force of circumstance.*

. . . It is time that we should recur to the maxim delivered at our entrance upon this subject, that individuals are everything, and society, abstracted from the individuals of which it is composed nothing. An immediate consequence of this maxim is, that the internal affairs of the society are entitled to our principal attention, and the external are matters of inferior and subordinate consideration. The internal affairs are subjects of perpetual and hourly concern, the external are periodical and precarious only. . . .

If therefore it should appear that, of these two articles, internal and external affairs, one must, in some degree be sacrificed to the other, and that a democracy will in certain respects be less fitted for the affairs of war than some other species of government, good sense will not hesitate in the alternative.We shall have sufficient reason to be satisfied, if, together with the benefits of justice and virtue at home, we have no reason to despair of our safety from abroad. A confidence in this article will seldom deceive us, if our countrymen, however little trained to formal rules, and the uniformity of mechanism, have studied the profession of

6. P. 148.
7. P. 366.

man, understand his attributes and his nature, and have their necks unbroken to the yoke of blind credulity and abject submission. Such men, inured, as we are now supposing them, to a rational state of society, will be full of calm confidence and penetrating activity, and these qualities will stand them instead of a thousand lessons in the school of military mechanism. If democracy can be proved adequate to wars of defence, and other governments be better fitted for wars of a different sort, this would be an argument, not of its imperfection, but of its merit.[8]

The duty of individuals, in their political capacity, is, in the first place, to endeavour to meliorate the state of society in which they exist, and to be indefatigable in detecting its imperfections. But, in the second place, it behoves them to recollect, that their efforts cannot be expected to meet with instant success, that the progress of knowledge has, in all cases, been gradual, and that their obligation to promote the welfare of society during the intermediate period, is certainly not less real, than their obligation to promote its future and permanent advantage. Even the future advantage cannot be effectually procured, if we be inattentive to the present security. But, as long as nations shall be so far mistaken, as to endure a complex government, and an extensive territory, coercion will be indispensably necessary to general security. It is therefore the duty of individuals, to take an active share upon occasion, in so much coercion, and in such parts of the existing system, as shall be sufficient to counteract the growth of universal violence and tumult. It is unworthy of a rational enquirer to say, "These things are necessary, but I am not obliged to take my share in them." If they be necessary, they are necessary for the general welfare; of consequence, are virtuous, and what no just man will refuse to perform.

The duty of individuals is, in this respect, similar to the duty of independent communities, upon the subject of war. It is well known what has been the prevailing policy of princes under this head. Princes, especially the most active and enterprising among them, are seized with an inextinguishable rage for augmenting their dominions. The most innocent and inoffensive conduct on the part of their neighbours, will not, at all times, be a sufficient security against their ambition. They indeed seek to disguise their violence under plausible pretences; but it is well known that, where no such pretences occur, they are not, on that account, disposed to relinquish the pursuit. Let us imagine then a land of freemen invaded by one of these despots. What conduct does it behove

8. Pp. 176–8.

them to adopt. We are not yet wise enough, to make the sword drop out
of the hands of our oppressors, by, the mere force of reason. Were we
resolved, like quakers, neither to oppose, nor, where it could be avoided,
to submit to them, much bloodshed might perhaps be prevented: but
a more lasting evil would result. They would fix garrisons in our country, and torment us with perpetual injustice. Supposing it were even
granted, that, if the invaded nation should demean itself with unalterable constancy, the invaders would become tired of their fruitless usurpation, it would prove but little. At present we have to do, not with nations of philosophers, but with nations of men whose virtues are alloyed
with weakness, fluctuation and inconstancy. At present it is our duty to
consult, respecting the procedure which, to such nations, may be attended with the most favourable result. It is therefore proper, that we
should choose the least calamitous mode, of obliging the enemy speedily
to withdraw himself from our territories.[9]

. . . the system of a standing army is altogether indefensible, and
. . . a universal militia is a much more formidable defence, as well as
more agreeable to the principles of justice and political happiness. . . .
what would be the real situation of a nation, surrounded by other nations, in the midst of which standing armies were maintained, that
should nevertheless, upon principle, wholly neglect the art military in
seasons of peace. In such a nation it will probably be admitted, that, so
far as relates to mere numbers, an army may be raised upon the spur of
occasion, nearly as soon; as in a nation the citizens of which had been
taught to be soldiers. But this army, though numerous, would be in
want of many of those principles of combination and activity, which are
of material importance in a day of battle. There is indeed included in
the supposition, that the internal state of this people, is more equal and
free, than that of the people by whom they are invaded. This will infallibly be the case, in a comparison between a people with a standing
army, and people without one; between a people who can be brought
blindly and wickedly to the invasion of their peaceful neighbours, and
a people who will not be induced to fight but in their own defence. The
latter therefore will be obliged to compare the state of society and government, in their own country, and among their neighbours, and will not
fail to be impressed with great ardour in defence of the inestimable advantages they possess. Ardour, even in the day of battle, might prove
sufficient. A body of men, however undisciplined, whom nothing could

9. Pp. 363–5.

induce to quit the field, would infallibly be victorious over their veteran adversaries, who, under the circumstances of this case, could have no accurate conception of the object for which they were fighting, and therefore could not entertain an inextinguishable love for it. It is not certain that activity and discipline, opposed to ardour, have even a tendency to turn the balance of slaughter against the party that wants them.[10]

. . . Treaties of alliance, if we examine and weigh the history of mankind, will perhaps be found to have been, in all cases, nugatory, or worse. Governments, and public men, will not, and ought not, to hold themselves bound to the injury of the concerns they conduct, because a parchment, to which they or their predecessors were a party, requires it. If the concert demanded in time of need, approve itself to their judgment, and correspond with their inclination, it will be yielded, though they are under no previous engagement for that purpose. Treaties of alliance serve to no other end, than to exhibit, by their violation, an appearance of profligacy and vice, which unfortunately becomes too often a powerful encouragement to the inconsistency of individuals. Add to this, that if alliances were engines as powerful, as they are really impotent, they could seldom be of use to a nation uniformly adhering to the principles of justice. They would be useless, because they are, in reality, ill-calculated for any other purposes than those of ambition. They might be pernicious, because it would be beneficial for nations, as it is for individuals, to look for resources at home, instead of depending upon the precarious compassion of their neighbours.[11]

In another section of his treatise Godwin elaborated the distinction between just and unjust war. He sought to restrict the justification of war by confining it to the defense of liberty. But so great was his love of liberty that he gave a wide definition to its defense, asserting that a nation had a right to assist another people in revolution.

. . . we may venture to enquire what are the justifiable causes and rules of war.

It is not a justifiable reason, "that we imagine our own people would be rendered more cordial and orderly, if we could find a neighbour with whom to quarrel, and who might serve as a touchstone to try the characters and dispositions of individuals among ourselves." We are not at

10. Pp. 170–1.
11. Pp. 173–4.

liberty to have recourse to the most complicated and atrocious of all mischiefs, in the way of an experiment.

It is not a justifiable reason, "that we have been exposed to certain insults, and that tyrants, perhaps, have delighted in treating with contempt, the citizens of our happy state who have visited their dominions." Government ought to protect the tranquillity of those who reside within the sphere of its functions; but, if individuals think proper to visit other countries, they must then be delivered over to the protection of general reason. Some proportion must be observed, between the evil of which we complain and the evil which the nature of the proposed remedy inevitably includes.

It is not a justifiable reason, "that our neighbour is preparing or menacing hostilities." If we be obliged to prepare in our turn, the inconvenience is only equal; and it is not to be believed, that a despotic country is capable of more exertion than a free one, when the task incumbent on the latter is indispensable precaution.

It has sometimes been held to be sound reasoning upon this subject "that we ought not to yield little things, which may not, in themselves, be sufficiently valuable to authorise this tremendous appeal, because a disposition to yield, only invites further experiments." Much otherwise; at least when the character of such a nation is sufficiently understood. A people that will not contend for nominal and trivial objects, that adheres to the precise line of unalterable justice, and that does not fail to be moved at the moment that it ought to be moved, is not the people that its neighbours will delight to urge to extremities.

The vindication of "national honour," is a very insufficient reason for hostilities. True honour is to be found only in integrity and justice. It has been doubted, how far a view to reputation, ought, in matters of inferior moment, to be permitted to influence the conduct of individuals; but, let the case of individuals be decided as it may, reputation, considered as a separate motive in the instance of nations, can perhaps never be justifiable. In individuals, it seems as if I might, consistently with the utmost real integrity, be so misconstrued and misrepresented by others, as to render my efforts at usefulness almost necessarily abortive. But this reason does not apply to the case of nations. Their real story cannot easily be suppressed. Usefulness and public spirit, in relation to them, chiefly belong to the transactions of their members among themselves; and their influence in the transactions of neighbouring nations, is a consideration evidently subordinate— The question which respects the justifiable causes of war, would be liable to few difficulties, if we were accustomed, along with the word, strongly to call up to our minds the thing which that word is intended to represent.

Accurately considered, there can probably be but two causes of war that can maintain any plausible claim to justice; and one of them, is among those which the logic of sovereigns, and the law of nations, as it has been termed, have been thought to proscribe: these are the defence of our own liberty, and of the liberty of others. The well-known objection to the latter of these cases, is, "that one nation ought not to interfere in the internal transactions of another." But certainly every people is fit for the possession of any immunity, as soon as they understand the nature of that immunity, and desire to possess it; and it is probable that this condition may be sufficiently realized, in cases, where, from the subtlety of intrigue, and the tyrannical jealousy of neighbouring kingdoms, they may be rendered incapable of effectually asserting their rights. This principle is capable of being abused by men of ambition and intrigue; but, accurately considered, the very same argument that should induce me to exert myself for the liberties of my own country, is equally cogent, so far as my opportunities and ability extend, with respect to the liberties of any other country. But what is my duty in this case, is the duty of all; and the exertion must be collective, where collective exertion can be effectual.[12]

The balance of power incurred Godwin's particular condemnation, for although this doctrine merely dealt with the power relations of states —which were not worthy objects of attention—it was often the means by which peoples were lured into war. Godwin thought that war was justifiable against the oppressive use of power but not against its mere accumulation.

The celebrated topic of the balance of power is a mixed consideration, having sometimes been proposed as the cause for beginning a war, and sometimes as an object to be pursued in a war already begun. A war, undertaken to maintain the balance of power, may be either of defence as to protect a people who are oppressed, or of prevention, to counteract new acquisitions or to reduce the magnitude of old possessions. We shall be in little danger of error, however, if we pronounce wars undertaken to maintain the balance of power to be universally unjust. If any people be oppressed, it is our duty, as has been already said, as far as a favourable opportunity may invite us, to fly to their succour. But it would be well if, in such cases, we called our interference by the name

12. Pp. 147–52.

which justice prescribes, and fought against the oppression and not the power. All hostilities against a neighbouring people, because they are powerful, or because we impute to them evil designs which they have not begun to carry in execution, are incompatible with every principle of morality. . . . The pretence of the balance of power, has, in a multitude of instances, served as a veil to the intrigue of courts; but it would be easy to show, that the present independence of the different states of Europe, has, in no instance, been materially assisted, by the wars undertaken for that purpose. The fascination of a people desiring to become the appendage of a splendid despotism, will rarely occur; and, when it does, can justly be counteracted only by peaceable means. The succouring a people in their struggle against oppression must always be just, with this limitation, that to attempt it without an urgent need on their part, may uselessly extend the calamities of war, and has a tendency to diminish those energies among themselves, the exertion of which might contribute to their virtue and happiness. Add to this, that the object itself, the independence of the different states of Europe, is of an equivocal nature.[13]

Godwin's benevolence led him to urge the utmost moderation in actual warfare and in the making of peace. In particular Godwin argued that war should be fought for limited objects, that it should be regarded as an instrument to achieve definite policy objectives. Once these were achieved, the method should be abandoned. "Nothing," he wrote, "can be a sufficient object of war, that is not a sufficient cause for beginning it." [14]

The utmost benevolence ought to be practised towards our enemies. We should refrain from the unnecessary destruction of a single life, and afford every human accommodation to the unfortunate. The bulk of those against whom we have to contend, are comparatively speaking, innocent of the projected injustice. Those by whom it has been most assiduously fostered, are entitled to our kindness as men, and to our compassion as mistaken. It has already appeared that all the ends of punishment are foreign to the transactions of war. It has appeared, that the genuine melioration of war, in consequence of which it may be expected absolutely to cease, is by gradually disarming it of its ferocity. The horrors of war have sometimes been attempted to be vindicated, by a supposition, that the more intolerable it was made, the more quickly

13. Pp. 155–7.
14. P. 155.

would it cease to infect the world. But the direct contrary of this is truth. Severities beget severities. It is a most mistaken way of teaching men to feel that they are brothers, by imbuing their minds with unrelenting hatred. The truly just man cannot feel animosity, and is therefore little likely to act as if he did.[15]

Let us pass, from the causes, to the objects of war. As defence is the only legitimate cause, the object pursued, reasoning from this principle will be circumscribed within very narrow limits. It can extend no further, than the repelling the enemy from our borders. It is perhaps desirable that, in addition to this, he should afford some proof that he does not propose immediately to renew his invasion; but this, though desirable, affords no sufficient apology for the continuance of hostilities. Declarations of war, and treaties of peace, were the inventions of a barbarous age, and would probably never have grown into established usages, if war had customarily gone no further than to the limits of defence.

The criminal justice, as it has been termed, of nations within themselves, has only three objects that it can be imagined to have in view, the reformation of the criminal, the restraining him from future excesses, and example. But none of these objects, whatever may be thought of them while confined to their original province, can sufficiently apply to the case of war between independent states. War, as we have already seen, perhaps never originates, on the offending side, in the sentiments of a nation, but of a comparatively small number of individuals; and, were it otherwise there is something so monstrous, in the idea of changing the principles of a whole country by the nose of military execution, that every man not lost to sobriety and common sense, may be expected to shrink from it with horror.

Restraint appears to be sometimes necessary, with respect to the offenders that exist in the midst of a community, because it is customary for such offenders to assail us with unexpected violence; but nations cannot move with such secrecy, as to make an unforeseen attack an object of considerable apprehension. The only effectual means of restraint in this case, is by disabling, impoverishing and depopulating the country of our adversaries; and, if we recollected that they are men as well as ourselves, and the great mass of them innocent of the quarrel against us, we should be little likely to consider these expedients with complacency.—The idea of making an example of an offending nation

15. Pp. 162–3.

is reserved for God, whom the church, as by law established, instructs us to adore.

Indemnification is another object of war, which the same mode of reasoning will not fail to condemn. The true culprits can never be discovered, and the attempt would only serve to confound the innocent and the guilty: not to mention that nations having no common umpire, the reverting, in the conclusion of every war, to the justice of the original quarrel, and the indemnification to which the parties were entitled, would be a means of rendering the controversy endless. The question respecting the justifiable objects of war would be liable to few difficulties, if we laid it down as a maxim, that, as often as the principle or object of a war already in existence was changed, it was to be considered as equivalent to the commencement of a new war. This maxim, impartially applied, would not fail to condemn objects of prevention, indemnification and restraint.[16]

The desire for a world composed of small autonomous communities naturally impelled Godwin to condemn colonialism. The practice of acquiring overseas possessions was a fruitful source of war which did not confer any corresponding advantages on either the colonists or the mother country.

The principles here delivered on the conduct of war, lead the mind to a very interesting subject, that of foreign and distant territories. Whatever may be the value of these principles considered in themselves, they become altogether nugatory, the moment the idea of foreign dependencies is admitted. But, in reality, what argument possessing the smallest degree of plausibility, can be alleged, in favour of that idea? The mode in which dependencies are acquired, must be either conquest, cession or colonization. The first of these no true moralist or politician will attempt to defend. The second is to be considered as the same thing in substance as the first, but with less openness and ingenuity. Colonization, which is by much the most specious pretence, is however no more than a pretence. Are these provinces held in a state of dependence, for our sake, or for theirs? If for ours, we must recollect that this is still an usurpation, and that justice requires we should yield to others, what we demand for ourselves, the privilege of being governed by the dictates of their own reason. If for theirs, they must be told, that it is the business of associations of men to defend themselves, or, if that be impracticable, to look for support to the confederation with their neighbours. They

16. Pp. 153–5.

must be told, that defence against foreign enemies is a very inferior consideration, and that no people were ever either wise or happy, who were not left to the fair development of their inherent powers. Can any thing be more absurd, than for the West India islands, for example, to be defended by fleets and armies to be transported across the Atlantic? The support of a mother country extended to her colonies, is much oftener a means of involving them in danger, than of contributing to their security. The connection is maintained, by vanity on one side, and prejudice on the other. If they must sink into a degrading state of dependence, how will they be the worse, in belonging to one state, rather than another? Perhaps the first step towards putting a stop to this fruitful source of war, would be to annihiliate that monopoly of trade which enlightened reasoners at present agree to condemn, and to throw open the ports of our colonies to all the world. The principle which will not fail to lead us right upon this subject of foreign dependencies, as well as upon a thousand others, is the principle delivered in entering upon the topic of war, that that attribute, however splendid, is not really beneficial to a nation, that is not beneficial to the great mass of individuals of which the nation consists.[17]

17. Pp. 164–6.

14. JEREMY BENTHAM

1748-1832

JEREMY BENTHAM *began his career as a lawyer. He quickly found himself in sharp disagreement with the principles of practicing lawyers and devoted the rest of his long life to "carrying on against them a guerilla war."* [1] *A man of great generosity and benevolence, he wished to promote the "greatest happiness of the greatest number." He believed that all law and government should be designed to the service of this great end. For this reason he revolted against the lawyers' devotion to precedent and made utility the test of social institutions: utility measured by efficiency in promoting the greatest happiness.*

For effecting his reforms Bentham relied on the force of an enlightened public opinion. He believed that there was no real conflict between individual interests rationally considered. By promoting the common happiness, the individual would be most effective in promoting his own. Bentham was confident that men could be made to understand this by education. Men's opinions would be decided by weight of evidence and, granted a fair presentation of the evidence, the majority would reach correct decisions. In accordance with this idea Bentham placed great emphasis on the need for free speech and a free press to mold a wise public opinion. Given this, progress was assured.

The principle of the greatest happiness of the greatest number was by no means original with Bentham, but he did most to win practical men over to the concept. In England he personally inspired a group that included James Mill and his son. This group became the nucleus of the Radical Liberals and had a great influence on the early British socialists. Abroad, Bentham counted John Quincy Adams and Richard Rush amongst his personal friends and carried on an amiable correspondence with Andrew Jackson. The French revolutionaries received

1. "Correspondence," *Works*, 9, 9.

The edition used is *The Works of Jeremy Bentham*, 10 vols. London and Edinburgh, Simpkin, Marshall, and Company, 1843.

frequent advice from Bentham. After 1815 the spate of nationalist up-
risings provided him with fresh outlets. Miranda and Bolivar acknowl-
edged their debts and Bentham's advice was sought from Russia to
New Granada.

His industrious mind did not neglect the external affairs of the state.
Indeed it was Bentham who coined the word "international." He ap-
plied to foreign affairs the same principle of the greatest happiness that
he did to domestic matters. The same essential community of interest
existed between nations as between individuals. Nations should there-
fore refrain from injury to each other and, in addition, they should
promote the welfare of other nations by positive aid. Such a mutual
adjustment of interests formed a beneficent "balance of forces."

Expressed in the most general manner, the end that a disinterested
legislator upon international law would propose to himself, would . . .
be the greatest happiness of all nations taken together.

In resolving this into the most primitive principles, he would follow
the same route which he would follow with regard to internal laws.
He would set himself to prevent positive international offences—
to encourage the practice of positively useful actions.

He would regard as a positive crime every proceeding—every arrangement, by which the given nation should do more evil to foreign
nations taken together, whose interests might be affected, than it should
do good to itself. For example, the seizing a port which would be of
no use except as the means of advantageously attacking a foreign nation;—the closing against other nations, or another nation, the seas and
rivers, which are the highways of our globe;—the employing force
or fraud for preventing a foreign nation from carrying on commerce
with another nation. But by their reciprocity, injuries may compensate one another.

In the same manner, he would regard as a negative offence every determination, by which the given nation should refuse to render positive
services to a foreign nation, when the rendering of them would produce more good to the last-mentioned nation, than it would produce
evil to itself.[2]

The feelings of benevolence are liable to be led astray from the
principle of general utility. This can only be prevented by instruction:
they cannot be commanded; they cannot be forced: they can only be

2. "Principles of International Law," *Works*, 2, 538-9.

persuaded and enlightened. Men are brought by little and little to distinguish the different degrees of utility; to proportion their benevolence to the extent of its object. The finest model is drawn by Fenelon in that saying, in which he has so well painted his own heart:—"I prefer my family to myself, my country to my family, and the human race to my country."

The objects sought in these public instructions should be, to direct the affections of the citizens to this object; to repress the wanderings of benevolence; to make them feel their own interest in the general interest; to make them ashamed of that spirit of family—of that *esprit de corps* which militates against the love of country—of that unjust love of country which turns to hatred against other nations . . .

The more we become enlightened, the more benevolent shall we become; because we shall see that the interests of men coincide upon more points than they oppose each other. In commerce, ignorant nations have treated each other as rivals, who could only rise upon the ruins of one another. The work of Adam Smith is a treatise upon universal benevolence, because it has shown that commerce is equally advantageous for all nations—each one profiting in a different manner, according to its natural means; that nations are associates and not rivals in the grand social enterprise.[3]

Balance of forces.—A case there is, in which this metaphor, this image, may be employed with propriety: this is the case of international law and international relations. Supposing it attainable, what is meant by a balance of forces, or a balance of power, is a legitimate object—an object, the effectuation of which is beneficial to all the parties interested. What is that object? It is, in one word, *rest*—rest, the absence of all hostile motion, together with the absence of all coercion exercised by one of the parties over another—that rest, which is the fruit of mutual and universal independence. Here then, as between nation and nation, that rest which is the result of well-balanced forces is peace and prosperity.[4]

Bentham was aware that in the existing state of international relations there were frequent disputes between nations. In their domestic affairs individuals had a comprehensive body of law to govern their disagreements. But "the customs which constitute what is called the law of nations can only be called laws by extending the meaning of the

3. "Principles of Penal Law," *Works, 1,* 563.
4. "The Book of Fallacies," *Works, 2,* 447.

term, and by metaphor." [5] *Nor was there any judiciary to pass on international disputes. In this situation the only way to settle disputes which could not be compromised was by war.*

All war was distasteful to Bentham, who was convinced that aggressive war never achieved its objects. Victory brought neither prosperity nor honor. But he conceded that a nation ought to defend itself against aggression. First in his list of sacrifices required of citizens were "General wants of the state for its defence against external enemies." [6] *Even in defensive war, however, a nation should weigh the costs of defense against the injury received or expected. Bentham saw no reason why a state should fight when defense seemed dearer than submission, the more so as frequent resort to war encouraged a spiral of mutual suspicion.*

War is, as has been said, a species of procedure by which one nation endeavours to enforce its rights at the expense of another nation. It is the only method to which recourse can be had, when no other method of obtaining satisfaction can be found by complainants, who have no arbitrator between them sufficiently strong, absolutely to take from them all hope of resistance. But if internal procedure be attended by painful ills, international procedure is attended by ills infinitely more painful—in certain respects in point of intensity, commonly in point of duration, and always in point of extent. . . . .

War is mischief upon the largest scale. It might seem at first sight, that to inquire into the causes of war would be the same thing as to inquire into the causes of criminality, and that in the one case as in the other, the source of it is to be looked for in the nature of man,—in the self-regarding, the dissocial, and now and then, in some measure, in the social affections. A nearer view, however, will show in several points considerable difference,—these differences turn on the magnitude of the scale. The same motives will certainly be found operating in the one case as in the other; but in tracing the process from the original cause to the ultimate effect, a variety of intermediate considerations will present themselves in the instance of war, which have no place in the quarrels of individuals. . . . .

The following may be enumerated among the inducements to war:—Apprehension of injustice—hope of plunder of moveables by individuals—hope of gain by raising contributions—hope of gain by sale or ran-

5. "View of a Complete Code of Laws," *Works, 3,* 162.
6. "Principles of The Civil Code," *Works, 1,* 313.

som of captives—national pride or glory—monarchical pride—national antipathy—increase of patronage—hope of preferment. . . . .

Wars may be:—

I. *Bonâ fide* wars. A remedy against these would be found in "The Tribunal of Peace".

II. Wars of passion. The remedy against these,— Reasoning, showing the repugancy betwixt passion on the one hand, and justice as well as interest on the other.

III. Wars of ambition, or insolence, or rapine. The remedies against these are—1. Reasoning, showing the repugnancy betwixt ambition and true interest; 2. Remedies of regulation, in the event of a temporary ascendency on the part of reason.

In all these cases, the utility with regard to the state which looks upon itself as aggrieved—the reasonableness in a word, of going to war with the aggressor—depends partly upon his relative force, partly upon what appears to have been the state of his mind with relation to the injury. If it be evident that there was no *mala fides* on his part, it can never be for the advantage of the aggrieved state to have recourse to war, whether it be stronger or weaker than the aggressor, and that in whatever degree;—in that case, be the injury what it will, it may be pronounced impossible that the value of it should ever amount to the expense of war, be it ever so short, and carried on upon ever so frugal a scale.

In case of *mala fides*, whether even then it would be worth while to have recourse to war, will depend upon circumstances. If it appear that the injury in question is but a prelude to others, and that it proceeds from a disposition which nothing less than entire destruction can satisfy, and war presents any tolerable chance of success, how small soever, prudence and reason may join with passion in prescribing war as the only remedy in so desperate a disease. For, though in case of perseverance on the part of the assailant, successful resistance may appear impossible; yet resistance, such as can be opposed, may, by gaining time, give room for some unexpected incident to arise, and may at any rate, by the inconvenience it occasions to the assailant, contribute in time or loss, to weaken the mass of inducements which prompt him to similar enterprises. Though the Spartans at Thermopylae perished to a man, yet the defence of Thermopylae was not without its use.

If on the other hand, the aggression, though too flagrant not to be accompanied with *mala fides*, appear to have for its origin some passion or caprice which has for its incentive some limited object, and promises to be contented with that object,—the option is now, not between ruin avenged and unavenged, but between the loss of the object, whatever it be, and the miseries of a more or less hopeless war.

The Dutch displayed prudence, while they yielded to the suggestions of indignation, in defending themselves against the force of Spain. The same people displayed their prudence in yielding to Britain the frivolous honours of the flag, at the end of the war of 1652; they would have displayed still more, if they had made the same concession at the beginning of it.

Lastly, if the aggression, how unjust soever it may appear, when viewed in the point of view in which it is contemplated by the state which is the object of it, does not appear accompanied with *mala fides* on the part of the aggressor nothing can be more incontestable than the prudence of submitting to it, rather than encountering the calamities of war. The sacrifice is seen at once in its utmost extent, and it must be singular indeed, if the amount of it can approach to that of the expense of a single campaign.[7]

. . . from the successes of war, come, say they, our prosperity, our greatness; thence the respect paid to us by Foreign Powers—thence our security. . . . . .

Respect is a term I shall beg leave to change; respect is a mixture of fear and esteem, but for constituting esteem, force is not the instrument, but justice. The sentiment really relied upon for security is fear. By respect then is meant, in plain English, fear. But in a case like this, fear is much more adverse than favourable to security. So many as fear you, join against you till they think they are too strong for you, and then they are afraid of you no longer;—meantime they all hate you, and jointly and severally they do you as much mischief as they can. You, on your part, are not behindhand with them. Conscious or not conscious of your own bad intentions, you suspect theirs to be still worse. Their notion of your intentions is the same. Measures of mere self-defence are naturally taken for projects of aggression. The same causes produce, on both sides, the same effects; each makes haste to begin for fear of being forestalled. In this state of things, if on either side there happen to be a minister or would-be minister, who has a fancy for war, the stroke is struck, and the tinder catches fire.[8]

7. "Principles of International Law," *Works, 2,* 538–45.
8. *Ibid.,* p. 559.

Bentham's interest in extending the principle of the greatest happiness to international relations prompted him to draw up a "plan for universal and perpetual peace." This plan rested on the emancipation of all colonies, disarmament, an international court, and open diplomacy.

The colonial question absorbed much of Bentham's attention. He believed that colonies were an abundant source of wars. Convinced by Adam Smith's arguments that colonies provided no economic advantages, Bentham viewed the expenses of colonial administration and defense as so much loss. Nor did the colonists benefit from the relationship, for they would prosper most under an independent government which understood their needs.

The object of the present Essay is to submit to the world a plan for an universal and perpetual peace. The globe is the field of dominion to which the author aspires,—the press the engine, and the only one he employs,—the cabinet of mankind the theatre of his intrigue.

The happiest of mankind are sufferers by war; and the wisest, nay, even the least wise, are wise enough to ascribe the chief of their sufferings to that cause.

The following plan has for its basis two fundamental propositions: —1. The reduction and fixation of the force of the several nations that compose the European system; 2. The emancipation of the distant dependencies of each state. Each of these propositions has its distinct advantages; but neither of them, it will appear, would completely answer the purpose without the other.

As to the utility of such an universal and lasting peace, supposing a plan for that purpose practicable, and likely to be adopted, there can be but one voice. The objection, and the only objection to it, is the apparent impracticability of it;—that it is not only hopeless, but that to such a degree that any proposal to that effect deserves the name of visionary and ridiculous. This objection I shall endeavour in the first place to remove; for the removal of this prejudice may be necessary to procure for the plan a hearing.

What can be better suited to the preparing of men's minds for the reception of such a proposal than the proposal itself?

Let it not be objected that the age is not ripe for such a proposal: the more it wants of being ripe, the sooner we should begin to do what can be done to ripen it; the more we should do to ripen it. A proposal of this sort, is one of those things that can never come too early nor too late. . . . .

Proposition— That it is not the interest of Great Britain to have any foreign dependencies whatsoever. . . . .

For maintaining colonies there are several avowed reasons, besides others which are not avowed: of the avowed reasons, by far the principal one is, the benefit of trade. If your colonies were not subject to you, they would not trade with you; they would not buy any of your goods, or let you buy any of theirs; at least, you could not be sure of their doing so: if they were subject to anybody else they would not do so; for the colonies of other nations are, you see, not suffered to trade with you. Give up your colonies, you give up so much of your trade as is carried on with your colonies. No; we do not give up any such thing,—we do not give up anything whatsoever. Trade with colonies cannot, any more than with anywhere else, be carried on without capital: just so much of our capital as is employed in our trade with the colonies—just so much of it is not employed elsewhere—just so much is either kept or taken from other trades. . . . .

The following is a summary of the reasons for giving up all the colonies:—

I. Interest of the mother-country.

1. Saving the expense of the establishments, civil and military.

2. Saving the danger of war—1. For enforcing their obedience; 2. On account of the jealousy produced by the apparent power they confer.

3. Saving the expense of defending them, in case of war on other grounds.

4. Getting rid of the means of corruption afforded by the patronage.— 1. Of their civil establishments; 2. Of the military force employed in their defence.

5. Simplifying the whole frame of government, and thereby rendering a competent skill in the business of government more attainable—1. To the members of administration; 2. To the people.

The stock of national intelligence is deteriorated by the false notions which must be kept up, in order to prevent the nation from opening its eyes and insisting upon the enfranchisement of the colonies.

At the same time, bad government results to the mother-country from the complication of interests, the indistinct views, and the consumption of time, occasioned by the load of distant dependencies.

II. Interest of the colonies.

Diminishing the chance of bad government resulting from—1. Opposite interest; 2. Ignorance.

The real interests of the colony must be sacrificed to the imaginary interests of the mother-country. It is for the purpose of governing it badly, and for no other, that you can wish to get or to keep a colony. Govern it well, it is of no use to you. Govern it as well as the inhabitants would govern it themselves,—you must choose those to govern it whom they themselves would choose. You must sacrifice none of its interests to your own,—you must bestow as much time and attention to their interests as they would themselves: in a word, you must take those very measures, and none others, which they themselves would take. But would this be governing? and what would it be worth to you if it were?

After all, it would be impossible for you to govern them so well as they would govern themselves, on account of the distance.[9]

General limitation of armaments was the second element in Bentham's scheme. The heart of the plan was that disarmament should be reached by mutual consultation. It must be made unmistakably clear that the proposition did not serve the particular purposes of any one nation. Acceptance or rejection of such a scheme would furnish a test of a nation's good will.

Proposition—that for the maintenance of such a pacification, general and perpetual treaties might be formed, limiting the number of troops to be maintained. . . . .

An agreement of this kind would not be dishonourable. If the covenant were on one side only, it might be so. If it regard both parties together, the reciprocity takes away the acerbity. . . .

On the contrary, whatsoever nation should get the start of the other in making the proposal to reduce and fix the amount of its armed force, would crown itself with everlasting honour. The risk would be nothing—the gain certain. This gain would be, the giving an incontrovertible demonstration of its own disposition to peace, and of the opposite disposition in the other nation in case of its rejecting the proposal.

The utmost fairness should be employed. The nation addressed should be invited to consider and point out whatever further securities it deemed necessary, and whatever further concessions it deemed just.

The proposal should be made in the most public manner;—it should be an address from nation to nation. This, at the same time that it conciliated the confidence of the nation addressed, would make it impracticable for the government of that nation to neglect it, or stave it off by shifts and evasions. It would sound the heart of the nation ad-

9. *Works,* 2, 546–8.

dressed. It would discover its intentions, and proclaim them to the world.[10]

Bentham hoped colonial emancipation and disarmament would greatly reduce international friction. To settle remaining disputes he designed a court to give equitable decisions in international disagreements. The habit of appealing to such a court would make it possible to accept even dubious decisions without loss of face.

As a last resort he envisaged the enforcement of the court's decisions by arms. But he believed the court would receive sufficient support from world public opinion to make recourse to arms largely unnecessary. The "Public Opinion Tribunal" would usually be sanction enough.

Proposition— That the maintenance of . . . pacification might be considerably facilitated, by the establishment of a common court of judicature . . .

It is an observation of somebody's that no nation ought to yield any evident point of justice to another. This must mean, evident in the eyes of the nation that is to judge,—evident in the eyes of the nation called upon to yield. What does this amount to? That no nation is to give up anything of what it looks upon as its rights—no nation is to make any concessions. Wherever there is any difference of opinion between the negotiators of two nations, war is to be the consequence.

While there is no common tribunal, some thing might be said for this. Concession to notorious injustice invites fresh injustice.

Establish a common tribunal, the necessity for war no longer follows from difference of opinion. Just or unjust, the decision of the arbiters will save the credit, the honour of the contending party. . . . .

There might, perhaps, be no harm in regulating, as a last resource, the contingent to be furnished by the several states for enforcing the decrees of the court. But the necessity for the employment of this resource would, in all human probability, be superseded for ever by having recourse to the much more simple and less burthensome expedient, of introducing into the instrument by which such court was instituted, a clause guaranteeing the liberty of the press in each state, in such sort, that the diet might find no obstacle to its giving, in every state, to its decrees, and to every paper whatever which it might think proper to sanction with its signature, the most extensive and unlimited circulation.[11]

10. *Ibid.*, pp. 550–1.
11. *Ibid.*, pp. 552–4.

Bentham considered that a free press and open diplomacy was needed in every country if the public opinion tribunal was to be effective. He admitted, however, that in the past public opinion had often been more aggressive than statesmen. His whole scheme therefore rested on his faith in the power of education to enlighten the public as to its true interests.

Proposition—that secresy in the operations of the foreign department in England ought not to be endured, being altogether useless, and equally repugnant to the interests of liberty and peace. . . . .

I take at once the boldest and the broadest ground—I lay down two propositions:—

1. That in no negociation, and at no period of any negociation, ought the negociations of the cabinet in this country to be kept secret from the public at large; much less from parliament and after inquiry made in parliament.

2. That whatever may be the case with preliminary negociations, such secresy ought never to be maintained with regard to treaties actually concluded.

In both cases, to a country like this, such secresy is equally mischievous and unnecessary.

It is mischievous. Over measures of which you have no knowledge, you can apply no controul. Measures carried on without your knowledge you cannot stop,—how ruinous soever to you, and how strongly soever you would disapprove of them if you knew them. . . . .

It is admitted that ministers ought not to have it in their power to impose taxes on the nation against its will. It is admitted that they ought not to have it in their power to maintain troops against its will. But by plunging it into war without its knowledge they do both. . . . .

Under the present system of secresy, ministers have, therefore, every seduction to lead them into misconduct; while they have no check to keep them out of it. And what species of misconduct? That in comparison of which all others are but peccadillos. . . . This is the department of all others in which the strongest checks are needful; at the same time, thanks to the rules of secresy of all the departments, this is the only one in which there are no checks at all. I say, then, the conclusion is demonstrated. The principle which throws a veil of secresy over the proceedings of the foreign department of the cabinet is pernicious in the highest degree, pregnant with mischiefs superior to everything to which the most perfect absence of all concealment could possibly give rise. . . . .

Hitherto war has been the national rage: peace has always come too soon—war too late. To tie up the ministers' hands and make them continually accountable, would be depriving them of numberless occasions of seizing those happy advantages that lead to war: it would be lessening the people's chance of their favourite amusement. For these hundred years past, ministers, to do them justice, have generally been more backward than the people—the great object has rather been to force them into war, than to keep them out of it. . . .

It admits of no doubt, if we are really for war, and fond of it for its own sake, we can do no better than let things continue as they are. If we think peace better than war, it is equally certain that the law of secresy cannot be too soon abolished.[12]

12. *Ibid.*, pp. 554–9.

15. RICHARD COBDEN

1804-1865

RICHARD COBDEN'S *speeches, pamphlets, and other political activities made him Britain's foremost proponent of free trade. He used the House of Commons, which he entered in 1841, as a sounding board for his theories of trade and politics. His work as a leader of the Anti-Corn Law League earned him chief credit for the repeal of the Corn Laws in 1846, an event which signified the defeat of the protectionist landed interests. During the next twenty years Cobden continued to expound the benefits of free trade. By 1860, when Cobden negotiated a commercial treaty with France, British protectionism was, in the words of Disraeli, "not only dead but damned."*

Cobden believed that the only way for a nation to increase its welfare was by increasing its productivity and improving its government: "fostering the accumulation of capital, the growth of cities, and the increase of civilisation and freedom. These are the only sources of power and wealth in an age of improvement." [1] *Such development also served to increase national power, for power ultimately rested on wealth.*

The best way to promote a nation's prosperity was laissez-faire at home and free trade abroad. As Cobden saw it, "the intercourse between communities is nothing more than the intercourse of individuals in the aggregate." [2] *International trade is conducted on the same basis of mutual profit as domestic commerce. For this reason "the only way in which we can protect our commerce is the cheapness of our manufactures."* [3] *He therefore rejected both protectionism and the attempt to secure markets forcibly by imperialism.*

1. "Russia," *Writings*, 1, 180.
2. *Speeches*, 2, 161.
3. "Russia," *Writings*, 1, 289.

The editions used are *Political Writings of Cobden*, 2 vols. London, William Ridgway, New York, D. Appleton, 1867; *Speeches on Questions of Public Policy*, ed. John Bright and James E. Thorold Rogers, 2 vols. London, Macmillan, 1870.

Cobden thought that free trade would minimize the risk of war. He maintained that most wars were fought for mercantilist ends. Experience of free trade would teach the world the true facts of international commerce. It would become apparent that "the honest and just interests of this country, and of her inhabitants, are the just and honest interests of the whole world." [4] *Furthermore, a flourishing international trade would prove a deterrent even to those wars which were not the result of commercial rivalry, for all the interests which benefited from trade would be violently opposed to its dislocation by hostilities. Frequent international intercourse would also breed friendship: "Free Trade! What is it? Why, breaking down the barriers that separate nations; those barriers, behind which nestle the feelings of pride, revenge, hatred, and jealousy, which every now and then burst their bounds, and deluge whole countries with blood."* [5] *Thus commerce was the "grand panacea" and Britain's free trading example a "beacon" for other nations.*

In a word, our national existence is involved in the well-doing of our manufacturers. If our readers . . . should ask, as all intelligent and reasoning minds ought to do, To what are we indebted for this commerce?—we answer, in the name of every manufacturer and merchant of the kingdom— The *cheapness* alone of our manufactures. Are we asked, How is this trade protected, and by what means can it be enlarged? The reply still is, By the *cheapness* of our manufactures. Is it inquired how this mighty industry, upon which depends the comfort and existence of the whole empire, can be torn from us?—we rejoin, Only by the *greater cheapness* of the manufactures of another country. . . . .

. . . his Majesty's speech . . . refers to the necessity of giving adequate protection to the *"extended"* commerce of the country. By which we are to infer, that it is the principle of the government, that the extension of our trade with foreign countries, demands for its protection, a corresponding augmentation of the royal navy. This, we are aware, was the policy of the last century, during the greater part of which, the motto, "Ships, Colonies, and Commerce," was borne upon the national escutcheon, became the watchword of statesmen, and was the favourite sentiment of public writers; but this, which meant, in other words— "Men of war to conquer colonies, to yield us a monopoly of their trade," must now be dismissed, like many other equally glittering but false

4. *Speeches*, 2, 27.
5. *Ibid.*, 1, 79.

adages of our forefathers, and in its place we must substitute the more homely but enduring maxim— *Cheapness*, which will command commerce; and whatever else is needful will follow in its train.

At a time when all beyond the precincts of Europe was colonial territory, and when the trade of the world was, with the exception of China, almost wholly forced into false channels, by the hand of violence, which was no sooner withdrawn than, by its own inherent law—the law of nature—it again sought its proper level course, the increase of the navy necessarily preceded and accompanied an extension of our commerce. . . .

Whilst our trade rested upon our foreign dependencies, as was the case in the middle of the last century—whilst, in other words, force and violence were necessary to command customers for our manufactures—it was natural and consistent that almost every king's speech should allude to the importance of protecting the commerce of the country, by means of a powerful navy; but whilst, under the present more honest principles of trade, *cheapness* alone is necessary to command free and independent purchasers, and to protect our commerce, it must be evident that such armaments as impose the smallest possible tax upon the cost of our commodities must be the best adapted for the protection of our trade. But, besides dictating the disuse of warlike establishments, free trade (for of that beneficient doctrine we are speaking) arms its votaries by its own pacific nature, in that eternal truth—*the more any nation trafficks abroad upon free and honest principles, the less it will be in danger of wars.*

. . . this commerce, unparalleled in magnitude, between two remote nations [England and America], demands no armament as its guide or safeguard: nature itself is both. And will one rational mind recognise the possibility of these two communities putting a sudden stop to such a friendly traffic, and, contrary to every motive of self-interest, encountering each other as enemies? Such a rupture would be more calamitous to England than the sudden drying up of the river Thames; and more intolerable to America than the cessation of sunshine and rain over the entire surface of one of her maritime states!

And if such is the character of free trade, (or, in other words, all trade between independent nations,) that it unites, by the strongest motives of which our nature is susceptible, two remote communities, rendering the interest of the one the only true policy of the other, and making each equally anxious for the prosperity and happiness of both; and if, moreover, every addition to the amount of traffic between two independent states, forges fresh fetters, which rivet more securely these amicable bonds—how can the extension of our commerce call for an increase in our armaments, or how can a government stand excused from the accusation of imposture, unless by the plea of ignorance, when it calls for an augmentation of the navy estimates under the pretence of protecting our extended commerce? [6]

. . . I defy you to show me how any Government or people on the Continent can strengthen themselves, even if they chose to carry on a war of conquest. . . . I defy you to show me any partition where an accession of territory has not been rather a source of weakness than of strength. Take the very worst that can happen:—suppose any power on the Continent is going to attack its neighbour, is there any reason why we should be armed to the teeth in order to take part in the struggle? In ancient times, when the people were counted as nothing, and when sovereigns told out their subjects as a shepherd would his flock; when a royal marriage united the crowns of two kingdoms, and the people of both became the willing subjects, or even serfs, of the one sovereign, there might have been danger in an acquisition of territory. But now that the people count everywhere for something, and we see on the Continent of Europe great lines of demarcation of race—the Italian Peninsula, for instance, one; Spain, another; Germany, another;—and when you find the great mosaic mass of Austrian dominion broken up, as it were, into Sclaves and Magyars, I see new limits assigned to conquest. I repeat, there is no longer any reason to fear that one empire will take possession, by force of arms, of it's neighbour's territory; but, if it should, the accession of territory would be a source of weakness, not of strength.[7]

. . . We are aware that no power was ever yet known, voluntarily, to give up the dominion over a part of its territory. But if it could be made manifest to the trading and industrious portions of this nation, who have no honours, or interested ambition of any kind, at stake in the matter, that, whilst our dependencies are supported at an expense to them, in direct taxation, of more than five millions annually, they serve but as gorgeous and ponderous appendages to swell our ostensible grandeur, but, in reality, to complicate and magnify our government expenditure, without improving our balance of trade—surely, under such circumstances, it would become at least a question for anxious inquiry with a

6. "Russia," *Writings, 1,* 287–95.
7. *Speeches, 1,* 483–4.

people so overwhelmed with debt, whether those colonies should not be suffered to support and defend themselves, as separate and independent existences.[8]

Cobden abominated war on humanitarian as well as economic grounds. It was the desire to "unite mankind in the bonds of peace" rather than any "pecuniary consideration," [9] *Cobden declared, which led him to struggle for free trade. He did not deny that a nation had the right to defend itself and that there might be legitimate occasions, in the last resort, for such defensive war. But Cobden did not believe that many wars actually partook of this defensive nature or were even concerned with important national interests. One fruitful and unnecessary cause of war, he thought, was the very existence of large scale military establishments which provoked other states and endowed a substantial part of the nation with a vested interest in international conflict. Cobden hoped that the spread of democracy and the rising influence of the "middle and industrious classes" would increasingly preserve the peace. As one direct means of aiding this progress he suggested international agreements for reciprocal disarmament and for arbitration as an economical and equitable method of resolving disputes.*

There is a large portion of the community which does not want peace. War is the profession of some men, and war, therefore, is the only means for their occupation and promotion in their profession. 15,000,-000 *l.* sterling are spent on military establishments. This is a considerable sum of money spent upon classes who are not very likely to be favourable to peace. Read the *United Service* and the *Army and Navy Gazette.* Do you think that these publications are intended to promote peace? Do they not seek the opportunity of exciting jealousies,—pointing to the ships of war of foreign countries, and saying, 'There are more guns there, and, therefore, we must have more?' Do they not endeavour to produce that rivalry of establishments and armaments which is always tending of necessity to hostile feelings and hostile acts? Again, there is a large portion of the continental community which is similarly situated to the portion of which I have just spoken in this country. Four millions of men—the flower of Europe—from twenty to thirty-three years of age, are under arms, living in idleness. . . . Thus there is a large body of men who do not desire peace. I do not believe that peace is their object. I do not know why they entered the army if they

8. "England, Ireland and America," *Writings, 1,* 30–1.
9. *Speeches, 2,* 421.

did not want war. That is their employment, and they must be idle
if they have not war; and, therefore, it is not unfair to argue that they
are not altogether favourable to peace, whatever they may say; and
consequently, I do not believe that all those men who use these cant
phrases about peace care for it.[10]

. . . I have latterly felt another motive for wishing for an extension
of the franchise, in what I have seen going on upon the Continent
within the last eighteen months, which has convinced me that the great
masses of mankind are disposed for peace between nations. You have
the fact brought out in strong relief that the people themselves, however they may be troubled with internal convulsions, have no desire
to go abroad and molest their neighbours. You have seen Louis Philippe
driven from the throne. We were told that he kept the French nation
at peace; but we find the masses of the people of France only anxious
to remain at home, and diminish, if possible, the pressure of taxation.

Where do we look for the black gathering cloud of war? Where do we
see it rising? Why, from the despotism of the North, where one man
wields the destinies of 40,000,000 of serfs. If we want to know where is
the second danger of war and disturbance, it is in that province of Russia—that miserable and degraded country, Austria—next in the stage
of despotism and barbarism, and there you see again the greatest danger
of war; but in proportion as you find the population governing themselves—as in England, in France, or in America—there you will find
that war is not the disposition of the people, and that if Government
desire it, the people would put a check upon it. Therefore, for the
security of liberty, and also, as I believe, that the people of every country, as they acquire political power, will cultivate the arts of peace, and
check the desire of their governments to go to war—it is on these
grounds that I wish to see a wide extension of the suffrage, and liberty
prevail over despotism throughout the world.[11]

Why do I assume that England arms against France, and France
against England? I am prepared to show that it is the avowed policy of
both countries to arm themselves, so as to be prepared to meet the
armaments provided by the other country. . . . .

I have two objections to that policy: first, it is an irritating policy,
having a constant tendency to increase the evil, and to which I see no
remedy, unless it is in some way met; and secondly, it is a proceeding

10. *Ibid.*, pp. 416–17.
11. *Ibid.*, pp. 432–3.

on exaggerated reports and ideas spread upon the subject of the armaments of the two countries. . . . .

. . . I would ask, then, whether it is not possible to devise some plan,
if not by actual convention . . . yet by some communication with a
Power like France, and say, "We are mutually building so many vessels
each in the year; our relative force is as three to two, and if we increase
it tenfold, still the relations will be the same. Will it not be possible, by
a friendly understanding, to agree that we shall not go on in this rivalry,
but that we shall put a mutual check upon this mutual injury?" . . . .

. . . while the spirit of rivalry is maintained by two countries so
equal in point of resources, taking the army and navy together, it is
impossible that one could ever gain a permanent advantage over the
other. If one were exceedingly weak and the other strong, and the strong
could have some extraordinary motive to oppress the weaker, I might
despair to convince by argument; but the case of England and France
is very different. Whenever England increases her armaments and fortifications France does the same, and *vice versa*. We are pursuing a
course, therefore, which holds out to neither country a prospect of any
permanent gain. We are not actuated by motives of ambition or aggression, but are simply acting for self-defence, and no rational mind in
either country supposes anything else, than that a war between the
two countries must be injurious to both. Every country will have an
interest in putting an end to this mutual rivalry and hostility by the
course which I recommend.[12]

. . . I assume, moreover, that there is not a man in this House who
would not repudiate war, if those objects—the just interests and honour of the country—could be preserved by any other means. My object
is to see if we cannot devise some better method than war for attaining those ends; and my plan is, simply and solely, that we should
resort to that mode of settling disputes in communities, which individuals resort to in private life. . . . I want to know why there may
not be an agreement between this country and France, or between this
country and America, by which the nations should respectively bind
themselves, in case of any misunderstanding arising which could not
be settled by mutual representation or diplomacy, to refer the dispute
to the decision of arbitrators. By arbitrators I do not mean necessarily
crowned heads, or neutral states . . . I do not confine myself to the
plan of referring disputes to neutral Powers. I see the difficulty of two

12. *Ibid.*, 1, 517–26.

independent states, like England and France, doing so, as one might prefer a republic for the arbitrator, and the other a monarchy. I should prefer to see these disputes referred to individuals, whether designated commissioners, or plenipotentiaries, or arbitrators, appointed from one country to meet men appointed from another country, to inquire into the matter and decide upon it; or, if they cannot do so, to have the power of calling in an umpire, as is done in all arbitrations. I propose that these individuals should have absolute power to dispose of the question submitted to them.

. . . what I propose is no novelty, no innovation; it has been practised, and practised with success; I only want you to carry the principle a little farther, and resort to it, in anticipation, as a mode of arranging all quarrels.

. . . a treaty binding two countries to refer their disputes to arbitration, is just as likely to be observed as any other treaty. Nay, I question very much whether it is not more likely to be observed; because, I think there is no object which other countries will be less likely to seek than that of having a war with a country so powerful as England. Therefore, if any provision were made by which you might honourably avoid a war, that provision would be as gladly sought by your opponents as by yourselves. But I deny that, as a rule, treaties are violated; as a rule, they are respected and observed. I do not find that wars, generally, arise out of the violation of any specific treaty—they more commonly arise out of accidental collisions; and, as a rule, treaties are observed by powerful States against the weak, just as well as by weak States against the powerful. I, therefore, see no difficulty specially applying to a treaty of this kind, greater than exists with other treaties. There would be this advantage, at all events, in having a treaty binding another country to refer all disputes to arbitration. If that country did not fulfil its engagement, it would enter into war with the brand of infamy stamped upon its banners. It could not proclaim to the world that it was engaged in a just and necessary war. On the contrary, all the world would point to that nation as violating a treaty, by going to war with a country with whom they had engaged to enter into arbitration. I anticipate another objection which I have heard made: they say, 'You cannot entrust the great interests of England to individuals or commissioners.' That difficulty springs out of the assumption, that the quarrels with foreign countries are about questions involving the whole existence of the empire. On the contrary, whenever these quarrels take place, it is generally upon the most minute and absurd pretexts—so trivial that it is almost impossible, on looking back for the last hundred years, to tell precisely what any war was about. . . .

. . . to return to the point whether or not commissioners might be entrusted with the grave matters which form the subjects of dispute between nations, I would draw the attention of the House to the fact, that already you do virtually entrust these matters to individuals. Treaties of peace, made after war, are entrusted to individuals to negotiate and carry out. . . . Why not depute to a plenipotentiary the same powers before a conflict as you give him after? . . . All I want is, that this should be done before, and not after, engaging in a war—done to avert the war, rather than to make up the difference after the parties are exhausted by the conflict. . . . .

. . . I see no limit to the increase of our armaments under the existing system. Unless you can adopt some such plan as I propose, unless you can approach foreign countries in a conciliatory spirit, and offer to them some kind of assurance that you do not wish to attack them, and receive the assurance that you are not going to be assailed by them, I see no necessary or logical end to the increase of our establishments. For the progress of scientific knowledge will lead to a constant increase of expenditure. . . . At all events, arbitration is more rational, just, and humane than the resort to the sword. . . . .

I do not anticipate any sudden or great change in the character of mankind, nor do I expect a complete extinction of those passions which form part of our nature. But I do not think there is anything very irrational in expecting that nations may see that the present system of settling disputes is barbarous, demoralising, and unjust; that it wars against the best interests of society, and that it ought to give place to a mode more consonant with the dictates of reason and humanity.[13]

As Cobden saw it, the greatest obstacle to the reduction of armaments was the traditional pursuit of the balance of power. To him the balance was a "mere chimera." The term "balance" was used because, "The phrase was found to please the public ear; it implied something of equity." [14] *But in reality every nation sought not a balance but its own preponderance. Such a policy was fatal to any lasting equilibrium.*

Cobden presented another reason for deriding the balance of power policy. The statesmen who jealously watched over the balance thought solely in terms of frontiers and armaments, ignoring the developments

13. *Ibid.*, 2, 161–76.
14. "Russia," *Writings, 1,* 256–7.

in industry and commerce which wrought the most significant changes in relative national power. The devotees of the balance of power were therefore courting failure even by their own standards.

To maintain what is denominated the true balance of European power, has been the fruitful source of wars from the earliest time; and it would be instructive, if the proposed limits of this work permitted it, to bring into review all the opposite struggles into which England has plunged, for the purpose of adjusting, from time to time, according to the ever-varying theories of her rulers, this national equilibrium. Let it suffice to say, that history exhibits us, at different periods, in the act of casting our sword into the scale of every European state. In the meantime, events have proclaimed, but in vain, how futile must be our attempts to usurp the sceptre of the Fates. Empires have arisen unbidden by us: others have departed, despite our utmost efforts to preserve them. All have undergone a change so complete that, were the writers who only a century ago lauded the then existing state of the balance of Europe to reappear, they would be startled to find, in the present relations of the Continent, no vestige of that perfect adjustment which had been purchased at the price of so much blood. And yet we have able writers and statesmen of the present day, who would advocate a war to prevent a derangement of what we now choose to pronounce the just equipoise of the power of Europe.[15]

We talk of this [Crimean] as a war which affects the interests of all Europe; and we hear the phrases "Balance of Power" and "International Law" frequently repeated, as though we were enforcing the edicts of some constituted authority. For a century and a half we have been fighting, with occasional intermissions, for the Balance of Power, but I do not remember that it has ever been made the subject of peaceful diplomacy, with a view to the organization of the whole of Europe. Now, if such a pact or federation of the States of Europe as is implied by the phrases "Balance of Power" or "International Law" should ever be framed, it must be the work of peace, and not of war. In the present case, our government has entered into war on the assumption that the European Balance has been, and still is, endangered by the ambition of Russia. Has the rest of Europe ever been, as a whole, consulted in a time of peace, and in a deliberate manner, upon this danger, and invited to take a part in averting it? If not, what shall we say of our government, or our governing class, or diplomacy in general? Now, assum-

15. "England, Ireland and America," *Writings, 1,* 5–6.

ing again that I occupied the position of our government, and were in earnest in my fears for Europe, and attached a real meaning to those phrases just quoted, I should appeal not only to Germany, but to all the States, small as well as great, of the Continent, for such a union as would prevent the possibility of any act of hostility from the common enemy. This is the work of peace; and to this end, with the views and responsibilities of the government, I should address myself. If I found that I failed to impart my apprehensions to the other nations of Europe,—if they declined to form part of a league, or confederation against Russian encroachments, I should be disposed to reconsider my own views on the subject, and to doubt whether I might not have been led away by an exaggerated alarm. In that case, at least, I would forego the quixotic mission of fighting for the liberties of Europe, and pursue a policy more just towards the interests, and more consistent with the prosperity, of the people whose welfare I was more especially charged to promote.[16]

. . . we should . . . expect to find that the "balancing system" had, at some period of modern history, been recognised and agreed to by all the Continental states; and that it had created a spirit of mutual concession and guarantee, by which the weaker and more powerful empires were placed upon a footing of equal security, and by which any one potentate or state was absolutely unable "to predominate over the others." But, instead of any such self-denial, we discover that the balance of Europe has merely meant (if it has had a meaning) that which our blunt Dutch king openly avowed as his aim to his parliament—a desire, on the part of the great powers, to "hold the balance of Europe," England has, for nearly a century, held the European scales— not with the blindness of the goddess of justice herself, or with a view to the equilibrium of opposite interests, but with a Cyclopean eye to her own aggrandizement. The same lust of conquest has actuated, up to the measure of their abilities, the other great powers; and, if we find the smaller states still, in the majority of instances, preserving their independent existence, it is owing, not to the watchful guardianship of the "balancing system," but to the limits which nature herself has set to the undue extension of territorial dominion—not only by the physical boundaries of different countries, but in those still more formidable moral impediments to the invader—the unity of language, laws, customs, and traditions; the instinct of patriotism and freedom; the hereditary rights of rulers; and, though last not least, that homage to the re-

16. "What Next—and Next," *Writings, 2,* 205–6.

straints of justice which nations and public bodies have in all ages avowed, however they may have found excuses for evading it.

So far, then, as we can understand the subject, the theory of a balance of power is a mere chimera—a creation of the politician's brain—a phantasm, without definite form or tangible existence—a mere conjunction of syllables, forming words which convey sound without meaning. Yet these words have been echoed by the greatest orators and statesmen of England: they gingled successively from the lips of Bolingbroke, Chatham, Pitt, Burke, Fox, Sheridan, Grey, and Brougham;—ay, even whilst we were in the act of stripping the maritime nations of the Continent of their colonies, then regarded as the sole source of commercial greatness; whilst we stood sword in hand upon the neck of Spain, or planted our standard on the rock of Malta; . . . the tongues of our orators resounded most loudly with the praises of the "balance of power!" . . .

. . . There can be little doubt, however, that the idea [of the balance of power], by whomsoever or at whatever epoch conceived, sprang from that first instinct of our nature, fear, and originally meant at least some scheme for preventing the dangerous growth of the power of any particular state; *That power being always regarded, be it well remembered, as solely the offspring of conquest and aggrandizement:* notwithstanding . . . that labour, improvements, and discoveries, confer the greatest strength upon a people; and that, by these alone, and not by the sword of the conqueror, can nations, in modern and all future times, hope to rise to supreme power and grandeur.[17]

The expensive, ineffective and unnecessary policy of guarding the balance of power entailed entanglement in every European quarrel. Britain's best policy was to take advantage of her insular position and stand aloof from continental squabbles, building up her strength while other nations dissipated theirs in frequent wars. The principles of a wise British foreign policy were those of Washington's Farewell Address. Cobden carried this principle of nonintervention to the length of opposing the current British inclination to assist the suppressed nationalities of Europe. To counter charges of indifference to the cause of liberty he asserted that such intervention rarely succeeded in advancing the cause of democracy.

Hitherto, whenever a war has at any time been threatened between two or more European states, however remote or however insignificant, it has furnished a sufficient pretence for our statesmen to augment

17. "Russia," *Writings, 1,* 262–6.

our armaments by sea and by land, in order to assume an imposing attitude, as it is termed; forgetting, all the while, that by maintaining a strict neutrality in these continental brawls, and by diligently pursuing our peaceful industry, whilst our neighbours were exhausting themselves in senseless wars, we might be growing in riches, in proportion as they became poorer; and, since it is by wealth after all that the world is governed, we should, in reality, be the less in danger from the powers on the Continent, the more they indulged in hostilities with each other.[18]

I think it is a great mistake to suppose that, in order that you may display a great deal of power to the world, all the power should be put into the shape of cannons, muskets, and ships of war. Do not you think that, in these times of industry, when wealth and commerce are the real tests of a nation's power, coupled with worth and intelligence—do you not see that if you beat your iron into ploughshares and pruning-hooks, instead of putting it into swords and spears, it will be equally productive of power, and of far more force, if brought into collision with another country, than if you put all your iron into spears, and swords? It is not always necessary to hold up a scarecrow to frighten your neighbours. I believe a civilised nation will estimate the power of a country, not by the amount laid out in armaments, which may perhaps be the means of weakening that power, but it will measure your strength by your latent resources—what margin of taxation you have that you can impose in case of necessity, greater than another country, to which you are about to be opposed—what is the spirit of the people, as having confidence in the institutions or government under which they live— what is the general intelligence of the people—what is, in every respect, their situation and capacity to make an effort, in case an effort were required? These will be the tests which intelligent people will apply to countries; not what amount of horse, foot, and artillery, or how many ships you have afloat.[19]

I have not much faith in the power of any one country to go and settle the affairs of another country upon anything like a permanent basis; and there is the ground on which I am such a strong advocate of the principle of non-intervention; it is because intervention must almost, by its very nature, fail in its object. There are two things we confound when we talk of intervention in foreign affairs. The intervention is easy

18. "England, Ireland and America," *Writings, 1*, 135.
19. *Speeches, 1*, 427–8.

enough, but the power to accomplish the object is another thing. You must take possession of a country, in order to impress your policy upon it; and that becomes a tyranny of another sort. But if you go to intervene in the affairs of Poland, with a view to rescue them from the attacks of Russia, I maintain that so far as England is concerned, you are attempting an impossibility; and if you cannot do it by physical force, if you cannot do it by war, then I humbly submit that you are certain to do it more harm than good if you attempt to do it by diplomacy. . . . Some people will say, do you intend to leave these evils without a remedy? Well, I have faith in God, and I think there is a Divine Providence which will obviate this difficulty; but I don't think that Providence has given it into our hands to execute His behests in this world. I think, when injustice is done, whether in Poland or elsewhere, the very process of injustice is calculated, if left to itself, to promote its own cure; because injustice produces weakness—injustice produces injury to the parties who commit it.[20]

Nor do we think it would tend less to promote the ulterior benefits of our continental neighbours than our own, were Great Britain to refrain from participating in the conflicts that may arise around her. An onward movement of constitutional liberty must continue to be made by the less advanced nations of Europe, so long as one of its greatest families holds out the example of liberal and enlightened freedom. England, by calmly directing her undivided energies to the purifying of her own internal institutions, to the emancipation of her commerce . . . would, by thus serving as it were for the beacon of other nations, aid more effectually the cause of political progression all over the continent, than she could possibly do by plunging herself into the strife of European wars.[21]

20. *Ibid.*, 2, 110–11.
21. "England, Ireland and America," *Writings, 1,* 44.

16. JOHN STUART MILL

1806-1873

JOHN STUART MILL'S *father was Bentham's friend and disciple, James Mill, who gave his son an intense education beginning with Greek at the age of three and including psychology, logic, and economics before adolescence. The younger Mill was thus early set in the ways of Benthamism. In his late teens he formed a "Utilitarian Society" of young men and began a literary career. From 1823 until the East India Company lost its monopoly in 1858 Mill worked for the India Office and was its chief for the last two years. He was elected to Parliament in 1865 and served a single term of three years.*

In later years Mill modified his earlier convictions. He came to regard some utilitarian conclusions as over-simplified and he stressed the complexity and dynamic nature of human affairs. However he retained "utility," in promoting the greatest happiness, as the test of law and policy. He became more willing to allow the state a positive role in serving the common good but insisted on consideration for the individual. The same things were not good for all men. Mill's writings on government and liberty therefore emphasized the preservation of individual and minority rights, always providing they did not conflict with the good of the greater society. The subordination of law to utility and care for the rights of minorities formed a noticeable part of Mill's views of international politics.

Mill granted that in international affairs the first concern of every state is its own national security ". . . to act when England's safety is threatened, or any of her interests hostilely or unfairly endangered . . . . is no more than what all nations, sufficiently powerful for their

The editions used are *Dissertations and Discussions: Political, Philosophical, and Historical,* 4 vols. Boston, William V. Spencer, 1864–67; *Considerations on Representative Government,* New York, Henry Holt, 1875; *Views of Mr. John Stuart Mill on England's Danger through the Suppression of her Maritime Power,* London, "Diplomatic Review" Office, 1874.

own protection, do, and no one questions their right to do. It is the common right of self-defence." [1] *He referred to the doctrine that is "professed and acted on by all governments,—that self-preservation, in a State as in an individual, is a warrant for many things, which, at all other times, ought to be rigidly abstained from."* [2] *At one time he believed that free trade would bring an era of universal peace. Later he came to regard this as overoptimistic.*

Mill did not assert that wars were an absolute evil. He thought that it might be right, and even a duty, to fight whenever a good cause could not be furthered by any other means. Because injustices are often imposed by force, it may be right to use force to secure justice.

. . . war, in a good cause, is not the greatest evil which a nation can suffer. War is an ugly thing, but not the ugliest of things: the decayed and degraded state of moral and patriotic feeling which thinks nothing *worth* a war is worse. When a people are used as mere human instruments for firing cannon or thrusting bayonets, in the service and for the selfish purposes of a master, such war degrades a people. A war to protect other human beings against tyrannical injustice; a war to give victory to their own ideas of right and good, and which is their own war, carried on for an honest purpose by their free choice,—is often the means of their regeneration. A man who has nothing which he is willing to fight for, nothing which he cares more about than he does about his personal safety, is a miserable creature, who has no chance of being free, unless made and kept so by the exertions of better men than himself. As long as justice and injustice have not terminated *their* ever-renewing fight for ascendency in the affairs of mankind, human beings must be willing, when need is, to do battle for the one against the other.[3]

There seems to be no little need that the whole doctrine of non-interference with foreign nations should be reconsidered, if it can be said to have as yet been considered as a really moral question at all. We have heard something lately about being willing to go to war for an idea. To go to war for an idea, if the war is aggressive, not defensive, is as criminal as to go to war for territory or revenue; for it is as little justifiable to force our ideas on other people as to compel them to

1. "A Few Words on Non-Intervention," *Dissertations, 3*, 244.
2. "The Contest in America," *Dissertations, 3*, 9.
3. *Ibid., 1*, 25–6.

submit to our will in any other respect. But there assuredly are cases in which it is allowable to go to war, without having been ourselves attacked, or threatened with attack; and it is very important that nations should make up their minds in time as to what these cases are.[4]

Mill observed that the so-called law of nations was merely a set of moral rules. Nevertheless these rules could materially assist in establishing justice between states. Every citizen needed some knowledge of international law in order to judge the policies of his government and prevent their becoming selfish and corrupt.

However, no nation should blindly follow the letter of international law when its sense of equity dictates another course. International law may conflict with justice. Because there is no institution to create and revise international law, the only way to adapt it is to ignore it whenever it runs counter to equitable conduct. Mill believed that the frailty of treaties was largely attributable to the fact that many such compacts were made in perpetuity and thus crystallized arrangements which became outmoded by changes of circumstance. He thought that treaties, like the rest of international law, should be sensitive to progress and should therefore be concluded only for a term of years. No treaty should be made which attempts to establish permanent discrimination between nations.

. . . What is called the Law of Nations is not properly law, but a part of ethics; a set of moral rules, accepted as authoritative by civilized states. It is true that these rules neither are nor ought to be of eternal obligation, but do and must vary more or less from age to age, as the consciences of nations become more enlightened and the exigencies of political society undergo change. But the rules mostly were at their origin, and still are, an application of the maxims of honesty and humanity to the intercourse of states. They were introduced by the moral sentiments of mankind, or by their sense of the general interest, to mitigate the crimes and sufferings of a state of war, and to restrain governments and nations from unjust or dishonest conduct towards one another in time of peace. Since every country stands in numerous and various relations with the other countries of the world, and many, our own among the number, exercise actual authority over some of these, a knowledge of the established rules of international morality is essential to the duty of every nation, and therefore of every person in it who helps to make up the nation, and whose voice and

4. "Non-Intervention," *Dissertations*, 3, 251–63.

feeling form a part of what is called public opinion. . . . It depends on the habit of attending to and looking into public transactions, and on the degree of information and solid judgement respecting them that exists in the community, whether the conduct of the nation as a nation, both within itself and towards others, shall be selfish, corrupt, and tyrannical, or rational and enlightened, just and noble.[5]

. . . The law of nations is simply the custom of nations. It is a set of international usages, which have grown up like other usages, partly from a sense of justice, partly from common interest or convenience, partly from mere opinion and prejudice. Now, are international usages the only kind of customs, which, in an age of progress, are to be subject to no improvement? Are they alone to continue fixed, while all around them is changeable? . . . What is called the law of nations is as open to alteration, as properly and even necessarily subject to it when circumstances change or opinions alter, as any other thing of human institution.

And, mark, in the case of a real law, of anything properly called a law, it is possible to maintain (however erroneous may be the opinion) that there is never any necessity for disobeying it; that it should be conformed to while it exists, the alternative being open of endeavouring to get it altered. But in regard to that falsely called law, the law of nations, there is no such alternative; there is no ordinance or statute to repeal: there is only a custom; and the sole way of altering that is to act in opposition to it. A legislature can repeal laws; but there is no Congress of nations to set aside international customs, and no common force by which to make the decisions of such a Congress binding. The improvement of international morality can only take place by a series of violations of existing rules; by a course of conduct grounded on new principles, and tending to erect these into customs in their turn.

Accordingly, new principles and practices are, and have been, continually introduced into the conduct of nations towards one another.[6]

. . . Through the greater part of the present century, the conscience of Europe has been habituated to the demoralising spectacle of treaties made only to be broken. In 1814 and 1815, a set of treaties were made by a general Congress of the States of Europe, which affected to regu-

5. "Inaugural Address," *Dissertations, 4,* 439–41.
6. "Vindication of the French Revolution of February, 1848," *Dissertations, 3,* 49–50.

late the external, and some of the internal, concerns of the European
nations, for a time altogether unlimited. These treaties, having been
concluded at the termination of a long war, which had ended in the
signal discomfiture of one side, were imposed by some of the contracting parties, and reluctantly submitted to by others. Their terms were
regulated by the interests, and relative strength at the time, of the vic-
tors and vanquished; and were observed as long as those interests and
that relative strength remained the same. But as fast as any alteration
took place in these elements, the powers, one after another, without
asking leave, threw off, and were allowed with impunity to throw
off, such of the obligations of the treaties as were distasteful to them,
and not sufficiently important to the others to be worth a fight. The general opinion sustained some of those violations as being perfectly
right; and even those which were disapproved, were not regarded as
justifying a resort to war. . . .

. . . No honest man can see with indifference a condition in which
treaties do not bind; in which it rests with the party who deems himself aggrieved by them, to say whether they shall be observed or not;
in which nations cannot trust each other's pledged word. It does not
follow, however, that this evil is likely to be remedied by ignoring the
fact, that there are treaties which never will, and even which never
ought to be permanently observed by those who have been obliged to
submit to them; far less, therefore, to be permanently enforced. . . .

What means, then, are there of reconciling, in the greatest practicable degree, the inviolability of treaties and the sanctity of national faith,
with the undoubted fact that treaties are not always fit to be kept,
while yet those who have imposed them upon others weaker than themselves are not likely, if they retain confidence in their own strength,
to grant a release from them? To effect this reconcilement, so far as
it is capable of being effected, nations should be willing to abide by
two rules. They should abstain from imposing conditions which, on
any just and reasonable view of human affairs, cannot be expected
to be kept. And they should conclude their treaties, as commercial
treaties are usually concluded, only for terms of years.

To the first of these rules it is essential that the obligations should
be defined, which nations are not warranted in imposing on one another. I do not pretend to enter exhaustively upon so large a subject.
But one great principle one can clearly see, and it is the only one which
need concern us at present. The community of nations is essentially
a republic of equals. Its purposes require that it should know no dis-

tinction of grades, no rights or privileges enjoyed by some and refused to others. The basis of international law—without which the weak, for whose protection chiefly international law exists, would never be secure —is, that the smallest and least powerful nation, in its capacity of a nation, is the equal of the strongest. Whatever rights belong to one belong to all, and can only be temporarily forfeited, even by misconduct, unless the erring nation is to be treated as a savage, and thrust out of the communion of civilized nations altogether. Now, all treaties which bind a nation, within itself and in its own affairs, by restrictions not common to all the rest, violate this principle. Of this nature is a stipulation that a country shall maintain one form of government, or abjure another; that she shall abstain from fortifying places situated within her own territory; that she shall limit to a prescribed amount her army or her fleet, or the portion of each stationed in a particular part of her dominions, no equivalent limitation of armaments being consented to by the other parties to the treaty, or by nations in general. I do not say that some of these restrictions cannot ever be admissible as a temporary penalty for crimes committed against other states; though in general some penalty would be preferable which could be completed by a single act. The period, however, for which such exceptional disabilities can justly be imposed, ought not, I conceive, to exceed the length of a generation . . .[7]

Mill thought that particularly glaring examples of the blind devotion of international law to the status quo were those provisions which forbade intervention to assist a nation struggling for independence. In his opinion every national group had a right to self-government because it was only under self-government that a nation could enjoy the benefits of democracy and liberty. For this reason Mill approved of intervention, by force if need be, whenever such action seemed likely to result in the establishment of self-government for a suppressed nationality.

A portion of mankind may be said to constitute a nationality if they are united among themselves by common sympathies which do not exist between them and any others—which make them co-operate with each other more willingly than with other people, desire to be under the same government, and desire that it should be government by themselves or a portion of themselves exclusively. This feeling of nationality may have been generated by various causes. . . .

7. "Treaty Obligations," *Dissertations*, 5, 132–9.

Where the sentiment of nationality exists in any force, there is a *primâ facie* case for uniting all the members of the nationality under the same government, and a government to themselves apart. This is merely saying that the question of government ought to be decided by the governed. One hardly knows what any division of the human race should be free to do if not to determine with which of the various collective bodies of human beings they choose to associate themselves. But, when a people are ripe for free institutions, there is a still more vital consideration. Free institutions are next to impossible in a country made up of different nationalities. Among a people without fellow-feeling, especially if they read and speak different languages, the united public opinion necessary to the working of representative government cannot exist. The influences which form opinions and decide political acts are different in the different sections of the country. An altogether different set of leaders have the confidence of one part of the country and of another.[8]

. . . The customs, or falsely called laws of nations, laid down in the books, were made for an age like that of Louis XIV, to prevent powerful and ambitious despots from swallowing up the smaller States. For this purpose they were well adapted. But the great interests of civilized nations in the present age are not those of territorial attack and defence, but of liberty, just government, and sympathy of opinion. . . . There was once in Europe a time, when, as much as at present, the most important interests of nations, both in their domestic and in their foreign concerns, were interests of opinion: it was the era of the Reformation. Did any one then pay the least regard to the pretended principle of non-interference? Was not sympathy of religion held to be a perfectly sufficient warrant for assisting anybody? Did not Protestants aid Protestants wherever they were in danger from their own governments? Did not Catholics support all other Catholics in suppressing heresy? What religious sympathies were then, political ones are now: and every liberal government or people has a right to assist struggling liberalism, by mediation, by money, or by arms, whenever it can prudently do so; as every despotic government, when its aid is needed or asked for, never scruples to aid despotic governments.[9]

However, Mill admitted that indiscriminate intervention, even when well-intentioned, might do more harm than good. He recognized that

8. *Representative Government,* p. 308.
9. "Vindication of the French Revolution, *Dissertations,* 5, 51–2.

intervention could successfully establish liberty only under certain fav-
orable conditions. Mill thought that the definition of those conditions
was one of the most pressing tasks of political philosophy, and he went
to considerable pains to provide an answer.

. . . There are few questions which more require to be taken in hand
by ethical and political philosophers, with a view to establish some rule
or criterion whereby the justifiableness of intervening in the affairs of
other countries, and (what is sometimes fully as questionable) the justifiableness of refraining from intervention, may be brought to a definite
and rational test. Whoever attempts this will be led to recognise more
than one fundamental distinction, not yet by any means familiar to the
public mind, and, in general, quite lost sight of by those who write in
strains of indignant morality on the subject. There is a great difference
(for example) between the case in which the nations concerned are of
the same, or something like the same, degree of civilization, and that in
which one of the parties to the situation is of a high and the other of a
very low, grade of social improvement. To suppose that the same international customs, and the same rule of international morality, can
obtain between one civilized nation and another, and between civilized
nations and barbarians, is a grave error, and one which no statesman
can fall into, however it may be with those, who, from a safe and unre-
sponsible position, criticise statesmen. Among many reasons why the
same rules cannot be applicable to situations so different, the two following are among the most important. In the first place, the rules of
ordinary international morality imply reciprocity. But barbarians will
not reciprocate. They cannot be depended on for observing any rules.
Their minds are not capable of so great an effort, nor their will sufficiently under the influence of distant motives. In the next place, nations
which are still barbarous have not got beyond the period during which
it is likely to be for their benefit that they should be conquered and held
in subjection by foreigners. Independence and nationality, so essential
to the due growth and development of a people further advanced in
improvement, are generally impediments to theirs. . . . .

But among civilized peoples, members of an equal community of nations, like Christian Europe, the question assumes another aspect, and
must be decided on totally different principles. It would be an affront
to the reader to discuss the immorality of wars of conquest, or of conquest even as the consequence of lawful war; the annexation of any
civilized people to the dominion of another, unless by their own spon-

taneous election. Up to this point, there is no difference of opinion among honest people; nor on the wickedness of commencing an aggressive war for any interest of our own, except when necessary to avert from ourselves an obviously impending wrong. The disputed question is that of interfering in the regulation of another country's internal concerns,—the question whether a nation is justified in taking part, on either side, in the civil wars or party contests of another; and, chiefly, whether it may justifiably aid the people of another country in struggling for liberty; or may impose on a country any particular government or institutions, either as being best for the country itself, or as necessary for the security of its neighbours.

Of these cases, that of a people in arms for liberty is the only one of any nicety, or which, theoretically at least, is likely to present conflicting moral considerations. The other cases which have been mentioned hardly admit of discussion. Assistance to the government of a country in keeping down the people, unhappily by far the most frequent case of foreign intervention, no one writing in a free country needs take the trouble of stigmatizing. A government which needs foreign support to enforce obedience from its own citizens is one which ought not to exist; and the assistance given to it by foreigners is hardly ever anything but the sympathy of one despotism with another. A case requiring consideration is that of a protracted civil war, in which the contending parties are so equally balanced, that there is no probability of a speedy issue; or, if there is, the victorious side cannot hope to keep down the vanquished but by severities repugnant to humanity, and injurious to the permanent welfare of the country. In this exceptional case it seems now to be an admitted doctrine, that the neighboring nations, or one powerful neighbor with the acquiescence of the rest, are warranted in demanding that the contest shall cease, and a reconciliation take place on equitable terms of compromise. Intervention of this description has been repeatedly practised during the present generation, with such general approval, that its legitimacy may be considered to have passed into a maxim of what is called international law. . . .

With respect to the question, whether one country is justified in helping the people of another in the struggle against their government for free institutions, the answer will be different according as the yoke which the people are attempting to throw off is that of a purely native government, or of foreigners; considering as one of foreigners every government which maintains itself by foreign support. When the contest is only with native rulers, and with such native strength as those rulers can enlist in their defence, the answer I should give to the question of the legitimacy of intervention is, as a general rule, No. The reason is that there can seldom be anything approaching to assurance, that intervention, even if successful, would be for the good of the people themselves. The only test possessing any real value, of a people's having become fit for popular institutions, is, that they, or a sufficient portion of them to prevail in the contest, are willing to brave labor and danger for their liberation. I know all that may be said. I know it may be urged, that the virtues of freemen cannot be learnt in the school of slavery; and that, if a people are not fit for freedom, to have any chance of becoming so they must first be free. And this would be conclusive, if the intervention recommended would really give them freedom. But the evil is, that, if they have not sufficient love of liberty to be able to wrest it from merely domestic oppressors, the liberty which is bestowed on them by other hands than their own will have nothing real, nothing permanent. . . .

It can seldom, therefore,—I will not go so far as to say never,—be either judicious or right, in a country which has a free government, to assist, otherwise than by the moral support of its opinion, the endeavours of another to extort the same blessing from its native rulers. We must except, of course, any case in which such assistance is a measure of legitimate self-defence. If (a contingency by no means unlikely to occur) this country, on account of its freedom, which is a standing reproach to despotism everywhere, and an encouragement to throw it off, should find itself menaced with attack by a coalition of Continental despots, it ought to consider the popular party in every nation of the Continent its natural ally: the Liberals should be to it what the Protestants of Europe were to the Government of Queen Elizabeth. . . .

But the case of a people struggling against a foreign yoke, or against a native tyranny upheld by foreign arms, illustrates the reasons for non-intervention in an opposite way; for, in this case, the reasons themselves do not exist. A people the most attached to freedom, the most capable of defending and of making a good use of free institutions, may be unable to contend successfully for them against the military strength of another nation much more powerful. To assist a people thus kept down is not to disturb the balance of forces on which the permanent maintenance of freedom in a country depends, but to redress that balance when it is already unfairly and violently disturbed. The doctrine of non-intervention to be a legitimate principle of morality, must be accepted by all governments. The despots must consent to be bound by it as well as the free

States. Unless they do, the profession of it by free countries comes but
to this miserable issue,—that the wrong side may help the wrong, but
the right must not help the right. Intervention to enforce non-intervention is always rightful, always moral, if not always prudent. Though it
be a mistake to *give* freedom to a people who do not value the boon, it
cannot but be right to insist, that, if they do value it, they shall not be
hindered from the pursuit of it by foreign coercion.[10]

Not all national groups met Mill's standards of eligibility for self-
government. Many backward nations lacked the self-discipline and cul-
ture necessary for the formation of a successful state. In such cases Mill
approved of more advanced nations assuming dominion over the back-
ward areas. This dominion should be exercised solely with a view to pre-
paring the subject races for self-government. At the proper time the
governing power should grant independence to its colonies.

Mill did not object to colonies remaining in permanent voluntary as-
sociation with their former rulers, for this would reduce the points of
possible international friction and war.

Whatever really tends to the admixture of nationalities, and the
blending of their attributes and peculiarities in a common union, is a
benefit to the human race. Not by extinguishing types . . . but by soft-
ening their extreme forms, and filling up the intervals between them.
The united people, like a crossed breed of animals (but in a still greater
degree, because the influences in operation are moral as well as physical), inherits the special aptitudes and excellencies of all its progenitors,
protected by the admixture from being exaggerated into the neighboring vices. But, to render this admixture possible, there must be peculiar
conditions. The combinations of circumstances which occur, and which
affect the result, are various.

The nationalities brought together under the same government may
be about equal in numbers and strength, or they may be very unequal.
If unequal, the least numerous of the two may either be the superior in
civilization, or the inferior. Supposing it to be superior, it may either,
through that superiority, be able to acquire ascendancy over the other,
or it may be overcome by brute strength and reduced to subjection.
This last is a sheer mischief to the human race, and one which civilized
humanity with one accord should rise in arms to prevent. . . .

If the smaller nationality, supposed to be the more advanced in improvement, is able to overcome the greater, as the Macedonians, re-

10. "Non-Intervention," *Dissertations*, 3, 251–63.

inforced by the Greeks, did Asia, and the English India, there is often
a gain to civilization, but the conquerors and the conquered cannot
in this case live together under the same free institutions. The absorption of the conquerors in the less advanced people would be an evil:
these must be governed as subjects, and the state of things is either a
benefit or a misfortune, according as the subjugated people have or
have not reached the state in which it is an injury not to be under a free
government, and according as the conquerors do or do not use their
superiority in a manner calculated to fit the conquered for a higher
stage of improvement. . . .

When the nationality which succeeds in overpowering the other is
both the most numerous and the most improved, and especially if the
subdued nationality is small, and has no hope of reasserting its independence, then, if it is governed with any tolerable justice, and if
the members of the more powerful nationality are not made odious
by being invested with exclusive privileges, the smaller nationality is
gradually reconciled to its position, and becomes amalgamated with
the larger. . . .

The cases in which the greatest practical obstacles exist to the blending of nationalities are when the nationalities which have been bound
together are nearly equal in numbers and in the other elements of
power. In such cases, each, confiding in its strength, and feeling itself
capable of maintaining an equal struggle with any of the others, is unwilling to be merged in it; each cultivates with party obstinacy its
distinctive peculiarities; obsolete customs, and even declining languages, are revived, to deepen the separation; each deems itself tyran-
nized over if any authority is exercised within itself by functionaries
of a rival race; and whatever is given to one of the conflicting nationalities is considered to be taken from all the rest. When nations
thus divided are under a despotic government which is a stranger to
all of them, or which, though sprung from one, yet feeling greater interest in its own power than in any sympathies of nationality, assigns
no privilege to either nation, and chooses its instruments indifferently
from all; in the course of a few generations identity of situation often
produces harmony of feeling, and the different races come to feel
towards each other as fellow-countrymen, particularly if they are
dispersed over the same tract of country. But if the era of aspiration
to free government arrives before this fusion has been effected, the
opportunity has gone by for effecting it. From that time, if the un-
reconciled nationalities are geographically separate, and especially if

their local position is such that there is no natural fitness or convenience in their being under the same government . . . there is not only an obvious propriety, but, if either freedom or concord is cared for, a necessity for breaking the connection altogether.[11]

But, though Great Britain could do perfectly well without her colonies, and though, on every principle of morality and justice, she ought to consent to their separation, should the time come when, after a full trial of the best form of union, they deliberately desire to be dissevered, there are strong reasons for maintaining the present slight bond of connection so long as not disagreeable to the feelings of either party. It is a step, as far as it goes, towards universal peace and general friendly co-operation among nations. It renders war impossible among a large number of otherwise independent communities, and, moreover, hinders any of them from being absorbed into a foreign state, and becoming a source of additional aggressive strength to some rival power, either more despotic or closer at hand, which might not always be so unambitious or so pacific as Great Britain. It at least keeps the markets of the different countries open to one another, and prevents that mutual exclusion by hostile tariffs which none of the great communities of mankind except England have yet completely outgrown.[12]

Following such reasoning, Mill looked favorably on the federal system as one answer to the problem of combining unity with diversity. But he observed that this form of government could succeed only under certain circumstances.

Portions of mankind who are not fitted or not disposed to live under the same internal government may often, with advantage, be federally united as to their relations with foreigners, both to prevent wars among themselves, and for the sake of more effectual protection against the aggression of powerful States.

To render a federation advisable several conditions are necessary. The first is that there should be a sufficient amount of mutual sympathy among the populations. . . . The sympathies available for the purpose are those of race, language, religion, and, above all, of political institutions, as conducing most to a feeling of identity of political interest. When a few free states, separately insufficient for their own defense,

11. *Representative Government,* pp. 315–19.
12. *Ibid.,* p. 342.

are hemmed in on all sides by military or feudal monarchs, who hate and despise freedom even in a neighbor, those states have no chance for preserving liberty and its blessings but by a federal union. . . .

The second condition of the stability of a federal government is that the separate states be not so powerful as to be able to rely for protection against foreign encroachment on their individual strength. If they are, they will be apt to think that they do not gain, by union with others, the equivalent of what they sacrifice in their own liberty of action; and consequently, whenever the policy of the confederation, in things reserved to its cognizance, is different from that which any one of its members would separately pursue, the internal and sectional breach will, through absence of sufficient anxiety to preserve the Union, be in danger of going so far as to dissolve it.

A third condition, not less important than the two others, is that there be not a very marked inequality of strength among the several contracting States. They can not, indeed, be exactly equal in resources; in all federations there will be a gradation of power among the members; some will be more populous, rich, and civilized than others. . . . The essential is, that there should not be any one State so much more powerful than the rest as to be capable of vying in strength with many of them combined. If there be such a one, and only one, it will insist on being master of the joint deliberations; if there be two, they will be irresistible when they agree; and whenever they differ, everything will be decided by a struggle for ascendancy between the rivals. . . . . .

When the conditions exist for the formation of efficient and durable federal unions, the multiplication of such is always a benefit to the world. It has the same salutary effect as any other extension of the practice of co-operation, through which the weak, by uniting, can meet on equal terms with the strong. By diminishing the number of those petty States which are not equal to their own defense, it weakens the temptations to an aggressive policy, whether working directly by arms, or through the *prestige* of superior power. It of course puts an end to war and diplomatic quarrels, and usually also to restrictions on commerce, between the states composing the Union; while, in reference to neighboring nations, the increased military strength conferred by it is of a kind to be almost exclusively available for defensive, scarcely at all for aggressive purposes. A federal government has not a sufficiently concentrated authority to conduct with much efficiency any war but one of self-defense, in which it can rely on the voluntary cooperation of every citizen; nor is there anything very flattering to national vanity or ambition in acquiring, by a successful war, not subjects, nor even fellow-citizens, but only new, and perhaps troublesome independent members of the confederation.[13]

13. *Ibid.*, pp. 320–32.

17. HERBERT SPENCER

1820-1903

HERBERT SPENCER *was born the son of a family of dissenting radicals. An uncle gave him some instruction in science, but at no time in his life did Spencer receive any formal education. After a brief period as a schoolmaster he became a railway surveyor. He did not find this work very absorbing and as early as 1842 began to write articles for the* Nonconformist. *At the same time he made a little money from inventions. By 1844 he was devoting all his time to writing. For a few years he was a subeditor of the* Economist *and while engaged in that work published* Social Statics, *his first book. The success of the book and a small legacy encouraged him to give up his job with the* Economist *and become a free-lance writer. From then on, the course of his life is marked by almost nothing but the publication of his books. He died in 1903.*

Spencer's greatest achievement was the Synthetic Philosophy, *a nine-volume attempt to unify knowledge of man and society. Accompanying the work was the* Descriptive Sociology, *an immense compilation of data on the behavior and institutions of various races and eras. Spencer supervised the production of eight volumes of this and the task was continued under the terms of his will.*

By applying the laws of biology to all human activities Spencer believed he could unify knowledge. The unifying principle was that of evolution. He achieved a tentative formulation of the "development hypothesis" in his Social Statics, *eight years before the* Origin of Species *was published. He did not, however, anticipate the concept of natural*

The editions used are *Facts and Comments*, New York, D. Appleton and Co., 1902, reprinted by permission of Appleton-Century-Crofts, Inc.; *Man versus the State*, New York, D. Appleton and Co., 1884; *Principles of Ethics*, 2 vols. New York, D. Appleton and Co., 1892; *Principles of Sociology*, 3 vols. New York, D. Appleton and Co., 1899; *Social Statics*, New York, D. Appleton and Co., 1892; *Various Fragments*, New York, D. Appleton and Co., 1898.

selection. Spencer asserted that society evolved like an individual organism and that evolution meant progress. His sociology was thus an optimistic one.

In his social and political theories Spencer carried individualism to an extreme. His ideal was liberty. Progress depended on struggle and "survival of the fittest"—a phrase coined by Spencer. Government must not interfere with the struggle. Education, mail, sanitation, even coinage should be left to private enterprise. The state should be limited to national defense, suppression of internal violence, and rigid enforcement of contract. Society developed from anarchy through militarism to an "industrial society" where men turned more and more to voluntary cooperation in producing the means to a full and pleasant life. This last stage of society, thought Spencer, was already emerging but the process was far from complete.

For Spencer the beginning of international relations coincides with the beginning of organized society. "Having spread wherever there is food, groups of men have come to be everywhere in another's way." [1] *This collision brings conflict. The men who survive this conflict are those who do most to consolidate themselves into a compact society: "government is initiated and developed by the defensive and offensive actions of a society against other societies."* [2] *This process of conflict, which inspires organization, also permits a society to gain sufficient size to sustain a high degree of organization. The first step is usually the simple selection of a fighting leader. This leader acquires control over all aspects of the society. The "militant society" must always be firmly disciplined. All members of the society have a part in the fighting forces or in supplying the materials for war. Such a society breeds men who place the highest value on bravery and warlike virtues. As long as international conflict continues, at least a residue of these militant characteristics will remain in the various societies.*

If to preserve the lives of its units, and to maintain that freedom to pursue the objects of life which is ordinarily possessed by unconquered peoples, a society has to use its corporate action chiefly for dealing with environing societies; then its organization must be such as will bring into play the effectually-combined forces of its units at specific times and places. It needs no proof that if its units are left to act without concert they will be forthwith subjugated; and it needs no proof that to produce concerted action, they must be under direction. Con-

1. *Ethics*, 2, 22.
2. *Ibid.*, p. 204.

formity to such direction must be insured by compulsion; the agency which compels must issue consistent orders; and to this end the orders must emanate from a single authority. Tracing up the genesis of the militant type leads irresistibly to the conclusion that for efficient external action of a society against other societies, centralisation is necessary; and that establishment of it becomes more decided the more habitual is such external action. Not only does the fighting body itself become subject to despotic rule, but also the community which supports it.[3]

. . . The members of a primitive horde, loosely aggregated, and without distinctions of power, cooperate for immediate furtherance of individual sustentation, and in a comparatively small degree for corporate sustentation. Even when, the interest of all being simultaneously endangered, they simultaneously fight, they still fight separately—their actions are uncoordinated; and the only spoils of successful battle are such as can be individually appropriated. But in the course of the struggles for existence between groups thus unorganized, there comes, with the development of such political organization as gives tribal individuality, the struggle to incorporate one another, first partially and then wholly. Tribes which are larger, or better organized, or both, conquer adjacent tribes and annex them, so that they form parts of a compound whole. And as political evolution advances, it becomes a trait of the large and stronger societies that they acquire appetites prompting them to subjugate and incorporate weaker societies. . . . .

. . . in more advanced stages the struggle between societies is, not to appropriate one another's means of sustentation and multiplication, but to appropriate one another bodily. Which society shall incorporate other societies with itself, becomes the question. Under one aspect, the history of large nations is a history of successes in such struggles; and down to our own day nations are being thus enlarged. . . .

Thus then, with social organisms as with individual organisms, it is the struggle for existence, first, by appropriating one another's means of growth, and then by devouring one another, that there arise those great aggregations which at once make possible high organization, and require high organization.[4]

Certain conditions, manifest *à priori*, have to be fulfilled by a society fitted for preserving itself in presence of antagonist societies. To be in

3. *Ibid.*, pp. 188–9.
4. *Sociology*, 2, 266–8.

the highest degree efficient, the corporate action needed for preserving the corporate life must be joined in by every one. Other things equal, the fighting power will be greatest where those who cannot fight, labour exclusively to support and help those who can: an evident implication being that the working part shall be no larger than is required for these ends. The efforts of all being utilized directly or indirectly for war, will be most effectual when they are most combined; and, besides union among the combatants, there must be such union of the non-combatants with them as renders the aid of these fully and promptly available. To satisfy these requirements, the life, the actions, and the possessions, of each individual must be held at the service of the society. This universal service, this combination, and this merging of individual claims, pre-suppose a despotic controlling agency. That the will of the soldier-chief may be operative when the aggregate is large, there must be sub-centres and sub-sub-centres in descending grades, through whom orders may be conveyed and enforced, both throughout the combatant part and the non-combatant part. As the commander tells the soldier both what he shall not do and what he shall do; so, throughout the militant community at large, the rule is both negatively regulative and positively regulative: it not only restrains, but it directs: the citizen as well as the soldier lives under a system of compulsory cooperation. Development of the militant type involves increasing rigidity, since the cohesion, the combination, the subordination, and the regulation, to which the units of a society are subjected by it, inevitably decrease their ability to change their social positions, their occupations, their localities. . . . . .

. . . the men who compose militant societies. . . . are led to identify goodness with bravery and strength. Revenge becomes a sacred duty with them; and acting at home on the law of retaliation which they act on abroad, they similarly, at home as abroad, are ready to sacrifice others to self: their sympathies, continually deadened during the war, cannot be active during peace. They must have a patriotism which regards the triumph of their society as the supreme end of action; they must possess the loyalty whence flows obedience to authority; and that they may be obedient they must have abundant faith.[5]

The "militant society" is a transient stage in social history. As they grow, societies place increasing value on qualities of character which facilitate free cooperation between men. Moreover, although the in

5. *Ibid.*, pp. 600–2.

*creasing size of societies makes wars larger, the reduced number of
independent units decreases the occasions for war. Spencer believed
that the "militant society" had served its purpose. In its place there was
emerging an "industrial society" which favored the development of
benevolent, cooperative, men. Ultimately there might emerge a world
society. The speed of this progress would depend on the decline in
warfare. Emergence of the industrial society and the extension of peace
thus appear reciprocal. "Inevitably the established code of conduct in
the dealings of Governments with citizens, must be allied to their code
of conduct in their dealings with one another." [6]*

Savage as have been the passions commonly causing war, and great
as have been its horrors, it has, throughout the past, achieved certain
immense benefits. From it has resulted the predominance and spread
of the most powerful races. Beginning with primitive tribes it has
welded together small groups into larger groups, and again at later
stages has welded these larger groups into still larger, until nations
have been formed. At the same time military discipline has habituated
wild men to the bearing of restraints, and has initiated that system of
graduated subordination under which all social life is carried on. But
though, along with detestation of the cruelties and bloodshed and
brutalisation accompanying war, we must recognize these great incidental benefits bequeathed by it heretofore, we are shown that henceforth there can arise no such ultimate good to be set against its enormous evils. Powerful types of men now possess the world; great
aggregates of them have been consolidated; societies have been organized; and throughout the future the conflicts of nations, entailing
on larger scales than ever before death, devastation, and misery, can
yield to posterity no compensating advantages. Henceforth social
progress is to be achieved, not by systems of education, not by the
preaching of this or that religion, not by insistence on a humane creed
daily repeated and daily disregarded, but only by cessation from these
antagonisms which keep alive the brutal elements of human nature,
and by persistence in a peaceful life which gives unchecked play to the
sympathies. In sundry places, and in various ways, I have sought to
show that advance to higher forms of man and society essentially depends on the decline of militancy and the growth of industrialism. This
I hold to be a political truth in comparison with which all other political truths are insignificant.[7]

6. *Man versus the State,* p. 45.
7. *Various Fragments,* pp. 141–2.

. . . In proportion as, with the advance of society to a peaceful state, there increases the form of social life which consists in mutual exchange of services—in proportion as it becomes to the advantage of the individual, and to the prosperity of the society, to regard others' claims and fulfil contracts—in proportion as the individual comes to be aided in leading a more complete life, by possessing a nature which begets friendship and kindly offices from all around; in such proportion does there continuously tend to take place both a strengthening of the altruistic emotions directly in the individual, and the increase of those individuals who inherit most largely the altruistic nature. And in proportion as there goes on this individual modification, conducing ever to the prosperity of the society after the peaceful [stage] has been reached, in that same proportion does it also happen that among societies those among whom that modification has gone on most effectually will be those to [survive and grow, so as gradually to replace those societies] in which the individual nature is not so adapted to social requirements. . . .[8]

. . . All that has gone before unites to prove that political institutions, fundamentally determined in their forms by the predominance of one or other of the antagonist modes of social action, the militant and the industrial, will be moulded in this way or in that way according as there is frequent war or habitual peace. Hence we must infer that throughout approaching periods, everything will depend on the courses which societies happen to take in their behaviour to another—courses which cannot be predicted. On the one hand, in the present state of armed preparation throughout Europe, an untoward accident may bring about wars which, lasting perhaps for a generation, will redevelop the coercive forms of political control. On the other hand, a long peace is likely to be accompanied by so vast an increase of manufacturing and commercial activity, with accompanying growth of the appropriate political structures within each nation, and strengthening of those ties between nations which mutual dependence generates, that hostilities will be more and more resisted and the organization for the carrying them on will decay.[9]

Spencer observed that however peaceful the ultimate future of mankind might be, the international relations of his time were still full of conflict and violence. In such a world even the most advanced society must stand ready to defend itself. Even a nation which is well on the

8. *Ethics*, 1, 302.
9. *Sociology*, 2, 648.

way to becoming an "industrial society" is fully justified in resorting to war in self-defense. It has, indeed, a duty to do so. Only by maintaining its rights is a nation capable of fulfilling its duties. In fighting the invading aggressor "soldiers are policemen who act in concert." Defensive warfare "must therefore be tolerated as the least of two evils."

. . . History, which is little more than the Newgate Calendar of nations, describing political burglaries and their results, yields illustrations on every page: "arms and the man" supply the universal theme. . . . War, even unprovoked war, was supported by a pro-ethical sentiment.

Nor is it essentially otherwise even now. Thinly veiled by conventional respect for the professed religious creed, the old spirit continually discloses itself. . . . Lord Wolseley says of the soldier:—"He must believe that his duties are the noblest that fall to man's lot. He must be taught to despise all those of civil life:" a sentiment which is not limited to the "duties" of the soldier as a defender of his country, which in our day he never performs, but is extended to his "duties" as an invader of other countries, and especially those of weak peoples: the appetite for aggression transforms baseness into nobility. . . . when with arms of precision, with shells, with rockets, with far-reaching cannon, peoples possessed only of feeble weapons are conquered with as great facility as a man conquers a child, there comes applause in our journals, with titles and rewards to the leaders! The "duties" of the soldier so performed are called "noble;" while, held up in contrast with them, those of the peaceful citizen are called despicable!

Beyond question, then, the sentiment which rejoices in personal superiority, and, not asking for equitable cause, is ready, under an authority it willingly accepts, to slaughter so-called enemies, is still dominant. The social sanction, and the reflected inner sanction due to it, constitute a pro-ethical sentiment which, in international relations, remains supreme.[10]

. . . Protection,—this is what men seek by political combination; and whether it be against internal or external enemies matters not. Unquestionably war is immoral. But so likewise is the violence used in the execution of justice; so is all coercion. Ethical law is as certainly broken by the deeds of judicial authorities as by those of a defensive army. There is, in principle, no difference whatever between the blow of a policeman's baton and the thrust of a soldier's bayonet. Both are infractions of the law of equal freedom in the persons of those injured.

10. *Ethics, 1,* 345–7.

In either case we have force sufficient to produce submission; and it matters not whether that force be employed by a man in red or by one in blue. Policemen are soldiers who act alone; soldiers are policemen who act in concert. Government employs the first to attack in detail ten thousand criminals who separately make war on society; and it calls in the last when threatened by a like number of criminals in the shape of drilled troops. Resistance to foreign foes and resistance to native ones having consequently the same object—the maintenance of men's rights, and being effected by the same means—force, are in their nature identical; and no greater condemnation can be passed on the one than on the other. The doings of the battlefield merely exhibit in a concentrated form that immorality which is inherent in government, and attaches to all its functions. What is so manifest in its military acts is true of its civil acts,—it uses wrong to put down wrong.

Defensive warfare (and of course it is solely to this that the foregoing argument applies) must therefore be tolerated as the least of two evils. There are indeed some who unconditionally condemn it, and would meet invasion by non-resistance. To such there are several replies.

First, consistency requires them to behave in like fashion to their fellow-citizens. They must not only allow themselves to be cheated, assaulted, robbed, wounded, without offering active opposition, but must refuse help from the civil power; seeing that they who employ force by proxy, are as much responsible for it as though they employed it themselves.

Again, such a theory makes pacific relationships between men and nations look needlessly Utopian. If all agree not to aggress, they must as certainly be at peace with each other as though they had all agreed not to resist. So that, while it sets up so difficult a standard of behaviour, the rule of non-resistance is not one whit more efficient as a preventive of war, than the rule of non-aggression.

Moreover, this principle of non-resistance is not deducible from the moral law. The moral law says— Do not aggress. It cannot say— Do not resist; for to say this would be to presuppose its own precepts broken. As explained at the outset, Morality describes the conduct of perfect men; and cannot include in its premises circumstances that arise from imperfection. . . .

Lastly, it can be shown that non-resistance is absolutely wrong. We may not carelessly abandon our dues. We may not give away our birthright for the sake of peace. . . . No: we may not be passive under aggression. In the due maintenance of our claims is involved the practicability of our duties.[11]

The duty to provide for national security sanctions those minimum interferences with liberty necessary to the state for organizing defense. One such interference is the regulation of trade to ensure sufficient supplies in wartime. This is the only ground on which any interference with international trade can be justified. As the "industrial society" emerges, barriers to trade fall and international intercourse becomes more free and a powerful encouragement to the development of a world society.

. . . a society of the militant type tends to evolve a self-sufficient sustaining organization. With its political autonomy there goes what we may call an economic autonomy. Evidently if it carries on frequent wars against surrounding societies, its commercial intercourse with them must be hindered or prevented: exchange of commodities can go on to but a small extent between those who are continually fighting. A militant society must, therefore, to the greatest degree practicable, provide internally the supplies of all articles needful for carrying on the lives of its members. Such an economic state as that which existed during early feudal times as in France, "the castles made almost all the articles used in them," is a state evidently entailed on groups, small or large, which are in constant antagonism with surrounding groups. If there does not already exist within any group so circumstanced, an agency for producing some necessary article, inability to obtain it from without will lead to the establishment of an agency for obtaining it within.

Whence it follows that the desire "not to be dependent on foreigners" is one appropriate to the militant type of society. So long as there is constant danger that the supplies of needful things derived from other countries will be cut off by the breaking out of hostilities, it is imperative that there shall be maintained a power of producing these supplies at home, and that to this end the required structure shall be maintained. Hence there is a manifest direct relation between militant activities and a protectionist policy.[12]

While hostile relations with adjacent societies continue, each society has to be productively self-sufficing; but with the establishment of peaceful relations, this need for self-sufficingness ceases. As the local

11. *Social Statics*, pp. 118–20.
12. *Ibid.*, pp. 577–8.

divisions composing one of our great nations, had, while they were at feud, to produce each for itself almost everything it required, but now permanently at peace with one another, have become so far mutually dependent that no one of them can satisfy its wants without aid from the rest; so the great nations themselves, at present forced in large measure to maintain their economic autonomies, will become less forced to do this as war decreases, and will gradually become necessary to one another. While, on the one hand, the facilities possessed by each for certain kinds of production, will render exchange mutually advantageous; on the other hand, the citizen of each will, under the industrial *régime*, tolerate no such restraints on their individualities as are implied by interdicts on exchange or impediments to exchange.

With the spread of industrialism, therefore, the tendency is towards the breaking down of the divisions between nationalities, and the running through them of a common organization: if not under a single government, then under a federation of governments.[13]

Spencer's conviction that nations had grown large enough for all the refinements of organized society and that future wars were a bar to progress led him naturally to condemn modern imperialism. In his view imperialism no more fulfilled the hopes of its exponents than it conduced to progress. The voluntary federation of widely scattered areas was unobjectionable but impracticable. Dependent empires imposed financial burdens without producing equivalent returns. The colonists usually fared worse than the mother country, and the natives fared worst of all. The support of imperial troops encouraged colonists to be inefficient in the management of their own affairs and overbearing toward the natives. Colonization should be left to private enterprise.

"You shall submit. We are masters and we will make you acknowledge it!" . . . this sentiment it is which . . . pervades indefinitely the political feeling now manifesting itself as Imperialism. Supremacy, where not clearly imagined, is vaguely present in the background of consciousness. Not the derivation of the word only, but all its uses and associations, imply the thought of predominance—imply a correlative subordination. Actual or potential coercion of others, individuals or communities, is necessarily involved in the conception.

There are those, and unhappily they form the great majority, who think there is something noble (morally as well as historically) in the exercise of command—in the forcing of others to abandon their own

13. *Sociology*, 2, 614–15.

wills and fulfil the will of the commander. I am not about to contest this sentiment. I merely say that there are others, unhappily but few, who think it ignoble to bring their fellow creatures into subjection, and who think the noble thing is not only to respect their freedom but also to defend it. Leaving this matter undiscussed, my present purpose is to show those who lean towards Imperialism, that the exercise of mastery inevitably entails on the master himself some form of slavery, more or less pronounced. . . .

Here is a prisoner with hands tied and a cord round his neck (as suggested by figures in Assyrian bas-reliefs) being led home by his savage conqueror, who intends to make him a slave. The one, you say, is captive and the other free? Are you quite sure the other is free? He holds one end of the cord, and unless he means to let his captive escape, he must continue to be fastened by keeping hold of the cord in such way that it cannot easily be detached. He must be himself tied to the captive while the captive is tied to him. In other ways his activities are impeded and certain burdens are imposed on him. A wild animal crosses the track, and he cannot pursue. If he wishes to drink of the adjacent stream, he must tie up his captive lest advantage be taken of his defenceless position. Moreover he has to provide food for both. In various ways, then, he is no longer completely at liberty; and these ways adumbrate in a simple manner the universal truth that the instrumentalities by which the subordination of others is effected, themselves subordinate the victor, the master, or the ruler.[14]

While the mere propensity to thieve, commonly known under some grandiloquent alias, has been the real prompter of colonizing invasions, from those of Cortez and Pizarro downwards, the ostensible purpose of them has been either the spread of religion or the extension of commerce. In modern days the latter excuse has been the favourite one. To obtain more markets—this is what people have said aloud to each other, was the object aimed at. And, though second to the widening of empire, it has been to the compassing of this object that colonial legislation has been mainly directed. Let us consider the worth of such legislation. . . .

. . . Trade is a simple enough thing that will grow up wherever there is room for it. But, according to statesmen, it must be created by a gigantic and costly machinery. That trade only is advantageous to a country which brings in return for what is directly and indirectly given,

14. *Facts and Comments*, pp. 157–9.

a greater worth of commodities than could otherwise be obtained. But statesmen recognize no such limit to its benefits. Every new outlet for English goods, kept open at no matter what cost, they think valuable. Here is some scrubby little island, or wild territory—unhealthy, or barren, or inclement, or uninhabited even—which by right of discovery, conquest, or diplomatic manoeuvring, may be laid hands on. Possession is forthwith taken; a high-salaried governor is appointed; officials collect round him; then follow forts, garrisons, guardships. From these by-and-bye come quarrels with neighbouring peoples, incursions, war; and these again call for more defensive works, more force, more money. And to all protests against this reckless expenditure, the reply is— "Consider how it extends our commerce." . . .

But not only do we expend so much to gain so little, we absolutely expend it for nothing: nay, indeed, in some cases to achieve a loss. All profitable trade with colonies will come without the outlay of a penny for colonial administration—must flow to us naturally; and whatever trade will not flow to us naturally, is not profitable, but the reverse. . . .

Passing from home interests to colonial interests, we still meet nothing but evil results. It is a prettily sounding expression, that of mother-country protection, but a very delusive one. If we are to believe those who have known the thing rather than the name, there is but little of the maternal about it. . . .

Great, however, as are the evils entailed by government colonization upon both parent State and settlers, they look insignificant when compared with those it inflicts on the aborigines of the conquered countries. . . .

No one can fail to see that these cruelties, these treacheries, these deeds of blood and rapine, for which European nations in general have to blush, are mainly due to the carrying on of colonization under State-management, and with the help of State-funds and State-force. . . . A schoolboy made overbearing by the consciousness that there is always a big brother to take his part, typifies the colonist, who sees in his mother-country a bully ever ready to back and defend him. Unprotected emigrants, landing among a strange race and feeling themselves the weaker party, are tolerably certain to behave well; and a community of them is likely to grow up in amicable relationship with the natives. But let these emigrants be followed by regiments of soldiers —let them have a fort built and cannons mounted—let them feel that they have the upper hand; and they will no longer be the same men. . . .

As though to round off the argument, history gives proof that while Government-colonization is accompanied by endless miseries and abominations, colonization naturally carried on is free from these. To William Penn belongs the honour of having shown men that the kindness, justice and truth of its inhabitants, are better safeguards to a colony than troops and fortifications and the bravery of governors. In all points Pennsylvania illustrates the equitable, as contrasted with the inequitable, mode of colonizing. It was founded not by the State but by private individuals. It needed no mother-country protection, for it committed no breaches of the moral law.[15]

15. *Social Statics*, pp. 190–9.

18. ALFRED THAYER MAHAN

1840-1914

ALFRED THAYER MAHAN *was born at West Point. At the age of sixteen he joined the navy as an acting midshipman; his father thought this choice of career ill-advised—an opinion in which Mahan later concurred. His progress as a line officer was undistinguished. He saw service during the Civil War and rose slowly to the rank of Captain by 1885. He retired at that rank in 1896. It was his naval career, however, which gave him his start as a writer and publicist.*

While on a three-year cruise to Asia, Mahan began to read history. In 1884, when the Naval War College was founded, Mahan joined the staff, and two years later became its president. This experience lifted him out of the rut of naval routine and gave him an opportunity to apply his study of history. His lectures on sea power in history had a resounding and unexpected popularity, so much so that they were published with slight revision in 1890 under the title The Influence of Sea Power on History, 1660–1783. *Mahan was now eagerly devoted to writing and soon gained some energetic disciples in Theodore Roosevelt and Henry Cabot Lodge. This enthusiasm was not wholly shared by Mahan's naval superiors, however, and in 1893 despite much wire-pulling, Mahan was taken from his college post and placed in command of the U. S. S.* Chicago, *flagship in European waters.*

Strangely enough, this assignment gave Mahan the fame he had been denied in his own country. His works had made a great impression in Europe, especially in naval-minded Britain. Queen Victoria gave Mahan a reception and both Oxford and Cambridge conferred honor-

---

The editions are *Armaments and Arbitrations*, New York and London, Harper and Bros., 1911, copyright 1940, Lyle E. Mahan; *From Sail to Steam*, New York and London, Harper and Bros., 1907; *Lessons of the War with Spain*, Boston, Little Brown, and Co., 1898; *Retrospect and Prospect*, Boston, Little, Brown, and Co., 1902; *Some Neglected Aspects of War*, Boston, Little, Brown, and Co., 1907; *The Interest of America in International Conditions*, Boston, Little, Brown, and Co., 1910; *The Interest of America in Sea Power*, Boston, Little, Brown, and Co., 1898.

*ary degrees. These respects drew the attention of Americans and en-
sured him a wide audience in the future.*

*Mahan returned to the United States and in 1896 retired to devote
himself to writing. He continued to perform occasional services for the
government, notably on the Naval War Board in the war with Spain
and as American delegate to the First Hague Conference. In 1906 he
was promoted Rear-Admiral on the retired list.*

Before retiring, Mahan had added a Life of Nelson *and several magazine articles to his publications. In retirement he concentrated on
popular writings. As a publicist he ranged over a wide field, writing
over a hundred articles, nearly all of which were eventually welded into
books. In these articles he sought to arouse American interest in naval
affairs and international politics. He challenged isolationism and urged
America to take an active part in world affairs.*

*In his political writings he tried to apply the method he advocated
for strategical studies: "the examination of extant conditions, and the
appreciation of their probable and proper effect upon future events
and present action." ¹ His works blended an emphasis on force and
a strong moralism, reflecting his character as a devout Christian.*

*For Mahan international relations chiefly consisted of contentions
between independent nations. Common traditions and the concept of
a balance provided some sense of community between nations of European origin. But even this community was tenuous. On closer examination the balance proved to be a "coincident struggle toward preponderance" ² in which self-restraint played a minor part. Mahan repeatedly warned that America could no longer escape involvement
in this struggle.*

*As the trustees of their nations' welfare, governments rightly made
the national interest their first concern. It was, declared Mahan, "vain
to expect nations to act consistently from any other motive than that of
interest." ³ This zealous pursuit of self-interest brought nations into
frequent collision. For this reason "the study of interests, is the one
basis of sound and provident policy for statesmen." ⁴ The interests
which governed national conduct were mainly geographical and economic. These were the inelastic facts of foreign politics. But these facts
were also combined with moral and emotional forces which had a far*

1. From Sail to Steam, p. 324.
2. The Interest of America in International Conditions, p. 35.
3. Ibid., pp. 80–1.
4. Ibid., p. 81.

greater influence on immediate conduct. Therefore, although economic forces were dominant, actual international conflicts were usually touched off by emotional impulses.

. . . It is a mistake to argue that because nations and peoples are largely animated by self-interest, self-interest alone moves them; and it is a blunder to infer that there is inconsistency in maintaining the predominance of interested motive, and at the same time affirming the existence of other and competing impulses. Both classes exist. If there be inconsistency here, as is sometimes asserted, the inconsistency is not in the statement, but in the human nature concerning which the statement is made.[5]

. . . In long-settled countries race and territory tend to identity of meaning, but we need scarce a moment's recollection to know that race does not bind as do border lines, nor even they as do economical facts. . . . Race, yes; territory—country—yes; the heart thrills, the eyes fill, self-sacrifice seems natural, the moral motive for the moment prevails; but in the long run the hard pressure of economical truth comes down upon these with the tyranny of the despot. . . .

. . . We shall not see aright the political movement of the world at large, the course of history past and present, until we discern under-lying all, consciously, or blindly, these primitive physical necessities, directing the desires of the peoples, and through them the course of their governments. Rightly do we call them economical—household—for they come home to the many firesides whence their stern exactions have exiled politics and sentiment; and herein, in the weight of struggling numbers, lies the immensity of their strength. Race and country but furnish a means for organizing and fortifying their action, bringing to it the sanction and inspiration of the loftier motives embodied in these consecrated words. But these holy names, while facilitating and intensifying local action, by the same means separate nation from nation, setting up hearthstone against hearthstone. Hence implicit war is perennial; antagonism lurks beneath the most smiling surface and the most honest interchanges of national sympathies.[6]

. . . the inciting causes of war in our day are moral; a statement which includes of course immoral, as both adjectives though opposite in meaning, as are "good" and "bad," belong to the same category of motives. . . .

5. *Armaments and Arbitration*, pp. 108–9.
6. *Some Neglected Aspects of War*, pp. 78–80.

. . . Nations are under no illusion as to the unprofitableness of war in itself; but they recognize that different views of right and wrong in international transactions may provoke collision, against which the only safeguard is armament. Unarmed, or inadequately armed, the nation is exposed to the perils of commercial disintegration and consequent popular suffering . . .

. . . The two motives, moral and interested, will co-exist; but self-interest, even when recognized, does not possess the impelling power which is supplied by the sympathies, or by the sense of right and wrong. "Thrice is he armed who hath his quarrel *just.*" Self-interest is also less easily perceived by the mass, because its connection with a dispute is often indirect. Bismarck *may* have engineered the wars of his day with a sole view to the material interest of Germany, but the force behind him was the passions and enthusiasm of the people. . . . .

Argument must proceed necessarily upon the recognition . . . that with nations, as with men, absolute singleness of motive is rarely found. Mixed motive is the rule, not the exception. . . .

. . . To regard mankind, in individuals or in states, as so dominated by material self-interest that the appeal of other motives—ambition, self-respect, resentment of injustice, sympathy with the oppressed, hatred of oppression—is by it overbalanced and inoperative, is not only to misread history, but to ignore it. Almost every war of the past half-century contradicts the assertion. Nations will fight for such reasons more readily than for self-interest.

. . . That war between two great nations injures both, and that the injury is felt by the whole international community, has become a commonplace of modern political thought, testified almost yearly by the anxiety of governments to localize disputes by confining them within a given area. . . . But when the conclusion is pressed to the point of maintaining that a disproportion between the welfare of two states may not be produced by war, to the permanent advantage of one, so that it may even advance to a position of economic supremacy, the proposition appears contestable. I had occasion several years ago to look somewhat extensively into the economical and financial conditions of Great Britain toward the end of the Napoleonic wars. They were dismal; but it is true none the less that those of the Continent were so much worse that Great Britain owed the long start which she held and kept to this cause largely, though of course not solely. A single reason rarely accounts for all the phenomena of a social order.[7]

7. *Armaments,* pp. 126–32.

The period in which Mahan wrote was the heyday of those who ad-
vocated compulsory arbitration as the proper means of settling those
conflicts which he believed to be an inevitable feature of international
relations. Mahan emphatically opposed this notion. He conceded that
nations might occasionally submit specific disputes to arbitration but
denied they could successfully make general undertakings to do so.
Arbitration confined to the application of existing law would be hope-
lessly rigid, for the law frequently contravened the clear demands of
equity. To allow arbitration to change the law would throw into ques-
tion infinite matters on which nations could allow no debate. Even
in cases where there was applicable law, each party to the dispute fre-
quently believed itself to be in the right and no nation could agree
to subordinate its conscience to the judgment of arbitrators. In other
instances there was frequently no real question of right at all but
merely conflicting claims capable of resolution only by force.

Throughout all the agitations and governmental movements [in international politics] there is to be discerned ultimately a simple contest of forces, determined by considerations of conflicting national interests. Whether regulated by diplomacy, or brought to the arbitrament
of war, whether between two communities, or between groups of states,
it is power arrayed against power; power not in the sense of physical
force only, but in a wide estimate of the advantages and disadvantages
attendant upon the course of action. In place of such balance of power,
which suggests necessarily two opposite scales, that is, an equilibrium
dependent on essential antagonism, and therefore liable to frequent
fluctuations, the last century witnessed the growth of the idea of
concert, whereby all or some of the great states, with other communities immediately affected, act together, in accord, for the solution of
questions upon a basis of right, or of compromise, which when reached
has the binding force of a contract. All general treaties, in a congress
of nations, partake of this character; but the present conception of "concert" applies the method of general consultation and arrangement,
whether by correspondence or by congress, to particular settlements,
of matters minor but important. . . . In such cases the result reached
represents, in form at least, agreement, not a balance of antagonisms.

In endeavoring to put aside force, substituting for it reason and
mutual concession, this resort is in idea cognate to arbitration, as balance of power is to forcible settlement. Unhappily, such agreements in
form represent also, too often a mere resultant of forces, and are liable

to disturbance as the forces vary. . . . When such an outcome is reached, the last state is worse than the first. The antagonism of forces revives, intensified by the evidence that a formal concert is liable to be cast aside, at the arbitrary decision of one of the parties, whenever convenience or imagined necessity occurs. Mutual confidence has been shaken, if not destroyed.

Whether inevitable or not, such a result illustrates that the states of the world are not yet in a condition to dispense with the institution of organized force. There are contentions which a state will not submit to either the deliberation of a concert or the adjudication of a tribunal; in which its action is maintained, or is checked, as the case may be, only by force.[8]

. . . To be consistent—perhaps not the highest of qualities—arbitration should undertake not merely to settle disputes which directly threaten war, but also to rectify the concrete inequalities, deriving from existing law of prescription, which place nations on different planes of advantage, and thus constitute the jealousies and antagonisms in which wars find their origin; just as social inequalities are provoking a demand for state regulation as against individual possession or achievement. . . .

Is the arbitration tribunal which the nations have set up to become thus a central power resembling a national government clothed with executive authority—with power such as a civil court now has to enforce its mandates? Or will it continue, as at present, limited to purely judicial functions? Can it remain simply a court of appeal? Or will it become one of, so to say, original jurisdiction, passing upon cases without previous reference to diplomacy? Must both, or all, the states interested in a particular dispute always agree to arbitrate, before the cause can be brought before the tribunal? Or will it become possible for a single state which feels itself aggrieved to obtain a decision at the mouth of the court upon the merits of the case? Probably, so long as the necessity for concurrent agreement holds, the dangers of war will incline states of nearly equal strength to seek arbitration; but where there is great disparity may not the weaker still go to the wall?

. . . A scheme of arbitration which cannot work in such cases is so ignobly defective that the disposition must be for very shame to seek to remedy the defect; to enable the court to intervene on the presentation of the case by one party. It is well to note the defect, because the

8. *International Conditions*, pp. 89–94.

remedy, if applied, will bring into litigation a great part of the existing political status of the planet, which rests, and in my judgment rests beneficially, upon force. Doubtless, the defects of a scheme must not induce forgetfulness of its good points, but the tendency indicated is one that requires watching.

Again . . . it is evident that the inducing motive in arbitration schemes, as at present propounded, is not love of right and of essential justice, but the wish to escape the material damage of war. It will not be questioned that the avoidance of the evils of war is a great and worthy object; but in the present desire to reach that end by the institution of a superior authority over the nations of the world, instead of by diplomatic processes, it is well that nations realize whither they are moving and count the cost not merely to themselves individually, but to the community of states at large. It will not be possible to stop on this incline at any such purely artificial landing as that of mutual consent or prescriptive rights. If mutual consent be of the essence of arbitration, it is an avowal that force remains the determining factor. For the state that possesses markedly superior organized force may consent to arbitrate, but it will remain the judge in its own case as to whether it will do so or not.

In brief, the question between armaments and arbitration in the present stage of the development of the world is that between reaching an ultimate equilibrium by the play of natural forces, of which armaments are the ultimate expression, or by an artificial method based upon law and equity, or custom, which often will have ceased to be applicable. . . .

It is evident that Arbitration and Force represent diametrically opposed ideas. It does not follow, however, that they are mutually destructive, any more than are centripetal and centrifugal. The opposition may result in the ultimate disappearance of armed forces, as an element of international relations; but force, the organized force of the community as the means of assuring its will, is and must remain the basis of social order so long as evil exists to be repressed. . . .

. . . In the writer's appreciation, armament represents the aggregation of the natural forces inherent in any community. This is especially true to-day, because in the strong rivalry and oppositions internal to the system of European civilization the armaments are a gage of the capacities of the people not only to do, in all the phases of national activity, but to bear—a no less important element of national power. Arbitration on the other hand, connotes law as its ultimate expression; for, although it often deals merely with facts, as a jury does, its decision has the force of law, while in many cases the decision itself must depend upon points of law. There is an element of truth in the phrase, "Law instead of War"; for this is the antithesis between arbitration and armament. The trouble with law is that, being artificial and often of long date, it frequently is inapplicable to a present dispute; that is, its decision is incompatible with existing conditions, although it may rest on grounds legally unimpeachable. The settlement, therefore, is insecure, its foundations are not solid; whereas in the long run the play of natural forces reaches an adjustment corresponding to the fundamental facts of the case.[9]

Mahan's belief that war is a necessary means of settling international disputes impelled him to an elaborate effort to prove that war could be morally justified and in particular that it could be reconciled to Christian ethics. Though he occasionally deplored the need for war and professed a hope for its ultimate abolition, his hopes were always qualified and remote.

Part of Mahan's faith in the coincidence of victory and justice stemmed from the conviction that military power reflected "national efficiency." This led him very close to the position that might makes right, a thesis he explicitly repudiated. Also closely related was his somewhat unusual argument that in a dispute the larger nation was equivalent to a democratic majority: "In the questions of great import to nations or to the world, the wishes, or interests, or technical rights of minorities must yield, and there is not necessarily any more injustice in this than in their yielding to a majority at the polls."[10]

. . . At a recent gathering an eminent American has said that war decides only which nation is the stronger. If by this was meant, as probably was, that war is not a moral arbiter, does not settle an ethical question, it is incontestable. We should have long outlived the idea underlying the ordeal of battle, that war is an appeal to the God of Hosts to judge a quarrel. We retain the expression, perhaps; but it is an archaic poeticism, better abandoned because misleading. War now is, and historically long has been, waged on a basis of asserted right or need; and what it does help to determine is that which is known in physics as the resultant of forces, of which itself is one; the others being the economical and political necessities or desires of the con-

9. *Armaments*, pp. 5–12.
10. *Interest of America in Sea Power*, p. 144.

tending parties. The other forces exist, aggressive, persistent; unless controlled by the particular force we call war, *in posse* or *in esse*, they reach a solution which is just as really one of force, and may be as unrighteous, and more so, than any war. . . . This is actually the state of the world at the present moment; and while a better balance-wheel than war may be conceived, it is at present doing its work fairly well. . . .[11]

. . . Dynastic wars, wars of conquest, wars clearly unrighteous, with these I have nothing to do. I affirm merely the general proposition: that in the present imperfect and frequently wicked state of mankind, evil easily may, and often does, reach a point where it must be controlled perhaps even destroyed, by physical force; and if the evil-doer has the means to resist, and does resist, by force, the obligation to destroy the evil, and the evil-doer, if need be, still exists. The result then is War.

. . . I affirm that War, under conditions that may and do arise, is righteous; and, further, that under such conditions it is distinctly an *unrighteous* deed to refrain from forcibly redressing evil, when it is in the power of thine hand to do so.

On the other hand, to clear the ground of bootless discussion, I admit willingly that War is—not evil—but *an* evil; a very different thing. Amputation is an evil, but it is not evil. I admit that, were the universal world living a life of Christian perfection, War would be unnecessary and wrong; and, finally, as the world is doubtless progressing, I gladly concede the duty of minimizing the frequency of War. . . . .

I have affirmed that under some conditions it is unrighteous not to use force to the extent of War. It will be asked, What conditions—from the Christian standpoint? In reply, I apply St. Paul's words: "Whatsoever is not of faith—of conviction—is sin." For the nation, as for the individual, conscience must be the judge; nor, in my judgment, is the national conscience justified in turning a case over to arbitration until it is satisfied that the matter is such that the decision either way will not violate its conscientious conviction of right.[12]

Believing war to be an indispensable instrument of national policy, Mahan was naturally a supporter of preparedness. He did not believe that armaments increased the chances of war. On the contrary, the ability to fight acted as a deterrent to other states.

11. *Aspects of War,* pp. 86–7.
12. *Ibid.,* pp. 98-102.

The extent of a nation's defense measures should be determined by its national interests. It was therefore essential that statesmen and even the public keep this relationship in mind. In particular, Mahan insisted that military policy must be subservient to political interests.

. . . the possession and exertion of organized force do not necessarily mean war. Such force may exert, and often does exert, its full proportional effect without striking a blow; and the more indisputably effective it is, the surer and more peaceful the result. It may be righteously used, or it may not be; but the organization and possession of it do not necessarily mean even an inclination to war, nor does its absence constitute a guarantee of peace. The War of Secession in the United States is an instance in point. No belligerents in modern times have been more utterly unprepared for war, in any ordinary sense of preparation, than were the two parties to that conflict. Yet they fought, the most prolonged war since Waterloo; prolonged just because the absence of preparation on either side constituted for the moment an equality, which, however destined ultimately to disappear before the greater resources of the North, permitted the South—justly from a military point of view—to hope that she could achieve separation through the failure of perseverance, of staying power, in her adversary.

. . . that security which organized force gives, even when ultimately inferior. . . . not only imposes respectful consideration beforehand, disinclining the adversary to a rupture for less than imperative reasons; it also, in case of hostilities, obtains delay, allowing time for skill, or for the chapter of accidents, to reverse conditions.[13]

To provide a force adequate to maintain the nation's cause, and to insure its readiness for immediate action in case of necessity, are the responsibility of the government of a state in its legislative and executive functions. Such a force is a necessary outcome of the political conditions which affect, or, as can be foreseen, probably may affect, the international relations of the country. Its existence at all and its size are, or should be, the reflection of the national consciousness that in this, that, or the other direction lie clear national interests—for which each generation is responsible to futurity—or national duties, equally clear from the mere fact that the matter lies at the door, like Lazarus at the rich man's gate. The question of when or how action shall be taken which may result in hostilities, is indeed a momentous one, having regard to the dire evils of war; but it is the question of a moment,

13. *International Conditions,* pp. 156–8.

of the last moment to which can be postponed a final determination of such tremendous consequence. To this determination preparation for war has only this relation: that it should be adequate to the utmost demand that then can be made upon it, and, if possible, so imposing that it will prevent war ensuing, upon the firm presentation of demands which the nation believes to be just. Such a conception, so stated implies no more than defence,—defence of the nation's rights or of the nation's duties, although such defence may take the shape of aggressive action, the only safe course in war.

Logically, therefore, a nation which proposes to provide itself with a naval or military organization adequate to its needs, must begin by considering, not what is the largest army or navy in the world, with the view of rivalling it, but what there is in the political status of the world, including not only the material interests but the temper of nations, which involves a reasonable, even though remote, prospect of difficulties which may prove insoluble except by war. The matter, primarily, is political in character. It is not until this political determination has been reached that the data for even stating the military problem are in hand; for here, as always, the military arm waits upon and is subservient to the political interests and civil power of the state.

It is not the most probable of dangers, but the most formidable, that must be selected as measuring the degree of military precaution to be embodied in the military preparations thenceforth to be maintained. The lesser is contained in the greater; if equal to the most that can be apprehended reasonably, the country can view with quiet eye the existence of more imminent, but less dangerous complications. Nor should it be denied that in estimating danger there should be a certain sobriety of imagination, equally removed from undue confidence and from exaggerated fears. . . . When British writers, realizing the absolute dependence of their own country upon the sea, insist that the British navy must exceed the two most formidable of its possible opponents, they advance an argument which is worthy at least of serious debate; but when the two is raised to three, they assume conditions which are barely possible, but lie too far without the limits of probability to affect practical action.[14]

Mahan asserted that the domination of civilized nations over backward races was fully justified: "there is no inalienable right in any community to control the use of a region when it does so to the detri-

14. *Sea Power,* pp. 178–81.

ment of the world at large." [15] *He insisted, however, that imperial nations had a sacred duty to their subject populations: "where the relations
are those of trustee to ward, as are those of every state which rules
over a weaker community not admitted to the full privileges of home
citizenship, the first test to which measures must be brought is the
good of the ward."* [16] *Colonialism further recommended itself to Mahan
as a means of gaining time for white peoples to educate the colored
for peaceful admission to the world community before the onset of
the struggle which he feared was impending between Asia and the
West.*

. . . we stand at the opening of a period when the question is to
be settled decisively, though the issue may be long delayed, whether
Eastern or Western civilization is to dominate throughout the earth
and to control its future. The great task now before the world of
civilized Christianity, its great mission, which it must fulfil or perish,
is to receive into its own bosom and raise to its own ideals those ancient
and different civilizations by which it is surrounded and outnum-
bered,—the civilizations at the head of which stand China, India, and
Japan. . . .

. . . Time and staying power must be secured for ourselves by that
rude and imperfect, but not ignoble, arbiter, force—force potential
and force organized—which so far has won, and still secures, the greatest triumphs of good in the checkered history of mankind. Our material advantages, once noted, will be recognized readily and appropriated with avidity; while the spiritual ideas which dominate our
thoughts, and are weighty in their influence over action, even with
those among us who do not accept historic Christianity or the ordinary
creeds of Christendom, will be rejected for long. The eternal law, first
that which is natural, afterwards that which is spiritual, will obtain
here, as in the individual, and in the long history of our own civilization. Between the two there is an interval, in which force must be ready
to redress any threatened disturbance of an equal balance between
those who stand on divergent planes of thought, without common
standards.[17]

. . . The commerce of our day has brought up children, nourished
populations, which now turn upon the mother, crying for bread. "The

15. *Ibid.*, p. 167.
16. *Lessons of the War with Spain*, p. 246.
17. *Sea Power*, pp. 243–5.

place is too strait for us; give place where we can sell more." The provision of markets for the production of an ever-increasing number
of inhabitants is a leading political problem of the day, the solution of
which is sought by methods commercial and methods political, so essentially combative, so offensive and defensive in character, that direct
military action would be only a development of them, a direct consequent; not a breach of continuity in spirit, however it might be in form.
As the interaction of commerce and finance shows a unity in the modern civilized world, so does the struggle for new markets, and for predominance in old, reveal the unsubdued diversity. Here every state
is for itself; and in every great state the look for the desired object is
outward . . . Beyond the seas, now as then, are to be found regions
scantily populated where can be built up communities with wants to
be supplied; while elsewhere are teeming populations who may be
led or manipulated to recognize necessities of which they have before been ignorant, and stimulated to provide for them through a higher
development of their resources, either by themselves, or, preferably,
through the exploitation of foreigners.

We are yet but at the beginning of this marked movement, much as has
been done in the way of partition and appropriation within the last
twenty years. The regions—chiefly in Africa—which the Powers of Europe have divided by mutual consent, if not to mutual satisfaction, await
the gradual process of utilization of their natural resources and consequent increase of inhabitants, the producers and consumers of a commerce yet to be in the distant future. The degree and rate of this development must depend upon the special aptitudes of the self-constituted
owners, whose needs meantime are immediate. Their eyes therefore
turn necessarily for the moment to quarters where the presence of a
population already abundant provides at once, not only numerous
buyers and sellers, but the raw material of labor, by which, under suitable direction and with foreign capital, the present production may be
multiplied. It is not too much to say that, in order further to promote
this commercial action, existing political tenure is being assailed; that
the endeavor is to supplant it, as hindering the commercial, or possibly
the purely military or political ambitions of the intruder. Commercial
enterprise is never so secure, nor so untrammelled, as under its own
flag; and when the present owner is obstructive by temperament, as
China is, the impulse to overbear its political action by display of
force tends to become ungovernable. At all events the fact is notorious;
nor can it be seriously doubted that in several other parts of the globe

aggression is only deterred by the avowed or understood policy of a powerful opponent, not by the strength of the present possessor. . . .

It seems demonstrable, therefore, that as commerce is the engrossing and predominant interest of the world today, so, in consequence of its acquired expansion, oversea commerce, oversea political acquisition, and maritime commercial routes are now the primary objects of external policy among nations.[18]

. . . the annexation, even, of Hawaii would be no mere sporadic effort, irrational because disconnected from an adequate motive, but a first-fruit and a token that the nation in its evolution has aroused itself to the necessity of carrying its life—that has been the happiness of those under its influence—beyond the borders which heretofore have sufficed for its activities. That the vaunted blessings of our economy are not to be forced upon the unwilling may be conceded; but the concession does not deny the right nor the wisdom of gathering in those who wish to come. Comparative religion teaches that creeds which reject missionary enterprise are foredoomed to decay. May it not be so with nations? Certainly the glorious record of England is consequent mainly upon the spirit, and traceable to the time, when she launched out into the deep—without formulated policy, it is true, or foreseeing the future to which her star was leading, but obeying the instinct which in the infancy of nations anticipates the more reasoned impulses of experience. Let us, too, learn from her experience. Not all at once did England become the great sea power which she is, but step by step, as opportunity offered, she has moved on to the world-wide pre-eminence now held by English speech, and by institutions sprung from English germs. How much poorer would the world have been, had Englishmen heeded the cautious hesitancy that now bids us reject every advance beyond our shore-lines! And can any one doubt that a cordial, if unformulated, understanding between the two chief states of English tradition, to spread freely, without mutual jealousy and in mutual support, would increase greatly the world's sum of happiness?

But if a plea of the world's welfare seem suspiciously like a cloak for national self-interest, let the latter be accepted frankly as the adequate motive which it assuredly is. Let us not shrink from pitting a broad self-interest against the narrow self-interest to which some would restrict us.[19]

18. *Retrospect and Prospect*, pp. 146–9.
19. *Sea Power*, pp. 49–51.

19. JOHN ATKINSON HOBSON

1858-1940

HOBSON's *career was that of a writer and teacher. He was at various times a schoolmaster and a lecturer in university extramural programs but his main energies were devoted to producing thirty-five books, in addition to numerous pamphlets and articles. These writings dealt chiefly with various aspects of economics. Hobson had a broad, humanist approach to economics. He wrote as a sociologist rather than an economic theorist and he refused to recognize any divorce between economics and politics. Even his theoretical researches were stimulated by social problems, for which he strove to present practicable remedies.*

Hobson's studies led him to many criticisms of existing capitalism. In the course of this work he broke much new theoretical ground. His most distinctive contribution was the theory of underconsumption, which he first presented in a collaborative work of 1889 entitled The Physiology of Industry. *He never condemned the capitalist system itself but took a middle ground between the old individualist economics and the rising collectivism. Nevertheless his political views and his unorthodox theories engendered some suspicion in established academic circles: despite his publications and growing reputation he was never offered a post at a British university, and London University even refused to allow him to participate in their extramural program. As the twentieth century progressed, however, his work gained increasing recognition, and the new "depression economics" of the thirties did much to lend credence to the theory of underconsumption. Hobson lived to receive a generous acknowledgement of debt from that most eminent of "new economists," Lord Keynes.*

A large part of Hobson's attention was devoted to international relations. He was a founder of the Union of Democratic Control and a member of the Bryce Committee to study a league of nations; but it is for his

Editions used: *Imperialism*, London, George Allen and Unwin, Ltd., and New York, The Macmillan Co., 1938; *The Open Door*, The Hague, Martinus Nijhoff, 1916.

study of imperialism that he is most famous and best remembered. So influential was this analysis of imperialism that the following readings are confined to that subject, excluding his other competent but not unusually distinguished writings on international affairs.

Hobson considered that the dominating characteristic of contemporary international relations was the existence of several competing imperialisms. The ambitions and fears of imperialist nations were accompanied by mutual suspicion, by arms races, and all too often by war. He believed that the driving force behind this imperialism was a quest for markets and investment opportunities. This search took the form of acquiring exclusive political control of territory as an answer to rampant protectionism stemming from the same preoccupation with markets. The truly novel feature of Hobson's analysis was his theory that the fundamental cause of the search for markets and openings for investment was chronic underconsumption in modern industrial economies, resulting in the excess accumulation of capital.

The book Imperialism *is the most complete presentation of Hobson's theories. It is a large volume, liberally illustrated with statistics, and does not lend itself to easy condensation. Moreover, Hobson lived to revise the book as recently as 1938, and it would seem unwise to neglect his maturer reflections. Fortunately, in issuing the 1938 edition he summarized his argument and his modifications in a preface. The following two extracts are a shortened version of that preface.*

. . . it may be convenient here to rehearse in bare terms the main argument of this book, and then to discuss such changes and modifications of the earlier argument as the current of recent history appears to demand.

That argument was to the effect that whereas various real and powerful motives of pride, prestige and pugnacity, together with the more altruistic professions of a civilising mission, figured as causes of imperial expansion, the dominant directive motive was the demand for markets and for profitable investment by the exporting and financial classes within each imperialist regime. The urgency of this economic demand was attributed to the growing tendency of industrial productivity, under the new capitalist technique of machinery and power, to exceed the effective demand of the national markets, the rate of production to outrun the rate of home consumption. This was not, of course the whole story. The rising productivity of industry required larger imports of some forms of raw materials, more imported foods for larger urban populations, and a great variety of imported consumption goods for a rising standard of living. These imports could only be purchased by a corresponding expansion of exports, or else by the incomes derived from foreign investments which implied earlier exports of capital goods.

But with these qualifications in mind, it is nevertheless true that the most potent drive towards enlarged export trade was the excess of capitalist production over the demands of the home market. Now, since it is manifest that everything that is produced belongs to someone connected with its production, who can either consume it or exchange it for some other consumable goods, it seems at first sight unreasonable to expect that an excess of goods requires a foreign market, unless some error has taken place in the apportionment of producing power as between the different industries. But when we find that at frequent intervals there is a general excess of production beyond the current demands of the home and foreign markets, it becomes manifest that the productive power of capital has been excessively fed. This in its turn means that the processes of saving and investment have proceeded too rapidly. In other words, there has been over-saving and under-spending. For while a certain and a growing quantity of saving and production of more and better capital goods belongs to every progressive national economy, there exists at any given time, having regard to the arts of industry, on the one hand, and the arts of consumption, on the other, a right balance or equilibrium between spending and saving. . . .

Now this argument signifies that the constant impulse to push for overseas markets in normal times and the periodic slumps of national trade in the home markets, are due to a chronic tendency to try to save a larger proportion of the national income than can find a useful expression in new capital. This is not due to the folly of individual savers, but to a distribution of the general income which puts too small a share in the hands of the working-classes, too large a share in the hands of the employing and owning classes. For it is to the latter that over-saving is attributable.

Now we are not here concerned with the important problems of equity and humanity involved in a maldistribution of income which places the vast bulk of purchasing power beyond the requirements of a bare living in the possession of a small proportion of the population in Great Britain, the United States and other advanced industrial countries. Our concern here is with the urgent drive this situation impels towards the acquisition of foreign markets and areas of lucrative overseas investment. Here we are confronted with the question to what extent this need for increased foreign markets and investment is a true cause of Imperialism. Now it may be admitted at the outset of any discussion of this question that other motives than trade-profits consciously occupy the mind of the statesmen who pursue an imperial policy, and that the term Empire does not connote commercial gain to the mind of the rank and file of imperialists. Power, pride, prestige are prevailing sentiments in an imperialist policy. Territorial expansion, the control over backward peoples, the mission of civilisation, the safe-guarding of existing colonial possessions, are not indeed dissociated from the belief that "trade follows the flag" and that by helping to establish order and develop the resources of the peoples and countries which come under our rule, we shall increase our trade and enlarge our national income. Indeed, the history of our empire, acquired, as Sir John Seeley once stated, "in a fit of absence of mind," attests clearly enough the confused sentiments and the opportunism which underlie the process of acquisition. But, when we study the particulars of the process, we recognise that "mind" in the sense of conscious motive was not entirely absent, and that trade played an important part in most of the early acquisitions. For though it is true that we do not need to own a country in order to trade with its people, the establishment of permanent trading arrangements with primitive or backward peoples generally involves some territorial holding which is likely to expand with the expanding importance of that trade. . . . If several advanced countries engage upon the same process, as in India, collisions of interest, partly political, partly commercial, are likely to arise in which the competing groups enlist native forces in their cause, and conduct a conflict which leads to the supremacy of that commercial group which can rally to its profitable cause the largest governmental and native support. It is a confused procedure widely differing in the older and populous civilisations of Asia and the more primitive and thinly peopled areas of Africa and North America. But, in nearly all cases where white peoples have brought under their sway lands peopled by coloured races, the earliest contacts have been of a commercial nature, and though considerations of political acquisition, colonial settlement and missionary services have been conscious supports, economic motives of trade and the exploitation of natural resources have been the dominant urges. Nor has this aggressive Imperialism been confined to the acquisition of backward countries. When this book was written the conquest of the Boer Republics and the incorporation of those territories in our South African Dominion furnished the latest and most striking example of the imperialist process. Here the directly economic factor was paramount over all the political and humanitarian considerations invoked to justify the forceful seizure. The mine-owners of the Transvaal had a definite interest in transferring the country from Boer to British rule, and the press and other political propaganda which secured this end were owned or controlled by these financial and industrial groups.

It will be said by those who controvert this economic causation of Imperialism that the Boer War was an exceptional case, and that the causation of the Great War lay outside the economic purview. It was power politics, not profit politics. But I am not here arguing the case for an exclusively or even a mainly economic causation of modern Wars. It is not yet clear how far and in what sense the enlargement of national territory or external control underlay the policy of Germany, Russia, or France, in loosing the forces of war. Still less is it reasonable to suppose that calculations of economic gains resulting from territorial changes governed the minds of the statesmen who were responsible for their country entering the war. But in the Peace arrangements the insane mentality of Versailles carried various illusions of an economic character. That annexation was profitable to the annexing country, that the extortion of huge reparation payments was possible and advantageous to the recipients, that national economic self-sufficiency, aided by tariffs and embargoes, was not only strategically but economically gainful—these and other related fallacies flowed from the heated atmosphere of a poisoned nationalism. Nor can it be held that the experience of the post-war period has altogether exploded these fallacies, and that we now know that territorial expansion does not increase the trade gains and the average wealth of the people of the imperialist power.

. . . under the urge of nationalist sentiment, supported by appeals to self-sufficiency for purposes of defence, most nations conserve their own markets for their own producers, or for producers in their colonies or allied countries. For in almost all branches of production, agricultural, mining, manufacturing, the technical advances have been so great that each country is afraid of being flooded by foreign goods in its own markets and of being excluded from foreign markets for the sale of its own export goods. It is idle to urge that such fears and the policies of restriction and aggression which they stimulate are unreasonable, and that the removal of all barriers to international trade and migration would at once assuage hostilities and restore prosperity. Those who hold this view either assume and assert that the political sentiments of nationalism are the real sources of the economic policy they hold to be irrational, or else that certain monetary disturbances are responsible for the unemployment, closing of markets and other interferences with the natural forces of free exchange. In fact we are confronted with three sorts of foolishness . . . political illusions . . . the financial fears and mistrusts which prevent sane monetary arrangements for internal and external marketing, and the tragic absurdity summarised as "poverty in plenty," the refusal to make full use of existing or attainable productive resources. It is the contest for priority in these three fields of causation that here concerns us. For each of them evidently figures in the process of imperialism. It may well be admitted that each disturbing factor has its own illusions and its own sentimental urges.[1]

Hobson conceded that the mere acquisition of territory made a strong emotional appeal to human nature. But he argued that these emotions were sustained and directed by economic motives stemming from maladjustments in the modern productive process. Certain economic interests called upon the state to provide exclusive markets for trade and investment. It was far from certain that capitalism as a whole benefited from these policies, but certain capitalists reaped handsome profits, for whereas the costs were borne by the nation, the returns were enjoyed by a select few.

. . . The distinctively political passion for greatness of territory acquired by a strong right hand is a manifestly potent driving force in all imperialisms though it is not always openly avowed. To extend the area of national ownership by seizure of neighbouring land or of distant colonies has a sentimental appeal which cannot be dispelled by citing the human or financial costs and risks of such virile procedure. The sort of patriotism that can be evoked in Italy, Germany or Japan for such aggression does not really proceed from the economic necessities cited in its defence. It is rooted in some ineradicable pugnacity and predacity of the animal man, intensified by herd appeals that repress any doubts or qualms of reason and humanity. But, though this patriotism has its own basic instinctive origins, it is fed and directed in its activities by economic motives. Are these economic motives equally irrational and based on miscalculations of business interests?

My contention is that the system prevailing in all developed countries for the production and distribution of wealth has reached a stage

1. *Imperialism*, pp. v–xii.

in which its productive powers are held in leash by its inequalities of distribution; the excessive share that goes to profits, rents and other surpluses impelling a chronic endeavour to oversave in the sense of trying to provide an increased productive power without a corresponding outlet in the purchase of consumable goods. This drive towards oversaving is gradually checked by the inability of such saving to find any profitable use in the provision of more plant and other capital. But it also seeks to utilise political power for outlets in external markets, and as foreign independent markets are closed or restricted, the drive to the acquisition of colonies, protectorates and other areas of imperial development becomes a more urgent and conscious national policy. If this reasoning is correct, capitalism to maintain its profitable character, by utilising its new productive powers as fully as possible, is impelled to seek the help of the State in the various ways that are now so much in evidence, tariffs, embargoes, subsidies, and the acquisition or retention of colonies where the home capitalist can have advantages both for his import and export trade, with such securities in monetary matters as can be provided by imperial control.

In such a policy the trades directly or indirectly connected with the production of armaments have a twofold function. On the one hand, they batten upon the public expenditure needed to sustain a spirited foreign policy. On the other hand, they evoke a corresponding "defensive" policy in other countries to which they contribute by profitable supplies of arms and ammunition—thus producing a growing competition in costs of "defence." . . .

But though it is incontestable that the armaments trades are naturally disposed to an international competition in the instruments of war which is itself provocative of war, it is often contended that actual war is detrimental to their interests, as it is to Capitalism in general. . . .

Now, though war, with its revolutionary aftermath, may well seem dangerous to the capitalist system, it is open to argument whether such risks may not appear worth running in view of the alternative piling up of unsaleable surpluses which the extension and improved methods of modern capitalism involve. . . .

But in arguing the case for maldistribution as the main cause of Imperialism and of the wars which accompany that policy, it is not necessary to contend that capitalism as "an economic system" benefits by war, but only that certain sections of capitalism with political influence at their disposal favour pushful foreign policies that involve the risk of war. This applies not merely to the armaments industries but to most other industries dependent largely upon export and import trades. . . . .

. . . While therefore . . . capitalism as a whole system and in the long run [may be] weakened and imperilled by such operations, it must be borne in mind that capitalism does not work as a single profitable system, and that capitalists often prefer a short to a long run in the pursuit of profit. . . .

. . . analysis of the various attempts to escape from the perils of excessive productivity shows that they fall under three heads. One consists in the policy of organized labour and the State, aiming to secure a more equal and equitable distribution of the money and real income of the community, by higher wages, shorter hours and other betterment of working and living conditions. The second consists in the business policy of restricted output . . . involving a close financial control of the major businesses in specified national or international industries, accompanied by a regulation of their markets and, when deemed desirable, by quotas and tariffs. The third method, and that most relevant to our present subject of Imperialism, is the combined or separate action of capital to obtain the help, financial, diplomatic, military, of the national government so as to secure preferential access to foreign markets and foreign areas of development by colonies, protectorates, spheres of preferential trade and other methods of a pushful economic foreign policy. It may be true that the people of the imperialist state are in the long, or even the short run losers by a policy so costly in money and in lives. But if, as is normally the case, the larger part of this expense falls upon the public as a whole, it may still be advantageous to those capitalist interests engaged in foreign trade and investments to promote a policy that is to their profit.[2]

The imperialism described by Hobson was, he asserted, the chief cause of international conflict and violence. Rivalries between certain dominant capitalists obscured the fact that the interests of the peoples of the world were compatible. Nations were deluded into preferring policies of expansion to the development and equitable distribution of their own resources. Hobson thought the expansionist urge could only be checked internally, by reforming the economic system which endowed a class with an interest in international friction or in policies leading to friction.

The contention of the *si pacem vis para bellum* school, that armaments alone constitute the best security for peace, is based upon the

2. *Ibid.*, pp. xii–xx.

assumption that a genuine lasting antagonism of real interests exists between the various peoples who are called upon to undergo this monstrous sacrifice.

Our economic analysis has disclosed the fact that it is only the interests of competing cliques of business men—investors, contractors, export manufacturers, and certain professional classes—that are antagonistic; that these cliques, usurping the authority and voice of the people, use the public resources to push their private interests, and spend the blood and money of the people in this vast and disastrous military game, feigning national antagonisms which have no basis in reality. . . .

War, however, represents not the success, but the failure of this policy; its normal and most perilous fruit is not war, but militarism. So long as this competitive expansion for territory and foreign markets is permitted to misrepresent itself as "national policy" the antagonism of interests seems real, and the people must sweat and bleed and toil to keep up an ever more expensive machinery of war.

Were logic applicable in such cases, the notion that the greater the preparation for war the smaller the probability of its occurrence might well appear a *reductio ad absurdum* of militarism, implying, as it does, that the only way to secure an eternal world peace is to concentrate the entire energy of all nations upon the art of war, which is thus rendered incapable of practice.

With such paradoxes, however, we need not concern ourselves. The patent admitted fact that, as a result of imperial competition, an ever larger proportion of the time, energy, and money of "imperialist" nations is absorbed by naval and military armaments, and that no check upon further absorption is regarded as practicable by Imperialists, brings "militarism" into the forefront of practical politics. . . . It is our mistaken annexation of tropical and sub-tropical territories, and the attempt to govern "lower races," that is driving us down the steep road to militarism.

If we are to hold all that we have taken since 1870 and to compete with the new industrial nations in the further partition of empires or spheres of influence in Africa and Asia, we must be prepared to fight. The enmity of rival empires, openly displayed throughout the South African war, is admittedly due to the policy by which we have forestalled, and are still seeking to forestall, these rivals in the annexation of territory and of markets throughout the world.[3]

3. *Ibid.*, pp. 127–9.

Everywhere the issue of quantitative *versus* qualitative growth comes up. This is the entire issue of empire. A people limited in number and energy and in the land they occupy have the choice of improving to the utmost the political and economic management of their own land, confining themselves to such accessions of territory as are justified by the most economical disposition of a growing population; or they may proceed, like the slovenly farmer, to spread their power and energy over the whole earth, tempted by the speculative value or the quick profits of some new market, or else by mere greed of territorial acquisition, and ignoring the political and economic wastes and risks involved by this imperial career. It must be clearly understood that this is essentially a choice of alternatives; a full simultaneous application of intensive and extensive cultivation is impossible. A nation may either, following the example of Denmark or Switzerland, put brains into agriculture, develop a finely varied system of public education, general and technical, apply the ripest science to its special manufacturing industries, and so support in progressive comfort and character a considerable population upon a strictly limited area; or it may, like Great Britain, neglect its agriculture, allowing its lands to go out of cultivation and its population to grow up in towns, fall behind other nations in its methods of education and in the capacity of adapting to its uses the latest scientific knowledge, in order that it may squander its pecuniary and military resources in forcing bad markets and finding speculative fields of investment in distant corners of the earth, adding millions of square miles and of unassimilable population to the area of the Empire.

The driving forces of class interest which stimulate and support this false economy we have explained. No remedy will serve which permits the future operation of these forces. It is idle to attack Imperialism or Militarism as political expedients or policies unless the axe is laid at the economic root of the tree, and the classes for whose interest Imperialism works are shorn of the surplus revenues which seek this outlet.[4]

At the time when Hobson wrote Imperialism *it was popular to invoke biological analogies supposed to demonstrate that international war served a useful and, indeed, indispensable function in the progress of mankind. This Hobson vehemently denied. He granted the value of competition but saw no reason why competition need be violent.*

4. *Ibid.*, pp. 92–3.

Instead he looked forward, although with no excessive optimism, to an
age of cultural and industrial competition based upon excellence and
efficiency of achievement rather than on force and fraud. In such a
world the common interests of mankind might even be reflected in
some international political organization.

. . . to ascribe finality to nationalism upon the ground that members of different nations lack "the common experience necessary to
found a common life" is a very arbitrary reading of modern history.
Taking the most inward meaning of experience, which gives most importance to the racial and traditional characters that mark the di-
vergences of nationality, we are obliged to admit that the fund of
experience common to peoples of different nationality is growing with
great rapidity under the numerous, swift, and accurate modes of intercommunication which mark the latest phases of civilisation. It is surely
true that the dwellers of large towns in all the most advanced European
States, an ever-growing proportion of the total population, have, not
merely in the externals of their lives, but in the chief formative influences of their reading, their art, science, recreation, a larger community
of experience than existed a century ago among the more distant members of any single European nation, whether dwelling in country or in
town. Direct intercommunication of persons, goods, and information
is so widely extended and so rapidly advancing that this growth of
"the common experience necessary to found a common life" beyond the
area of nationality is surely the most mark-worthy feature of the age.
Making, then, every due allowance for the subjective factors of national
character which temper or transmute the same external phenomena,
there surely exists, at any rate among the more conscious and more
educated sections of the chief European nations, a degree of true
"like-mindedness," which forms the psychical basis of some rudimen-
tary internationalism in the field of politics. Indeed it is curious and
instructive to observe that while some of those most insistent upon
"like-mindedness" and "common experience," as the tests of a true social
area, apply them in defence of existing nationalities and in repudiation
of attempts to absorb alien nationalities, others . . . apply them in the
advocacy of expansion and Imperialism.

Surely there is a third alternative to the policy of national independence on the one hand, and of the right of conquest by which the more
efficient nation absorbs the less efficient nation on the other, the alterna-

tive of experimental and progressive federation, which, proceeding on the line of greatest common experience, shall weave formal bonds of political attachment between the most "like-minded" nations, extending them to others as common experience grows wider, until an effective political federation is established, comprising the whole of "the civilized world," i.e. all those nations which have attained a considerable fund of that "common experience" comprised under the head of civilisation.

This idea does not conflict with the preservation of what is really essential and valuable in nationalism, nor does it imply a suspension or abolition of any form of struggle by which the true character of a nation may express itself in industry, in politics, in art or literature.[5]

Hobson realized that if the existing system of colonial annexations was abolished, some other method of exploiting underdeveloped areas would have to be found. He did not believe that civilized nations could or should be restrained from utilizing the resources of tropical areas or from introducing modern techniques. It was not feasible to leave this task purely in the hands of private capitalists. This method had been tried in the past and it led to oppression of the natives, to private warfare, and, ultimately and inevitably, to intervention by national governments. Having rejected this solution, Hobson proposed a system of international trusteeship by which colonial areas would be developed for the mutual benefit of natives and the whole community of civilized nations. Hobson first made this anticipation of the mandate system in Imperialism (1902). *The following extract presents the idea in somewhat more developed and compact form.*

The proposal that governments shall agree to a simple policy of 'Hands off,' leaving their nationals free to undertake any foreign trade or investments and work of development they choose entirely at their own discretion and their own risk, is quite impracticable.

An agreement of the Powers to proceed no further with the policy of political absorption of backward countries, and with the political assistance hitherto given to private businesses for purposes of trade and finance, could furnish no possible basis for a pacific future. For, since most of the desirable areas of profitable exploitation have already been appropriated, and are in actual process of economic absorption, no equality of opportunity could be provided by an arrangement that

5. *Ibid.,* pp. 168–9.

would divide the Powers into two groups, one satisfied the other un-
satisfied, and would preclude the latter for ever from obtaining satisfaction. . . .

No less impracticable would the proposal be as applied to the un-
absorbed portion of the earth. The notion that the governments of
the civilised states could safely or advantageously leave the further
processes of economic development to the free play of private profit-
eering enterprise among the trading and financial classes of their several nations must be rejected as soon as its meaning is realised. Such
a policy of naked *laissez faire* is quite inadmissible. A deliberate acceptance of the theory that bands of armed buccaneers calling themselves traders, were free to rob defenceless savages, to poison them
with alcohol or opium, to seize their lands, impose forced labour and
establish a slave-trade, is inconceivable. . . . The mere abstinence
from political intervention on the part of civilised states would plunge
every unappropriated country into sheer anarchy. But, even if the
governments or peoples of certain undeveloped countries were able
successfully to resist the entrance of foreign trade and capital, and to
refuse all access to strangers, this is not a policy in which other peoples,
or their governments, can or ought to acquiesce. No reasonable interpretation of rights of nationality or independence can justify the inhabitants of a country in refusing both themselves to develop the resources of the country and to permit others to do so. . . .

The problem is two-fold. First, how to secure the reasonable rights
of the inhabitants of such undeveloped countries against a policy of
plunder, extinction of life or servitude, imposed by the people of a
powerful aggressive state. Secondly, how to secure equal opportunities to the members of various advanced nations to participate in the
work and the gains of assisting to develop the natural resources and
the trade of these backward countries.

History shows that the former issue, primarily one of justice and humanity, is intimately bound up with the latter, the more distinctively
economic issue. The peace of the world is dependent upon both. The
most ruthless acts of annexation and the most wasteful practices of
exploitation have been due to the policy of exclusive possession and
protection imposed by the government of a colonising nation in the
short-sighted interest of particular groups of traders or syndicates of
capitalists. If the governments of all civilised nations would consent
to give equal rights of commerce and equal facilities of investment and

developmental work in their colonies and protectorates to members of all nations, this single agreement would go farther to secure a peaceful future for the world than any other measure, such as reduction of armaments, general arbitration or guarantees of national integrity. For not only would it greatly diminish the resentment and envy with which the older colonising powers are regarded by rising powers, such as Germany and Japan, but it would greatly modify the competition for further acquisition of territory. . . . It might then be a comparatively easy matter for friendly governments to agree among themselves what policy to adopt with regard to still unappropriated countries where dangerous disorder might prevail, or where the joint interests of all civilised peoples justified some interference of control. One method would be the establishment of a formal joint international protectorate, exercised by a Commission appointed by the permanent International Council, or whatever body was entrusted with the execution of the Treaty of International Relations. Another would be the delegation by this international authority to the government of some single nation of this duty of protection, where propinquity or other special circumstances rendered this course advisable. The prestige of such 'imperialism' would not arouse much jealousy, if the nationals of the power exercising it enjoyed no commercial or other advantages save such incidental ones as were unavoidably associated with the flag. Moreover, such incidental gains could be fairly apportioned by an international policy which distributed this work of protection and control fairly among the governments of the civilised nations. Such are the general principles for the realisation of "The Open Door." . . .

. . . if economic monopolies and preferences are once extracted, political imperialism becomes an empty shell, an illusion of quantitative power conceived in idle terms of area and population. Even if we suppose that some of the distinctively political and sentimental support of colonialism and imperialism survive, they will be greatly weakened in their hold of foreign policy and, lacking the pushful direction of the business man, will be unlikely to breed dangerous disputes. Once convert the Open Door into a genuinely constructive policy of international co-operation, for the peaceful development of the undeveloped resources of the world, administered by impartial internationally-minded men in the interest of the society of nations and with proper regard to the claims of the inhabitants of backward countries, a political support will have been found for that great and complex but hitherto, 'ungoverned' system of economic internationalism which has come into being during recent generations. The dangerous collisions between the forces of political nationalism and of economic internationalism would thus be obviated not by denial of the claims of the former, but by the political control of the latter.[6]

6. *The Open Door,* pp. 16–22.

20. WOODROW WILSON

1856-1924

THOMAS WOODROW WILSON *was born at Staunton, Virginia, in 1856. Following the peregrinations of his father's career as a Presbyterian minister, Wilson spent most of his youth in Georgia and the Carolinas. After graduating from Princeton University and experimenting in the practice of law, he became a teacher and author of works on politics and history. In 1902 Princeton selected him as its president. While serving in this capacity, his efforts to raise standards of scholarship and, in particular, to reduce the role of socially exclusive groups in favor of a more integrated university, won Wilson a national reputation. His campaign aroused powerful opposition, but before the contest reached a decision Wilson received the Democratic nomination for governor of New Jersey.*

Elected governor, Wilson proved an active leader who broke the old party machine and enacted a sweeping program of reform. This achievement won him a paramount position among progressive Democrats. In 1912 the Democratic Party nominated Wilson for president of the United States. The Republicans being split between Taft and Roosevelt, Wilson was easily elected.

Wilson had run on a progressive program dubbed the "New Freedom." This program concerned exclusively domestic affairs which Wilson expected to occupy his chief attention as President. During his presidency a very considerable number of reforms was indeed enacted, including some major departures in the field of finance, notably the Federal Reserve Act. But even before the European war erupted in 1914 Wilson was compelled to devote much attention to foreign policy. Faced with the constant trials which civil war and disorder in Mexico

The edition used is *The Public Papers of Woodrow Wilson*, ed. Ray Stannard Baker and William E. Dodd, 6 vols. New York and London, Harper and Brothers, 1925–27; copyright, 1925–27, Edith Bolling Wilson.

imposed upon the United States, he adopted a firm policy of sympathetic nonintervention intended to allow the Mexicans to reach their own solution. As further evidence of a conciliatory attitude he composed the Panama Tolls controversy with Britain and attempted to make restitution to Colombia for the high-handed diplomacy of Roosevelt in detaching Panama.

War in Europe forced Wilson to make foreign relations his chief concern. Steeped in the tradition of British as well as American political thought, he had by now developed a general outlook on politics which he believed was as relevant to the international scene as to the more familiar domestic arena. Perhaps foremost of his tenets were insistence on the need for moral—by which he meant Christian—conduct in public as well as private life and a profound faith in the considered judgment of the people through the democratic process. In his role as leader of the greatest neutral, later as a belligerent, and finally as an advocate of American participation in the League of Nations, Wilson displayed a remarkable capacity to advocate his policies and propound principles of international conduct. His name has in fact become the symbol of a certain idealistic attitude to foreign affairs. The abortive campaign for American ratification of the Treaty of Versailles broke his health in 1919 and he remained infirm until he died on February 3, 1924.

The speeches and state papers which form the chief repository of Wilson's ideas on international relations were of course almost exclusively directed to particular political problems. His thought is therefore not available in the coherent form of a political treatise. Yet he himself was always anxious to place his policies in the context of principle and frequently expressed the general theories which he applied to foreign affairs.

Wilson declared his belief "that character can be expressed upon a national scale and by a nation." [1] *He set great store by the extent to which nations afforded their citizens freedom and justice and to which they observed similar standards in their dealings with other nations. A nation ought not to pursue its interests to the detriment of another: "we wish nothing," Wilson asserted, "that can be had only at the expense of another people."* [2] *For him the personal and national duty to deal justly went beyond the observance of legal obligations and em-*

1. January 27, 1916; *Public Papers*, 4, 1.
2. March 5, 1917; *ibid.*, 5, 2–3.

*braced a Christian and positive concern for the welfare of others. He
believed that America, cosmopolitan in population and as yet relatively free from the trials of European politics, had a peculiarly favorable opportunity to offer a salutary example of honorable and peaceful
behavior toward other nations. During the early years of the war the
hope that determined American neutrality might "keep alive all the
wholesome processes of peace"³ and facilitate mediation strongly in-
fluenced Wilson's policy.*

I believe . . . that America, the country that we put first in our
thoughts, should be ready in every point of policy and of action to
vindicate at whatever cost the principles of liberty, of justice, and of
humanity to which we have been devoted from the first. [Cheers] You
cheer the sentiment, but do you realize what it means? It means that
you have not only got to be just to your fellow men, but that as a nation
you have got to be just to other nations. It comes high. It is not an
easy thing to do. It is easy to think first of the material interest of
America, but it is not easy to think first of what America, if she loves
justice, ought to do in the field of international affairs. I believe that
at whatever cost America should be just to other peoples and treat
other peoples as she demands that they should treat her. She has a
right to demand that they treat her with justice and respect, and she
has a right to insist that they treat her in that fashion, but she cannot
with dignity or with self-respect insist upon that unless she is willing
to act in the same fashion toward them. That I am ready to fight for
at any cost to myself.⁴

Our principles are well known. It is not necessary to avow them
again. We believe in political liberty and founded our great government to obtain it, the liberty of men and of peoples—of men to choose
their own lives and of peoples to choose their own allegiance. Our ambition, also, all the world has knowledge of. It is not only to be free
and prosperous ourselves, but also to be the friend and thoughtful
partisan of those who are free or who desire freedom the world over.
If we have had aggressive purposes and covetous ambitions, they were
the fruit of our thoughtless youth as a nation and we have put them
aside. We shall, I confidently believe, never again take another foot of
territory by conquest. We shall never in any circumstances seek to
make an independent people subject to our dominion; because we be-

3. February 2, 1916; *ibid., 4,* 105.
4. June 29, 1916; *ibid.,* pp. 213–14.

lieve, we passionately believe, in the right of every people to choose their own allegiance and be free of masters altogether. For ourselves we wish nothing but the full liberty of self-development; and with ourselves in this great matter we associate all the peoples of our own hemisphere. We wish not only for the United States but for them the fullest freedom of independent growth and of action, for we know that throughout this hemisphere the same aspirations are everywhere being worked out, under diverse conditions but with the same impulse and ultimate object.[5]

We are the mediating Nation of the world. I do not mean that we undertake not to mind our own business and to mediate where other people are quarreling. I mean the word in a broader sense. We are compounded of the nations of the world; we mediate their blood, we mediate their traditions, we mediate their sentiments, their tastes, their passions; we are ourselves compounded of those things. We are, therefore, able to understand all nations; we are able to understand them in the compound, not separately, as partisans, but unitedly as knowing and comprehending and embodying them all. It is in that sense that I mean that America is a mediating Nation. The opinion of America, the action of America, is ready to turn, and free to turn, in any direction. Did you ever reflect upon how almost every other nation has through long centuries been headed in one direction? That is not true of the United States. The United States has no racial momentum. It has no history back of it which makes it run all its energies and all its ambitions in one particular direction. And America is particularly free in this, that she has no hampering ambitions as a world power. . . . We do not want anything that does not belong to us. Is not a nation in that position free to serve other nations, and is not a nation like that ready to form some part of the assessing opinion of the world?

My interest in the neutrality of the United States is not the petty desire to keep out of trouble. To judge by my experience, I have never been able to keep out of trouble. I have never looked for it, but I have always found it. I do not want to walk around trouble. If any man wants a scrap that is an interesting scrap and worth while, I am his man. I warn him that he is not going to draw me into the scrap for his advertisement, but if he is looking for trouble that is the trouble of men in general and I can help a little, why, then, I am in for it. But I am interested in neutrality because there is something so much greater to

5. November 4, 1915; *ibid.,* 3, 385.

do than fight; there is a distinction waiting for this Nation that no nation has ever yet got. That is the distinction of absolute self-control and self-mastery.[6]

Wilson conceded that a policy of peaceful and aloof example was not always feasible. He observed that peace, though highly desirable, was not always "within the choice of the Nation." [7] *Innocent conduct could avert much of the risk of international conflict, but the most inoffensive nation might find violence the only defense of its legitimate interests. Moreover, every nation was concerned when gross violations of accepted national conduct menaced the whole structure of international community. Wilson therefore concluded that war might be a necessary and proper instrument of policy: "Some wars are to be regretted, some wars mar the annals of history, but some wars, contrasted with those make those annals distinguished . . ."* [8] *One of the causes justifying war was defense of a nation's independence and honor, without which it could not play a useful role in the world. Other just causes were defending the independence of small nations and preventing flagrant abuses of international law. The pressures of the European war convinced Wilson that, war being thus a possible contingency for all nations, they should maintain, physically as well as morally, a capability for a stout defense. He emphasized, however, that force could not of itself promote worthwhile values. It served merely to arrest threats to such values and to achieve conditions under which a just settlement might be constructed.*

. . . there is something that the American people love better than they love peace. They love the principles upon which their political life is founded. They are ready at any time to fight for the vindication of their character and of their honor. They will not at any time seek the contest, but they will at no time cravenly avoid it; because if there is one thing that the individual ought to fight for, and that the Nation ought to fight for, it is the integrity of its own convictions. We can not surrender our convictions. I would rather surrender territory than surrender those ideals which are the staff of life of the soul itself.

And because we hold certain ideals we have thought that it was right that we should hold them for others as well as for ourselves. America has more than once given evidence of the generosity and disin-

6. April 20, 1915; *ibid., 3*, 304–5.
7. January 29, 1916; *ibid., 4*, 43.
8. September 28, 1915; *ibid., 3*, 371.

terestedness of its love of liberty. It has been willing to fight for the liberty of others as well as for its own liberty. The world sneered when we set out upon the liberation of Cuba, but the world sneers no longer. The world now knows, what it was then loath to believe, that a nation can sacrifice its own interests and its own blood for the sake of the liberty and happiness of another people. Whether by one process or another, we have made ourselves in some sort the champions of free government and national sovereignty in both continents of this hemisphere; so that there are certain obligations which every American knows that we have undertaken.

The first and primary obligation is the maintenance of the integrity of our own sovereignty. That goes as of course. There is also the maintenance of our liberty to develop our political institutions without hindrance; and, last of all, there is the determination and the obligation to stand as the strong brother of all those in this hemisphere who mean to maintain the same principles and follow the same ideals of liberty.[9]

But there are other dangers . . . which are not past and which have not been overcome, and they are dangers which we can not control. We can control irresponsible talkers amidst ourselves. All we have got to do is to encourage them to hire a hall and their folly will be abundantly advertised by themselves. But we can not in this simple fashion control the dangers that surround us now and have surrounded us since this titanic struggle on the other side of the water began. . . .

Our thoughts are concentrated upon our own affairs and our own relations to the rest of the world, but the thoughts of the men who are engaged in this struggle are concentrated upon the struggle itself, and there is daily and hourly danger that they will feel themselves constrained to do things which are absolutely inconsistent with the rights of the United States. They are not thinking of us. I am not criticizing them for not thinking of us. I dare say if I were in their place neither would I think of us. They believe that they are struggling for the lives and honor of their nations, and that if the United States puts its interests in the path of this great struggle, she ought to know beforehand that there is danger of very serious misunderstanding and difficulty. So that the very uncalculating, unpremeditated, one might almost say accidental, course of affairs may touch us to the quick at any moment, and I want you to realize that, standing in the midst of these difficul-

9. January 27, 1916; *ibid.*, 4, 8–9.

ties, I feel that I am charged with a double duty of the utmost difficulty. In the first place, I know that you are depending upon me to keep
this Nation out of the war. So far I have done so, and I pledge you my
word that, God helping me, I will if it is possible. But you have laid
another duty upon me. You have bidden me see to it that nothing stains
or impairs the honor of the United States, and that is a matter not
within my control; that depends upon what others do, not upon what
the Government of the United States does. Therefore there may at any
moment come a time when I can not preserve both the honor and the
peace of the United States. Do not exact of me an impossible and contradictory thing, but stand ready and insistent that everybody who
represents you should stand ready to provide the necessary means for
maintaining the honor of the United States.[10]

. . . The present German submarine warfare against commerce is a
warfare against mankind.

It is a war against all nations. American ships have been sunk, American lives taken, in ways which it has stirred us very deeply to learn
of, but the ships and people of other neutral and friendly nations have
been sunk and overwhelmed in the waters in the same way. There has
been no discrimination. The challenge is to all mankind. Each nation
must decide for itself how it will meet it. The choice we make for ourselves must be made with a moderation of counsel and a temperateness
of judgment befitting our character and our motives as a nation. We
must put excited feeling away. Our motive will not be revenge or the
victorious assertion of the physical might of the nation, but only the
vindication of right, of human right, of which we are only a single
champion.

. . . There is one choice we cannot make, we are incapable of making: we will not choose the path of submission and suffer the most
sacred rights of our Nation and our people to be ignored or violated.
The wrongs against which we now array ourselves are no common
wrongs; they cut to the very roots of human life. . . . .

. . . We have no selfish ends to serve. We desire no conquest, no
dominion. We seek no indemnities for ourselves, no material compen-
sation for the sacrifices we shall freely make. We are but one of the
champions of the rights of mankind. We shall be satisfied when those
rights have been made as secure as the faith and the freedom of nations can make them. . . . .

10. January 31, 1916; *ibid.*, pp. 47–9.

. . . It is a fearful thing to lead this great peaceful people into war, into the most terrible and disastrous of all wars, civilization itself seeming to be in the balance. But the right is more precious than peace, and we shall fight for the things which we have always carried nearest our hearts,—for democracy, for the right of those who submit to authority to have a voice in their own Governments, for the rights and liberties of small nations, for a universal dominion of right by such a concert of free peoples as shall bring peace and safety to all nations and make the world itself at last free.[11]

. . . We regard war merely as a means of asserting the rights of a people against aggression. And we are as fiercely jealous of coercive or dictatorial power within our own nation as of aggression from without. We will not maintain a standing army except for uses which are as necessary in times of peace as in times of war; and we shall always see to it that our military peace establishment is no larger than is actually and continuously needed for the uses of days in which no enemies move against us. But we do believe in a body of free citizens ready and sufficient to take care of themselves and of the governments which they have set up to serve them. . . .

But war has never been a mere matter of men and guns. It is a thing of disciplined might. If our citizens are ever to fight effectively upon a sudden summons, they must know how modern fighting is done, and what to do when the summons comes to render themselves immediately available and immediately effective. And the government must be their servant in this matter, must supply them with the training they need to take care of themselves and of it. The military arm of their government, which they will not allow to direct them, they may properly use to serve them and make their independence secure,—and not their own independence merely but the rights also of those with whom they have made common cause, should they also be put in jeopardy. They must be fitted to play the great role in the world, and particularly in this hemisphere, which they are qualified by principle and by chastened ambition to play.[12]

Force will not accomplish anything that is permanent, I venture to say, in the great struggle which is going on on the other side of the sea. The permanent things will be accomplished afterwards, when the opinion of mankind is brought to bear upon the issues, and the only

11. April 2, 1917; *ibid.*, 5, 8–16.
12. December 7, 1915; *ibid.*, 3, 411–12.

thing that will hold the world steady is this same silent, insistent, all-powerful opinion of mankind.

Force can sometimes hold things steady until opinion has time to form, but no force that was ever exerted, except in response to that opinion, was ever a conquering and predominant force.[13]

With his belief that war alone could not achieve desirable ends Wilson combined a lively awareness of the difficulties of peacemaking. As a neutral and later as a belligerent he frequently asserted the need for a careful adjustment of conflicting views and claims if the coming peace was to last. A stable settlement, Wilson insisted, must be built upon the best possible satisfaction of all parties, not the unrestrained ambition of one side. Peacemaking must, in fact, be "removing the chief provocations to war." [14]

Very soon after the war in Europe broke out, Wilson predicted that peace would have to be "reached wholly by the force of reason and justice after the trial at arms is found futile." [15] *Even as a belligerent he retained the conviction that an "enduring peace . . . must be based upon justice and fairness and the common rights of mankind."* [16] *In defining the principles of justice on which a new international order was to be based, he insisted that the weak must enjoy the same rights as the strong, that "every territorial settlement . . . be made in the interest and for the benefit of the populations concerned" and that "well-defined national aspirations shall be accorded the utmost satisfaction"* [17] *within the limits of possibility. He showed mounting fear that the Allies, when victorious, might abandon all restraint and impose a punitive and therefore tenuous peace.*

The present war must first be ended; but we owe it to candor and to a just regard for the opinion of mankind to say that, so far as our participation in guarantees of future peace is concerned, it makes a great deal of difference in what way and upon what terms it is ended. The treaties and agreements which bring it to an end must embody terms which will create a peace that is worth guaranteeing and preserving, a peace that will win the approval of mankind, not merely a peace

13. June 30, 1916; *ibid., 4,* 219–20.

14. January 8, 1918; *ibid., 5,* 161.

15. Letter, October 4, 1914; quoted in Ray S. Baker, *Woodrow Wilson: Life and Letters* (8 vols. Garden City, N.Y., Doubleday Page, 1927–39), 5, 290.

16. August 27, 1917; *Public Papers, 5,* 95–6.

17. February 11, 1918; *ibid.,* p. 183.

that will serve the several interests and immediate aims of the nations engaged. . . .

No covenant of co-operative peace that does not include the peoples of the New World can suffice to keep the future safe against war; and yet there is only one sort of peace that the peoples of America could join in guaranteeing. The elements of that peace must be elements that engage the confidence and satisfy the principles of the American governments, elements consistent with their political faith and with the practical convictions which the peoples of America have once for all embraced and undertaken to defend. . . . .

. . . The question upon which the whole future peace and policy of the world depends is this: Is the present war a struggle for a just and secure peace, or only for a new balance of power? If it be only a struggle for a new balance of power, who will guarantee, who can guarantee the stable equilibrium of the new arrangement? Only a tranquil Europe can be a stable Europe. There must be, not a balance of power, but a community of power; not organized rivalries, but an organized common peace. . . . .

. . . it must be a peace without victory. It is not pleasant to say this. I beg that I may be permitted to put my own interpretation upon it and that it may be understood that no other interpretation was in my thought. I am seeking only to face realities and to face them without soft concealments. Victory would mean peace forced upon the loser, a victor's terms imposed upon the vanquished. It would be accepted in humiliation, under duress, at an intolerable sacrifice, and would leave a sting, a resentment, a bitter memory upon which terms of peace would rest, not permanently, but only as upon quicksand. Only a peace between equals can last. Only a peace the very principle of which is equality and a common participation in a common benefit. The right state of mind, the right feeling between nations, is as necessary for a lasting peace as is the just settlement of vexed questions of territory or of racial and national allegiance.

The equality of nations upon which peace must be founded if it is to last must be an equality of rights; the guarantees exchanged must neither recognize nor imply a difference between big nations and small, between those that are powerful and those that are weak. Right must be based upon the common strength, not upon the individual strength, of the nations upon whose concert peace will depend. Equality of territory or of resources there of course cannot be; nor any other sort of equality not gained in the ordinary peaceful and legitimate development of the peoples themselves. But no one asks or expects anything more than an equality of rights. Mankind is looking now for freedom of life, not for equipoises of power.

And there is a deeper thing involved than even equality of right among organized nations. No peace can last, or ought to last, which does not recognize and accept the principle that governments derive all their just powers from the consent of the governed, and that no right anywhere exists to hand peoples about from sovereignty to sovereignty as if they were property. . . .

I speak of this, not because of any desire to exalt an abstract political principle which has always been held very dear by those who have sought to build up liberty in America, but for the same reason that I have spoken of the other conditions of peace which seem to me clearly indispensable—because I wish frankly to uncover realities. Any peace which does not recognize and accept this principle will inevitably be upset. It will not rest upon the affections of or the convictions of mankind. The ferment of spirit of whole populations will fight subtly and constantly against it, and all the world will sympathize. The world can be at peace only if its life is stable, and there can be no stability where the will is in rebellion, where there is not tranquility of spirit and a sense of justice, of freedom, and of right.[18]

The wrongs, the very deep wrongs, committed in this war will have to be righted. That of course. But they cannot and must not be righted by the commission of similar wrongs against Germany and her allies. The world will not permit the commission of similar wrongs as a means of reparation and settlement. Statesmen must by this time have learned that the opinion of the world is everywhere wide awake and fully comprehends the issues involved. No representative of any self-governed nation will dare disregard it by attempting any such covenants of selfishness and compromise as were entered into at the Congress of Vienna. . . . . .

. . . Justice and equality of rights can be had only at a great price. We are seeking permanent, not temporary, foundations for the peace of the world and must seek them candidly and fearlessly. As always, the right will prove to be the expedient.[19]

. . . The peace of the world depends upon the just settlement of each of the several problems to which I adverted in my recent address to the

18. January 22, 1917; *ibid.*, 4, 408–12.
19. December 4, 1917; *ibid.*, 5, 133–5.

Congress [i.e. the Fourteen Points]. I, of course, do not mean that the peace of the world depends upon the acceptance of any particular set of suggestions as to the way in which those problems are to be dealt with. I mean only that those problems each and all affect the whole world; that unless they are dealt with in a spirit of unselfish and unbiased justice, with a view to the wishes, the natural connections, the racial aspirations, the security, and the peace of mind of the peoples involved, no permanent peace will have been attained. They cannot be discussed separately or in corners. None of them constitutes a private or separate interest from which the opinion of the world may be shut out. Whatever affects the peace affects mankind, and nothing settled by military force, if settled wrong, is settled at all. It will presently have to be reopened.

. . . There shall be no annexations, no contributions, no punitive damages. Peoples are not to be handed about from one sovereignty to another by an international conference or an understanding between rivals and antagonists. National aspirations must be respected; peoples may now be dominated and governed only by their own consent. "Self-determination" is not a mere phrase. It is an imperative principle of action, which statesmen will henceforth ignore at their peril. We cannot have general peace for the asking, or by the mere arrangements of a peace conference. It cannot be pieced together out of individual understandings between powerful states. All the parties to this war must join in the settlement of every issue anywhere involved in it; because what we are seeking is a peace that we can all unite to guarantee and maintain and every item of it must be submitted to the common judgment whether it be right and fair, an act of justice, rather than a bargain between sovereigns.[20]

If it be in deed and in truth the common object of the Governments associated against Germany and of the nations whom they govern, as I believe it to be, to achieve by the coming settlements a secure and lasting peace, it will be necessary that all who sit down at the peace table shall come ready and willing to pay the price, the only price, that will procure it. . . .

That price is impartial justice in every item of the settlement, no matter whose interest is crossed; and not only impartial justice, but also the satisfaction of the several peoples whose fortunes are dealt with. . . . . .

20. February 11, 1918; *ibid.*, pp. 179–80.

First, the impartial justice meted out must involve no discrimination between those to whom we wish to be just and those to whom we do not wish to be just. It must be a justice that plays no favorites and knows no standard but the equal rights of the several peoples concerned;

Second, no special or separate interest of any single nation or any group of nations can be made the basis of any part of the settlement which is not consistent with the common interest of all.[21]

Even before America entered the First World War, Wilson expressed the hope that the nation might participate in some organized effort to preserve the peace. Earlier, in the development of his Latin-American policy, he had broached the idea of such cooperation on a smaller scale, limited to the Americas. The progress of the war slowly convinced him that the world had reached a stage of political and technological development at which it both needed and was able to create a league of nations which would abolish the old system of alliances and by a new diplomacy unite the nations of the world against aggression in common defense of the fundamental rights of mankind. Only democracies, Wilson believed, could successfully form such a league, because it would rely heavily on its ability to bring issues before world opinion. He warned that it was impossible to create an elaborate and effective organization all at once and that there could be no absolute guarantees of peace. At the least, however, a league would provide a means of adjusting faults in the settlement of the World War.

. . . We are not mere disconnected lookers-on. The longer the war lasts, the more deeply do we become concerned that it should be brought to an end and the world be permitted to resume its normal life and course again. And when it does come to an end we shall be as much concerned as the nations at war to see peace assume an aspect of permanence, give promise of days from which the anxiety of uncertainty shall be lifted, bring some assurance that peace and war shall always hereafter be reckoned part of the common interest of mankind. We are participants, whether we would or not, in the life of the world. The interests of all nations are our own also. We are partners with the rest. What affects mankind is inevitably our affair as well as the affair of the nations of Europe and of Asia.

One observation on the causes of the present war we are at liberty to make, and to make it may throw some light forward upon the future, as well as backward upon the past. It is plain that this war could have

21. September 27, 1918; *ibid.*, pp. 256–7.

come only as it did, suddenly and out of secret counsels, without warning to the world, without discussion, without any of the deliberate movements of counsel with which it would seem natural to approach so stupendous a contest. It is probable that if it had been foreseen just what would happen, just what alliances would be formed, just what forces arrayed against one another, those who brought the great contest on would have been glad to substitute conference for force. If we ourselves had been afforded some opportunity to apprise the belligerents of the attitude which it would be our duty to take, of the policies and practices against which we would feel bound to use all our moral and economic strength, and in certain circumstances even our physical strength also, our own contribution to the counsel which might have averted the struggle would have been considered worth weighing and regarding.

And the lesson which the shock of being taken by surprise in a matter so deeply vital to all the nations of the world has made poignantly clear is, that the peace of the world must henceforth depend upon a new and more wholesome diplomacy. Only when the great nations of the world have reached some sort of agreement as to what they hold to be fundamental to their common interest, and as to some feasible method of acting in concert when any nation or group of nations seeks to disturb those fundamental things, can we feel that civilization is at last in a way of justifying its existence and claiming to be finally established. It is clear that nations must in the future be governed by the same high code of honor that we demand of individuals.

. . . Repeated utterances of the leading statesmen of most of the great nations now engaged in war have made it plain that their thought has come to this, that the principle of public right must henceforth take precedence over the individual interests of particular nations, and that the nations of the world must in some way band themselves together to see that that right prevails as against any sort of selfish aggression; that henceforth alliance must not be set up against alliance, understanding against understanding, but that there must be a common agreement for a common object, and that at the heart of that common object must lie the inviolable rights of peoples and of mankind. The nations of the world have become each other's neighbors. It is to their interest that they should understand each other. In order that they may understand each other, it is imperative that they should agree to co-operate in a common cause, and that they should so act that the guiding principle of that common cause shall be even-handed and impartial justice. . . . .

We believe these fundamental things: First, that every people has a right to choose the sovereignty under which they shall live. Like other nations, we have ourselves no doubt once and again offended against that principle when for a little while controlled by selfish passion as our franker historians have been honorable enough to admit; but it has become more and more our rule of life and action. Second, that the small states of the world have a right to enjoy the same respect for their sovereignty and for their territorial integrity that great and powerful nations expect and insist upon. And, third, that the world has a right to be free from every disturbance of its peace that has its origin in aggression and disregard of the rights of peoples and nations.

So sincerely do we believe in these things that I am sure that I speak the mind and wish of the people of America when I say that the United States is willing to become a partner in any feasible association of nations formed in order to realize these objects and make them secure against violation.

There is nothing that the United States wants for itself that any other nation has. We are willing, on the contrary, to limit ourselves along with them to a prescribed course of duty and respect for the rights of others which will check any selfish passion of our own, as it will check any aggressive impulse of theirs.

. . . I am sure that the people of the United States would wish their Government to move along these lines: . . . an universal association of the nations to maintain the inviolate security of the highway of the seas for the common and unhindered use of all the nations of the world, and to prevent any war begun either contrary to treaty covenants or without warning and full submission of the causes to the opinion of the world— a virtual guarantee of territorial integrity and political independence.[22]

Have you ever heard what started the present war? If you have, I wish you would publish it, because nobody else has, so far as I can gather. Nothing in particular started it, but everything in general. There had been growing up in Europe a mutual suspicion, an interchange of conjecture about what this Government and that Government was going to do, an interlacing of alliances and understandings, a complex web of intrigue and spying, that presently was sure to entangle the whole of the family of mankind on that side of the water in its meshes.

Now, revive that after this war is over and sooner or later you will have just such another war, and this is the last war of the kind or of any other

22. May 27, 1916; ibid., 4, 184–8.

kind that involves the world that the United States can keep out of.

I say that because I believe that the business of neutrality is over; not because I want it to be over, but I mean this, that war now has such a scale that the position of neutrals sooner or later becomes intolerable. Just as neutrality would be intolerable to me if I lived in a community where everybody had to assert his own rights by force and I had to go around among my neighbors and say: "Here, this cannot last any longer; let us get together and see that nobody disturbs the peace any more." That is what society is and we have not yet a society of nations.

We must have a society of nations, not suddenly, not by insistence, not by any hostile emphasis upon the demand, but by the demonstration of the needs of the time. The nations of the world must get together and say, "Nobody can hereafter be neutral as respects the disturbance of the world's peace for an object which the world's opinion cannot sanction." The world's peace ought to be disturbed if the fundamental rights of humanity are invaded, but it ought not to be disturbed for any other thing that I can think of, and America was established in order to indicate, at any rate in one Government, the fundamental rights of man. America must hereafter be ready as a member of the family of nations to exert her whole force, moral and physical, to the assertion of those rights throughout the round globe.[23]

. . . Self-governed nations do not fill their neighbor states with spies or set the course of intrigue to bring about some critical posture of affairs which will give them an opportunity to strike and make conquest. Such designs can be successfully worked out only under cover and where no one has the right to ask questions. Cunningly contrived plans of deception or aggression, carried, it may be, from generation to generation, can be worked out and kept from the light only within the privacy of courts or behind the carefully guarded confidences of a narrow and privileged class. They are happily impossible where public opinion commands and insists upon full information concerning all the nation's affairs.

A steadfast concert for peace can never be maintained except by a partnership of democratic nations. No autocratic government could be trusted to keep faith within it or observe its covenants. It must be a league of honor, a partnership of opinion. Intrigue would eat its vitals away; the plottings of inner circles who could plan what they would and render

23. October 27, 1916; *ibid.*, pp. 381–2.

account to no one would be a corruption seated at its very heart. Only free peoples can hold their purpose and their honor steady to a common end and prefer the interests of mankind to any narrow interest of their own. . . . .

. . . The world must be made safe for democracy. Its peace must be planted upon the tested foundations of political liberty.[24]

. . . [We have met at Versailles] for two purposes, to make the present settlements which have been rendered necessary by this war, and also to secure the peace of the world, not only by the present settlements, but by the arrangements we shall make at this conference for its maintenance. The League of Nations seems to me to be necessary for both of these purposes. There are many complicated questions connected with the present settlements which perhaps cannot be successfully worked out to an ultimate issue by the decisions we shall arrive at here. I can easily conceive that many of these settlements will need subsequent reconsideration, that many of the decisions we make shall need subsequent alteration in some degree; for, if I may judge by my own study of some of these questions, they are not susceptible of confident judgments at present.

It is, therefore, necessary that we should set up some machinery by which the work of this conference should be rendered complete. We have assembled here for the purpose of doing very much more than making the present settlements. We are assembled under very peculiar conditions of world opinion. I may say without straining the point that we are not representatives of Governments, but representatives of peoples. . . .

It is a solemn obligation on our part, therefore, to make permanent arrangements that justice shall be rendered and peace maintained. This is the central object of our meeting. Settlements may be temporary, but the action of the nations in the interest of peace and justice must be permanent. We can set up permanent processes. We may not be able to set up permanent decisions.[25]

24. April 2, 1917; *ibid.*, 5, 12–14.
25. January 25, 1919; *ibid.*, 5, 395–6.

INDEX

Aggression, 7, 14, 43–5, 51, 67, 100–1, 132, 152, 159, 164–5, 168, 170, 181–2, 184–5, 191, 207–8, 214, 227–9, 252–3, 270, 275–8

Alliances, 16, 32–4, 55–7, 59–61, 81, 129–30, 149, 170, 275–7; unreliability of, 5–6, 32–4, 149, 173; *see also* Treaties

America, in relation to Europe, 130–2, 145–6, 153–4, 162–3, 266, 269, 272–3, 275–8; *see also* European system, Isolation

Amity, international, 5–6, 42, 45, 79–80, 95, 110–12, 132, 181–2; *see also* Enmity

Appeasement, 13–15, 117, 119, 144, 146, 154, 269

Arbitration, 196, 198–200, 238–42

Armaments. *See* Disarmament; Military policy; Power, elements of; Preparedness; Sea power

BACON, Francis, 11–25
  appeasement, opposition to, 13–15
  balance of power, 12–16
  human nature, and international relations, 12–13
  imperialism, 17, 19–22, 23
  morality, international, 14
  parable of Perseus, 22–5
  power, as basis of security, 12–13; elements of, 17–21
  self-restraint, limits of, 13–14
  treaties, unreliability of, 12–13
  vigilance, 13, 15
  war, causes of, 14–16, 21–3; conduct of, 22–5; preventive, 14–15

Balance of power, 12–16, 29, 56–9, 61–2, 71–2, 79–82, 105–6, 108, 121–3, 127, 143–6, 153–4, 162–3, 175–6, 181–2, 185, 197–8, 200–3, 235, 238–42, 272

BENTHAM, Jeremy, 180–91
  amity, international, 181–2
  balance of power, 181–2
  colonies, as cause of war, 186–8
  defense, against aggression, 183–5; limits of, 183–5
  disarmament, 188–9
  international court, 189
  open diplomacy, 190–1
  peace, plan for perpetual, 186
  public opinion, 189–91
  war, just and unjust, 183–5; mischief of, 183–5

BOLINGBROKE, 55–62
  alliances, 59–61
  balance of power, Britain as the guardian of, 61–2; and the national interest, 56–61
  defense, 59–61
  foreign policy, as related to interest and power, 55–6
  isolation, and insularity, 59–61
  national interest, 55–6

BURKE, Edmund, 109–25
  amity, international, 110–12
  balance of power, and self-restraint, 121–3
  colonies, and self-determination, 123–5
  defense, 119–21
  European system, 110–12
  intervention, in internal affairs, 114–16
  morality, and the national interest, 112–14; the enforcement of, 112–14
  nations, as center of man's interest, 110–11
  neighborhood, law of, 113–14
  peacemaking, 119–21
  power, need for, 117; elements of, 117–19
  prudence, 115, 117, 119
  subversion, by Jacobins, 114–16

COBDEN, Richard, 192–205
  arbitration, 196–200

COBDEN, Richard (*continued*)
balance of power, as a chimera, 200–3
conquest, futility of, 195–6
democracy, and peace, 197
disarmament, 196–200
free trade, and peace, 193–5
insularity, 203–5
intervention, dangers of, 203–5
peace, popular desire for, 196–7
peaceful settlement of disputes, 196–200
treaties, observance of, 199–200
war, abomination of, 196; alternatives to, 198–200
Coercion, 43–5, 101–4, 142–3, 171, 226–8, 238–40, 241, 267, 270–1
Colonialism. *See* Colonies; Imperialism
Colonies, 7–8, 17, 20, 82, 90–3, 123–5, 130, 178–9, 186–8, 194–6, 213, 216–18, 230–3, 245–7, 249–62; as a trust, 125, 259–62; self-determination of, 92–3, 123–5, 130–2, 136–7; *see also* Imperialism
Commerce, 17, 49–50, 59, 69, 74–6, 79–82, 87–91, 130, 133–4, 136–7, 140–2, 161–3, 167, 179, 181–2, 187, 192–6, 207, 229–32, 237, 245–7, 249–57, 259–61; *see also* Free trade
Competition, peaceful, 75–6, 80–1, 87–9, 258–9
Conflict, 27–9, 59–60, 65–8, 96–100, 105, 134, 166–70, 182–3, 222–4, 226–7, 235–9, 246, 251, 255–7, 267; *see also* War
Conquest, 2, 4–5, 29, 49–54, 74–5, 105–8, 144–5, 167, 195, 202, 213–14, 216–17, 242, 265; *see also* Imperialism

Deception, 6, 9, 83, 102–3
Defense, 2, 13–15, 27, 29–33, 34–5, 39, 42–9, 67–8, 79–80, 85–6, 90, 96, 98, 100–2, 106, 114, 119–20, 138, 140, 143, 170–5, 178–9, 183–5, 196, 198, 223–4, 227–30, 242–3, 267–8; joint, 45–7, 57, 60–1, 112, 145, 202, 230, 274–8; *see also* War, preventive
Democracy, peace promoted by, 127, 132–6, 167, 195–7, 224–6, 275, 278–9; peaceful policies not guaranteed by, 74, 140–2

Deterrence, 9, 40, 45–7, 158, 185, 242–4
Diplomacy. *See* Foreign policy, Negotiation, Open diplomacy
Disarmament, 136–7, 186, 188–9, 196–200

Empire. *See* Colonies, Imperialism
Ends and means, 30–1, 39, 55–6, 101–5, 117–18, 174
Enmity, international, 12, 15, 27–32, 34, 36, 43, 57, 68–9, 79–81, 89, 95–8, 100, 127, 140, 142, 235–6, 246, 249; *see also* Amity
Ethics. *See* Morality; Self-restraint; War, just
European system, 59–60, 108, 110–15, 118, 122, 129, 131, 159, 226, 265; *see also* America

Federation, as cure for war, 142, 216–20, 259
FERGUSON, Adam, 94–108
balance of power, and empire, 105–8
conflict, international, 96; usefulness of, 97–100
conquest, and defense, 105–8
defense, self-restraint in, 100–2; right of, 102–5
national character, 95–6
nations, origin of, 95–6
war, causes of, 97–100; conduct of, 104–5
Foreign policy, conduct of, 2–5, 35–6, 48–9, 58, 154; *see also* Negotiation, Open diplomacy
Force. *See* Coercion, War
Free trade, 74–6, 87–91, 130, 136–7, 161–2, 167, 179, 187, 193–6, 229–32; limitations on, 88–90, 207, 229–30

Glory, national, 79, 127–8, 169, 195
GODWIN, William, 166–79
aggression, 170
alliances, uselessness of, 170, 173
balance of power, condemnation of, 175–6
conflict, imaginary, 166–9
defense, limited need for, 170–3; by free men, 170–3; of liberty, 173–5
imperialism, as cause of war, 178–9
individuals, as chief concern, 166–71
national interest, so-called, 166–9

nationalism, pernicious, 169
preparedness, through militia, 172
revolution, assistance to, 173–5
self-restraint, 176–8
war, just and unjust, 173–5; limitation and moderation of, 176–8
Government, origin of, 47, 67–8, 98, 143, 222–5
Governments. See Rulers
Great Britain, foreign policy of, 61–2, 72–3, 117

HAMILTON, Alexander, 139–54
aggression, difficulty of discerning, 152–3
alliances, 149
balance of power, 143–6, 153–4
compromise, and coercion, 142–3
conquest, 144–6
isolation, and its limits, 153–4
national interest, and morality, 146–9, 150–1
power, desire for, 143–4; elements of, 153–4
self-interest, and selfishness, 146–9
self-restraint, 146–52
vigilance, 149–52
war, causes of, 140–2; preventive, 143, 146
HOBBES, Thomas, 26–40
conflict, causes of, 27–9
conquest, love of, 29
defense, 29–31, 33–7
enmity, international, 29–30
human nature, and fear, 27–8; and desire for material things and power, 27–9
international law, and peace, 32–3
morality, international, 30–4
power, desire for, 27–9
preparedness, 36–7
self-restraint, in war, 38–40
state of nature, as a state of war, 27–9; similar to international relations, 26, 38
state of war, 29–30; and morality, 31; perpetual, 31–2
HOBSON, John Atkinson, 248–62
colonies, as a trust, 259–62
competition, peaceful, 258–62
conflict, and capitalist interests, 255–7; and economic reform, 255–7
economic motives, 253–5

imperialism, effects of, 249–53; underconsumption as cause of, 249–62
nationalism, and internationalism, 258–9, 261–2
open door, 261–2
war, and profits, 254–5; and progress, 257
Honor, national, 127–9, 150–1, 167, 174, 185, 267–9
Human nature, 3, 12, 27, 43, 64–8, 79, 95, 97, 110–11, 120, 133, 135, 140, 168, 181–3, 193, 226–7, 236–7, 253
HUME, David, 63–77
balance of power, 71–4
conquest, opposition to, 74–5
defense, and the establishment of government, 67–8
foreign policy, British conduct of, 72–4
human nature, 63–7
morality, different in international relations, 68–71; and self-interest, 64–71
power, and wealth, 74–6
self-restraint, in war, 70–1
small states, advantage of, 74, 76–7
state of nature, as a fiction, 64; and society without government, 64–7
war, causes of, 68–9, and morality, 68–9

Imperialism, 5, 17, 19–22, 23, 34, 59–60, 74–7, 105–8, 123, 140, 143–4, 167–8, 171, 178–9, 223, 227, 230–3, 245–7, 249–62, 265; see also Colonies, Conquest
Independence, 99–100, 105–8, 122, 176, 267–8
Insularity, 17, 50, 59–62, 130, 203
Intelligence, 22, 24, 35–7
Interest. See National interest
International court, 189
International law, 68–70, 79–82, 97, 157, 181–3, 201, 208–9, 211, 238, 240–1, 267
International organization, 132–3, 135–8, 186–91, 258–62, 272, 275–9
Intervention, 7, 14, 17, 56–62, 112–15, 160, 173–6, 203–5, 207, 211–16, 267–8; see also America, Isolation
Isolation, 59–62, 74, 129–31, 136, 153–4, 159–63, 195, 203, 275–8; see also America, Intervention

JEFFERSON, Thomas, 155–65
  aggression, 158–9
  balance of power, 162–3
  commerce, as cause of war, 163
  defense, 158–9
  foreign policy, moral and peaceful
    conduct of, 160
  isolation, from European politics,
    159–62; and geography, 159–61;
    limits of, 163; and sympathy for
    liberty, 162
  morality, international identical with
    individual, 156–9; and the national
    interest, 156–9
  peace, 159–62
  treaties, 156–9
  war, causes of, 163–5; and true in-
    terests of nations, 159; perpetual
    in Europe, 159–62
Justice, international. See Morality; Self-
    restraint; War, just

Law, international. See International
    law
Law of nature, 32, 38–40, 42–9, 51–4,
    97, 104, 159; see also State of
    nature, State of war
League of nations, 272, 275–9; see also
    International organization
Liberty, wars for, 17, 23, 167, 173
LOCKE, John, 41–54
  aggression, 43; punishment of, 45–6;
    and conquest, 51–2
  conquest, and commerce, 49; rights
    of, 45–54
  defense, right of, 43–5; through self-
    help, 47; as a purpose of govern-
    ment, 47–8; policy of, 48–9
  foreign policy, conduct of, 42, 45,
    48–9
  law of nature, 42; violation of, 43
  morality, 42–3, 50–4
  power, and wealth, 49–50
  state of nature, and peace, 41, 43;
    and state of war, 43–5

MAHAN, Alfred Thayer, 234–47
  arbitration and force, 240–1; opposi-
    tion to, 238–41
  conflict, and emotional impulses, 235–
    7
  imperialism, as a mission, 245–7
  national interest, as first concern, 235;

  geographical, economic, moral, and
    emotional, 235–8
  military policy, and political interest,
    243
  morality, international, 241–2
  war, just and unjust, 241–2; and
    morality, 241–2
Means. See Ends and means
Military policy, 18–19, 59, 74–5, 85–6,
    172–3, 204, 222–4, 243–4, 254,
    270; see also Preparedness, Sea
    power
MILL, John Stuart, 206–20
  colonies, 216–18; association with
    mother country, 218
  international law, so-called, 208–11;
    and morality, 208–9; and status
    quo, 211
  national self-determination, 211–12,
    216–18; and backward nations,
    216; and federation, 218–20; and
    mixed nationalities, 216–18
  nations, equality of, 208–11
  nonintervention, and the promotion
    of self-government, 211–16; rules
    of, 212–16
  treaties, observance of, 208–11
  war, just and unjust, 207–8
Moderation. See Self-restraint
Morale, national, 10, 14, 17–19, 22–3,
    73–4, 85–6, 99, 117, 120, 170–3,
    204
Morality, international, 1–6, 12, 14, 30–
    4, 42–3, 50–4, 64–71, 82–5, 110,
    112–14, 128, 143, 146–8, 156–9,
    164–5, 172, 203, 208–9, 226–9, 233,
    238–9, 241–2, 264–7, 269–76, 279;
    see also Self-restraint; War, just
MORE, Sir Thomas, 1–10
  alliances, uselessness of, 5–6
  amity, international, 5–6
  colonies, 7–8
  foreign policy, of war and conquest,
    2–5
  morality, and political practice, 1–5
  self-restraint, 2–5, in war, 8–10
  statesmanship, 1; and ideals of phi-
    losopher, 2–5
  war, conduct of, 7–10; hate of, 6–7;
    just and unjust, 6–7

National character, 95–6, 99–100, 108
National interest, 12–13, 55–7, 59–60,

79–81, 90, 96–8, 111–12, 131, 143, 145, 149–50, 166–9, 174, 181–4, 193–4, 206, 208–9, 235–6, 238, 243, 247, 258, 264–5, 268–9, 271–2, 274–5, 279; private interests may oppose, 88–9, 92, 127–8, 141, 252–7

National self-determination, 7, 156, 161–2, 203–5, 211–18, 265–6, 268, 271–4, 277–9

Nationalism, 55–6, 79–83, 89, 95–8, 108, 110, 169, 181–2, 195, 202, 211–12, 224, 236, 252–3, 255, 258–9, 262, 264, 266

Nationalities, mixture of, 216–20

Nations, 110–11, 156–7, 170, 211, 225; equality of, 156, 210–11, 265, 271–3, 277

Nature. See Human nature, Law of nature, State of nature

Negotiation, 83, 102–3, 149–52; see also Peaceful settlement

Neighborhood, enmity bred by, 89, 142; duties of, 113–14

Neutrality, 82–3, 131, 136–8, 160–1, 265–7, 278

Open diplomacy, 133, 136, 167–9, 186, 190–1, 274–9

Open Door, 259–62

PAINE, Thomas, 126–38
    colonies, self-determination of, 130–2, 136–7
    defense, 138
    democracy, and peace, 132–6
    international organization, 136–8
    isolation, from European politics, 129–32; and international organization, 136–8
    neutrality, unarmed, 137–8
    war, causes of, 127–8; prevention of, 132–6

Patriotism. See Nationalism

Peace, 12, 39, 42, 67–8, 133–4, 141, 153, 160, 186, 194–7, 224–6, 230, 261–2, 268–9

Peaceful settlement, 102, 148–52, 196, 198–200, 210, 270–1, 275–9; see also Peacemaking

Peacemaking, 9–10, 39–40, 73, 102–5, 119–22, 152–3, 176–8, 210, 267,

271–5, 277–9; see also Peaceful settlement

Power, 12–13, 55, 107, 116–17, 123, 154; desire for, 27–9, 141, 143–4; elements of, 17–21, 35–7, 49–50, 74–5, 87–90, 117–19, 153–4, 161, 203–4, see also Morale, Unity; estimates of, 17–23, 57–9, 118–9, 151, 201, 203; see also Balance of power, Sea power

Powers. See States

Preparedness, 6, 18, 22, 36–8, 49, 85–6, 144, 149, 151, 158, 170, 172, 237, 242–4, 255–6, 267, 269–70; see also Military policy, Sea power, Vigilance

Propaganda, 9, 114

Prudence, 56, 72, 114–15, 117, 119

Public opinion, 14, 83, 149, 158, 189–91, 208–9, 270–1, 275, 277–9

Reparation, 8, 38–9, 45–6, 52–3, 150, 273–4

Rulers, wars caused by, 88, 127, 134–5, 167, 169, 177, 197

Sanctions, economic, 137–8, 163–4

Sea power, 17–18, 20–1, 50, 59, 61–2, 89–90, 153–4, 158, 163–5, 193–5, 206–7, 227–8, 234–5, 244

Security. See Defense

Self-determination. See National self-determination

Self-help, 46–7

Self-restraint, in foreign policy, 2–5, 13–14, 52–3, 72–4, 100–2, 108, 112, 121–3, 145–6, 150–1, 153, 158–60, 165, 168, 174, 178, 235, 264–9, 271–2, 275, 277; in war, 8–10, 38–40, 45–7, 70–1, 100–2, 104–5, 112, 176–7; see also Morality

SMITH, Adam, 78–93
    colonies, and the national interest, 92–3; and trade, 90–3; and self-determination, 92–3
    defense, duty of, 85–7; more important than opulence, 90
    enmity, international, 79–81
    free trade, benefits of, 87–9; and strategic industries, 87, 89–90
    international law, and necessity, 82; and war, 82–5
    morality, international, 82–5

SMITH, Adam (*continued*)
    patriotism, savage and enlightened,
        79–81
    peace, and progress, 79–81
    power, and wealth, 87–90
    preparedness, 85–6
    war, conduct of, 82–4; and morality,
        82–5
SPENCER, Herbert, 221–33
    aggression, and defense, 227–9
    colonies, 230–3
    conflict, and the establishment of
        government, 222–4; and the "mili-
        tant society," 222–4
    defense, and the regulation of trade,
        229–30; right and duty of, 227–9
    imperialism, condemnation of, 230–3
    morality, international, 226–9
    peace, and the "industrial society,"
        225
State of nature, 26–34, 38–9, 41–8, 64,
    95; *see also* Law of nature, State
    of war
State of war, 27–33, 42–5, 95; *see also*
    Law of nature, State of nature
States, large, 76–7, 116–17, 202, 219
States, small, 74–7, 105–6, 116, 168–9,
    202, 219
Statesmanship, 1–5, 56, 81, 147
Subversion, 8–9, 21, 24–5, 114, 116, 278

Territorial expansion. *See* Colonies,
    Conquest, Imperialism
Treaties, 4, 6, 12–13, 34, 36, 69–70, 83,
    111, 128, 169, 199–200, 208–11,
    238; sanctity of, 43, 102–4, 156–8,
    169, 199; *see also* Alliances

Unity, 36, 68, 118–19, 151–2, 222–4
United States. *See* America

Vigilance, 4, 13–15, 17, 22, 27–30, 36–
    7, 58, 60–1, 100, 149; *see also* Pre-
    paredness
Violence. *See* Coercion, War

War, 2, 4–6, 32, 67–8, 97–9, 127–9,
    159–61, 167, 207, 225–6, 240–1,
    254–8, 271; aims in, 8–9, 102, 104,
    177–8, 269–70; as ultimate arbiter
    of disputes, 28, 97, 104, 140, 142–
    3, 170, 183, 238; causes of, 14–16,
    21–3, 29–30, 83–5, 97–8, 114, 119,
    127, 134–5, 140–1, 163–5, 178,
    183–6, 193–4, 196–7, 232, 236–7,
    252, 254–7, 268–9, 277; conduct
    of, 4, 7–10, 22–5, 68–71, 82, 85–6,
    102, 104–5, 120, 176, 222–4; just,
    6–8, 13–16, 20, 22, 38–9, 43–5,
    68–9, 82–5, 100–1, 114, 119, 150–
    2, 159, 163–5, 171–6, 183–5, 196,
    207–8, 227–9, 241–2, 267, 270;
    law of, 38–9, 68–71, 82–5, 97, 102,
    104–5, 176–7; preventive, 7, 14–16,
    84, 100–1, 143, 146, 174, 178, 185,
    214, 244; *see also* Conflict
Wealth, 18–19, 37, 49, 74–6, 88
Welfare, as aim of policy, 18, 48, 110–
    11, 171, 179, 202, 235, 257, 264
WILSON, Woodrow, 263–79
    aggression, 270, 277–8
    defense, duty of, 267–8
    foreign policy, honorable and peace-
        ful, 265
    league of nations, 275, 277
    morality, international, 264–7, 269–
        71; of peace settlement, 271–5
    national self-determination, 271–3,
        277–9
    nations, equality of, 271–3
    neutrality, 265–7; end of, 278
    open diplomacy, 274–9
    peace, and democracy, 279; and
        honor, 268–70; of justice and rea-
        son, 271–3
    peacemaking, and all-round satisfac-
        tion, 271; without victory, 272
    public opinion, 270–1, 275, 277–9
    self-restraint, 264–9, 271–2
    war, causes of, 277; just, 267–70; and
        the vindication of right, 269